T0339786

Empress Wu the Great

CHAPTER 1 THE CLIENT

EMPRESS WU THE GREAT

TANG DYNASTY CHINA

X. L. WOO

Algora Publishing
New York

Library of Congress Cataloging-in-Publication Data —

Woo, X. L.
  Empress Wu the Great / X L. Woo.
    p. cm.
  ISBN 978-0-87586-660-4 (trade paper: alk. paper) — ISBN 978-0-87586-661-1 (case
laminate: alk. paper) — ISBN 978-0-87586-662-8 (ebook) 1. Wu hou, Empress of China,
624-705 2. Empresses—China—Biography. 3. China—History—Tang dynasty, 618-907.
I. Title.
  DS749.42.W8W66 2008
  951'.017092—dc22
  [B]
                              2008031633

Front Cover: Empress Wu the Great

TABLE OF CONTENTS

PREFACE

In Europe, the idea of "ladies first" once held sway, and there have been many sovereign queens in Europe's history. In ancient China there was none of that. The social status of women was low. They were not allowed to do what men were doing and not allowed to interfere with what men were doing, especially politically. They were deemed at best ornaments in men's life and as reproduction machines to bear offspring for their husbands' families. It was their duty was to obey men and please men. Although in some particular families the husband might listen to the wife or might even be henpecked, that was hardly the prevailing trend. By tradition, a woman who did not bear any sons (daughters did not count) for the husband could be divorced for that reason alone. Actually, it was not even a "divorce." The husband could simply return the woman, like a defective product; he could send her back to her original family. The parents could not refuse to take their daughter back. But they were not obliged to welcome her warmly

Under such circumstances, it was not easy for a woman to climb all the way up to the throne. Yet one woman did it. Eventually known as Empress Wu Zetian the Great, she became the only female sovereign to rule in her own name in Chinese history.

Women occupied a low social status long before her time, the Tang Dynasty (AD 618–AD 907); it can be seen in records from the early Zhou Dynasty (1121 BC–476 BC), which is as far back as we can really go. The Chinese government boasts that China has an even longer history, going back five thousand years, but the first dynasty they include may be legendary. No archeological evidence has ever been found; there are only references to it in later written records. Thus some historians hold that China's history only goes back three thousand seven hundred years.

While readers may be more familiar with Greek, Roman, Egyptian or Indian history, a brief outline of Chinese history may help to set this story in context. The major dynasties in Chinese history were:

Xia Dynasty (2207 BC–1766 BC). Questionable.

Shang Dynasty (1765 BC–1122 BC). Many bronze utensils have been dated to this period.

Zhou Dynasty (1121 BC–476 BC)

War Period among Seven Kingdoms (475 BC–221 BC)

Qin Dynasty (220 BC–207 BC) conquers the other six kingdoms and forms imperial China.

Han Dynasty (206 BC–AD 220)

Three Kingdoms Period (AD 220–AD 280)

Jin Dynasty (AD 265–AD 420) conquers the other two kingdoms by 280 AD

War Period among many small separate kingdoms (AD 420–AD 589)

Sui Dynasty (AD 581–AD 618) wipes out all the other kingdoms by AD 589

Tang Dynasty (AD 618–AD 907)

War Period again (AD 907–AD 960)

Song Dynasty (AD 960–AD 1279)

Yuan Dynasty (AD 1271–AD 1368) is formed by a Mongolian tribe

Ming Dynasty (AD 1368–AD 1644)

Qing Dynasty (AD 1644–AD 1911), the last dynasty in China.

In writing this volume I have relied primarily on the most authoritative ancient Chinese record, *Zizhitongjian*, the foundational historical reference written by a prime minister in the Song Dynasty, Sima Guang, who was a great scholar. He began his chronicles with the late period of the Zhou Dynasty and went up to AD 959, a total of 294 volumes. Since he was writing shortly after the Tang Dynasty, the facts as he stated them are fairly reliable. But Sima Guang was a conservative man and abhorred anything that flew in the face of tradition; and he was certainly no less biased than any other writer of histories. One obvious example was that when Empress Wu had already established her new dynasty and become the sovereign empress, Sima in his book still referred to her as "empress dowager" (deriving her authority from her status as the widow of her husband), not as "empress." In his mind, the concept of a female sovereign was unthinkable.

The narrative flow of this book aims to follow certain major themes, within which events are arranged by year. Whenever an important person is introduced, a brief biography follows.

In accordance with Chinese usage, surnames are presented before given names in this book.

Chapter 1. Origins of a Future Sovereign

The Wu Family

Wu Shiyue (?–AD 635) was not a wealthy young man. His family lived in Wenshui (meaning Literary Water) Town in Bingchow (Chow means District) in the present Shanxi Province (Shan here means Mountain and Xi means West). He had two elder brothers, Wu Shiling and Wu Shiyi. The family business was to make and sell bean curd or tofu. They made the bean curd early every morning. Then the father took it out for sale. As their bean curd was of good quality, it sold well. So they made money.

Wu's Father Rises from a Merchant to a Nobleman

China was then under the reign of the Sui Dynasty (AD 581–AD 618). Emperor Yang (AD 560–AD 618), the second emperor of the Sui Dynasty, led a life of indulgence. He loved to travel and had an extra palace built wherever he would go. This created a large demand for lumber. Wu's father seized the opportunity to become a lumber merchant and accumulated wealth. But in feudal China, wealth did not equal status, and merchants were not held in esteem.

There were four social classes or castes in feudal China. The first class consisted of "scholars," including courtiers and officials. Peasants belonged to the second class because they produced grain to feed the people. The third class consisted of workers and craftsmen, who provided people with other necessities of life. The merchants were of the lowest class because they produced nothing and it was considered that they made money from the efforts of other people.

Wishing to improve his social status, Mr. Wu joined the army as a low-ranking officer. As he served well, he was promoted to staff officer in charge of arms keeping. Then he joined the army of Li Yuan (AD 566–AD 635, reigning AD 618–AD 626), who would be the first emperor of the Tang Dynasty in the years to come. He came to know Li Yuan personally. Several times when Li Yuan was commanded by the emperor to quench the fire of peasant revolts here and there and passed Wenshui Town, he would stay in the Wu residence. Their relationship developed cordially.

In AD 617, Li Yuan was appointed the prefect of Taiyuan (meaning extreme plateau) City by the emperor, who was a cousin of Li Yuan (his mother and the mother of Emperor Yang were sisters). At that time more and more peasants in more and more places were taking up arms against the corruption of the Sui Dynasty. Our man Wu Shiyue advised Li Yuan to raise his own banner against the Sui Dynasty. Li seems to have been thinking along the same lines; he did turn against the emperor and let Wu Shiyue know that if he should attain the throne, he "wouldn't forget him." Then Li Yuan began to recruit men and put Liu Hongji and Changsun Shunde in charge of the raw recruits and to train them.

Two vice prefects, Wang Wei and Gao Junya, had been appointed by Emperor Yang to serve under Prefect Li Yuan. They were loyal to the emperor and suspected Li Yuan of betrayal. They consulted Wu, saying, "Liu and Changsun were army deserters when His Majesty (denoting the second emperor of the Sui Dynasty) invaded Korea. Shall we arrest and interrogate them?"

Wu Shiyue was on Li's side, of course, and replied, "They are Prefect Li's men. It's not our place to arrest them." So no action was taken.

Emperor Yang of the Sui Dynasty had built Jinyang Palace (Jin here is the name of an ancient kingdom in China and Yang here means the sun) close by Taiyuan City. Li Yuan told Wu Shiyue to set an ambush at the eastern gate of the palace in case of any surprise attack. A soldier learned of this and wanted to report to vice prefect Wang Wei, but Wu Shiyue stopped him, and gave him an incentive to keep quiet.

In the fifth moon of the same year, Li Yuan killed both the vice prefects on some pretext and then in the seventh moon raised his banner against the Sui Dynasty. He appointed Wu Shiyue as his staff officer responsible for arms and materiel. At that time the army of the Sui Dynasty was struggling to fight the rebellious peasants. Li Yuan grasped the chance to besiege city after city, and he occupied them one by one.

In the ninth moon, they entered ChangAn ("everlasting safety") City, which was later made the capital of the Tang Dynasty. As now it seemed that the whole nation was up in arms against Emperor Yang, Li Yuan supported Yang You (AD 605–AD 619), the grandson of Emperor Yang, to be the emperor of the Sui Dynasty. He was called Emperor Gong, and he designated the present Emperor Yang an ex-emperor.

Li Yuan announced himself as general prime minister with the appellation Prince Tang. Why Tang? His grandfather had been Duke of TangGuo in a previous dynasty; hence, he was already drawing up a heritage for what he aimed to make the Tang Dynasty. Li Yuan granted Wu Shiyue a large manor house, three million coins, and five thousand scrolls of silk. He appointed Wu as the vice minister of the Etiquette Ministry with a title of Duke of Yiyuan. He also gave Wu two hundred blood horses and two thousand bushels of grain.

On the fourth day of the tenth moon in AD 618, Emperor Yang of the Sui Dynasty was killed by his general Yuwen (double surname) Huaji.

Then Li Yuan forced the young Emperor Gong to abdicate and declared himself emperor of a new dynasty, the Tang Dynasty. After a feast to celebrate the victory, the participants were rewarded in accordance with their service. Wu Shiyue was appointed a general and given an additional three hundred acres of arable land, three hundred slaves of both sexes, five hundred catties of gold and twenty thousand pieces of colored cloth. He even received a metal certificate of exemption from a death sentence in case he once committed a crime worthy of the death penalty.

In AD 620, Wu Shiyue was appointed head of the Construction Ministry. (There were six ministries in the Tang Dynasty: The Official Ministry, Military Ministry, Judicial Ministry, Household Ministry, Etiquette Ministry and Construction Ministry.) Wu again proved his competence and the emperor was so delighted that he conferred on Wu another title, Duke Yingguo. Wu modestly demurred. Anyway, he had risen from bean curd dealer and lumber merchant to nobleman in ChangAn City. He was satisfied and did not want to overreach.

Mr. Wu Marries Up

While Wu Shiyue was traveling with the troops, he suffered a tragic personal loss. He had four sons. However, during the time he was marching with the troops, two of his sons died of disease. A year later, his wife also died of disease. He never had a chance to see them for one last time or to say goodbye. He mourned for them in his heart and kept on working with single-minded determination. When the emperor Li Yuan learned of the situation, he was further impressed and gave Wu Shiyue great praise for his loyalty to his duties. Now, as Wu Shiyue's wife had died, the emperor thought he might again offer him an honor while finding him another wife.

The woman the emperor had in mind was a middle-aged spinster from a noble family. Her father, Yang Da, had been the vice minister of both the

Official Ministry and the Judicial Ministry in the Sui Dynasty. He had gone with Emperor Yang of the Sui Dynasty to invade Korea and had died in battle. Since her father died, she had stayed single, praying for his soul every day before a statuette of Buddha in a special room at home. She was the cousin of the brother-in-law of Prince Qin, namely Li Shiming, the second son of Li Yuan. So by marrying her Wu Shiyue would become a distant relative of the imperial Li family.

In AD 622, Emperor Li Yuan played matchmaker for Wu Shiyue. The woman was then forty-four years old and Wu was forty-six. The wedding expenses were all covered by the emperor. The woman became Lady Wu, née Yang, and despite her age she gave birth to two daughters for Wu Shiyue. The second daughter would grow up to be our chief character, Empress Wu.

On the twenty-third day of the first moon in AD 624, the young Miss Wu was born in ChangAn City (the present XiAn, meaning west safety), the capital of the Tang Dynasty, when her father was working there as the minister of the Construction Ministry (supposedly based on his having been a lumber merchant). Her father was by then forty-eight and her mother forty-six. As noted, she had two stepbrothers and an elder sister, still a child.

In AD 625, one year after her birth, Miss Wu's father left ChangAn City for Yangchow (Yang here means Raise and Chow means district) City under the command of the emperor. He took his wife and two daughters with him, leaving his two sons behind as they were already adults.

Yangchow City is situated to the north side of the Yangtze River, on the lower reaches, close to Nanking (meaning South Capital) City across the river. Back in AD 616, Emperor Yang of the Sui Dynasty had escaped to Yangchow City since revolts after revolts broke out almost everywhere in his empire, and when he was killed in AD 618 by his general Yuwen Huaji, the city was occupied by this general. In AD 619, a riotous army of the peasants took over the city. Then another peasant army conquered it. The city changed hands between peasant armies during the next several years.

The emperor, Li Yuan, sent his nephew, Prince Li Xiaogong, to attack Yangchow City in AD 624 and took it in the third moon. Then the emperor appointed Prince Li Xiaogong to be the governor of Yangchow City. Generally after war the government was expected to do something to restore agricultural activities, but the nephew turned his attention to his own merry-making and enjoyment. Therefore, the situation was just as bad as before. Then rumors spread that Prince Li Xiaogong was planning a mutiny. The emperor summoned him to the capital and imprisoned him.

Prince Shenfu was appointed the governor of Yangchow City. According to the regulations at the beginning of the Tang Dynasty, the position of governor should be given only to princes, but generally the princes only took the positions in name. They did not even go to live there, and so an administrator would be appointed at the same time to actually take charge of everything in the city and the surrounding area, generally the province of which the city was capital. Thus the position of Wu Shiyue was to be the administrator in Yangchow City. But later when Li Yuan abdicated and left the throne to his second son, Prince Qin, the second emperor of the Tang Dynasty, called Emperor Taizong (AD 599–AD 649 and AD 627–AD 649 on the throne), the rule was changed. Any courtier could be appointed a governor.

Mr. Wu Becomes a Governor

In the first moon of AD 627, General Li Yi, titled Prince Yanjun, rebelled in Jingchow (Jing here is the name of a river). The reason was that he was a pretty arrogant fellow, and once when Prince Qin had sent a messenger to him, he had beaten him for no reason at all. Now that Prince Qin was crowned to be the second emperor, he was afraid that the emperor would kill him. A sorcerer from Zaochow (Zao here is a surname) read his face and said to him, "Your Highness's face reading shows that Your Highness will reach a higher position soon." A position "higher than a prince" would appear to indicate "emperor." Therefore, at the advice of the sorcerer, he rebelled. He lied that he had received a secret imperial edict to lead his army to the capital. On his way there, he reached Youchow (You meaning secluded). The magistrate Zhao Cihao came out to meet him. General Li Yi occupied Youchow. The emperor sent Changsun Wuji (AD 594–AD 659), the minister of Official Ministry, as commander-in-chief to attack General Li Yi. When Zhao Cihao knew that the government army would come, he planned to attack General Li Yi, assisted by a junior general Yang Ji, who camped outside Youchow. When General Li Yi learned the plan, he imprisoned Zhao Cihao. Then junior general Yang Ji assaulted General Li Yi and put his warriors to rout. General Li Yi deserted his wife and children and escaped alone. He wanted to run away to the Tujue Clan, a minority to the north of the Tang territory, but was killed by his followers. His brother Li Shou, the governor of Lichow (meaning Benefit District), was executed. Then Li Xiaochang was sent to Lichow as a new governor. But in the twelfth moon, Li Xiaochang went to the capital. He stayed there and planned a revolt with some generals of different ranks. He wanted to seize the power and to be the emperor himself. But as a result, he failed and was executed together with his accomplices.

After his death, his followers in Lichow were uneasy and the situation there seemed in unrest. Emperor Taizong wanted to send someone there to assuage the followers. He weighed all his courtiers one by one to see who would be the more suitable person for that errand. Finally he decided on Wu Shiyue and then transferred him to the position of the governor of Lichow in

Sichuan (meaning Four Streams) Province, which is a beautiful mountain-ous region. Empress Wu spent her childhood there for four years.

In AD 629 when she was five years old, Empress Wu started to be edu-cated. In AD 630, she began to learn arts and music from her mother, who was an educated woman.

In AD 631, as the situation was under control in Sichuan Province, Wu Shiyue was once more transferred from Lichow to Jingchow (meaning Bram-ble District), as a general governor, the rank of which was a little higher than just a governor. He would govern seven districts, not just one as a governor did. Next year he arrived there with his family. Jingchow (present Jiangling, meaning River Hill) City in Hubei (Hu here means Lake and Bei means North) Province) was situated on the midstream of the Yangtze River. It was an important strategic place geographically for a war.

In AD 632 when Wu was eight years old, she began to study poetry and classics, and to learn etiquette exercised in the officialdom.

In AD 633, as Wu Shiyue did an excellent job there he was praised and rewarded by Emperor Taizong. That year Empress Wu made great progress in her studies. She liked to read history books, which was of great use for her later when she reigned over the country.

During the first moon of AD 635, just after the Spring Festival, Wu Shi-yue secured two low positions for his sons through his influence with the Official Ministry, whose duties were to appoint or remove, and promote or demote officials in various positions nationwide.

Mr. Wu Leaves His Family Bereft

On the sixth day of the fifth moon in AD 635, the first emperor Li Yuan died. The sad news came and Wu Shiyue fell ill, because he had a special feeling toward Li Yuan who had promoted him to a high position at the be-ginning of his political career. Before long, in the same year, he died, too, at the age of fifty-nine. His daughter, the future empress, was only eleven at the time.

In the twelfth moon, the bereaved wife and sons and daughters went with the coffin back to their home town, Wenshui in Bingchow, though the wife and her two daughters had never been there before. The capital of Bingchow then was Jinyang (Jin here is the name of an ancient kingdom and Yang here means the Sun) City, southwest to Taiyuan City in present Shanxi (meaning Mountain West) Province.

After the death of Wu Shiyue, the widow and her two daughters had a difficult life. Unlike the daughters of other families who learned to sew and cook, the daughter whose fate we are following spent her time studying the books from which the boys were taught. She also knew calligraphy and painting, music and dance.

According to tradition, the two sons inherited the estate. The bereaved wife, who was only the stepmother of the two sons, lived at their mercy, together with her two daughters. The sons hated their stepmother and also their two stepsisters, because their father had given all his love to them. So the sons treated them badly.

In the first moon of AD 636, the current emperor, Taizong, decided that since Wu Shiyue had been such a loyal person he ordered his funeral to be managed by the government. Li Ji (AD 594–AD 669), the governor of Bingchow, presided over the funeral and all the expenses were paid by the local government.

That Wu Shiyue could rise from a pedlar and merchant to the position of a minister and governor can be ascribed to the following conditions: 1) he had an extraordinary ambition to change his social status; 2) favorable situations offered themselves; and 3) he worked for a successful leader, in Li Yuan.

Firstly, if he had been contented with his life as a wealthy merchant, he would not have joined Li Yuan's army. Of course, he would not have met Li Yuan and helped him to establish the Tang Dynasty. Secondly, if he had lived in a peaceful time, no chaos at all, he could not have had the chance to meet Li Yuan because Li himself could have had no opportunity to rise up successfully against an uncorrupted government. Thirdly, if he had chosen the wrong man to serve, one who had failed after a series of fights, he would have perished too. After all, Chinese people would say that it was his fate that made him as he was.

THE ESTABLISHMENT OF THE TANG DYNASTY

The daughter of this successful man married twice, and both times auspiciously. Her first husband was the second emperor of the Tang Dynasty, Emperor Taizong, or Tang Taizong as Chinese people generally refer to him.

The first emperor, Li Yuan, had four sons. Emperor Taizong, his second son, was a man of talent. After the overthrow of the Sui Dynasty, there were many warlords all over the country. Some had been generals of the Sui Dynasty, controlling some troops. Others were ambitious persons who gathered riotous peasants to form troops and occupy a region. If Li Yuan wanted to put the whole country under his reign, he would have to conquer all the warlords. The second son was victorious in almost all the battles and became a great support in the establishment of the Tang Dynasty. Now let us look back to how Tang Dynasty was built up and how the second son succeeded to the throne.

In AD 617 when Li Yuan held up his own banner against the Sui Dynasty, he sent out messengers to cities and towns close by and wanted all the mayors to obey him. The mayor of Xihe (meaning West River) City refused. So

Li Yuan sent his two sons, Li Jiancheng (AD 589–AD 626), the elder, and Li Shiming, the second son, to besiege the city. He told Wen Dayou, the mayor of Taiyuan City, to go with his sons. He said to Wen Dayou, "My sons are still young and have no relevant. You will be their military counselor in all actions. This battle will test whether our cause can be victorious or not." Wen Dayou was born into a scholar's family. After the city was taken, he was made a secretary to Li Yuan in charge of secret documents. He thought the position unsuitable and wanted to resign, but Li Yuan would not permit it. However, he always kept these secrets at arm's length and his colleagues held a high opinion of him. He died early of disease.

Their army mostly consisted of new recruits and was inexperienced in fighting. Although they were from a family of nobility, the two sons lived with and had the same food as that of the soldiers. But when fighting, they rushed forth ahead of the soldiers. Their soldiers were forbidden to rob the people. They could, however, buy things from the locals. All these made both the soldiers and the people love the Li family and they were willing to do anything for them. Before long the city was taken by the brothers. When Li Yuan heard the news, he was proud of his sons.

Among the recruits of Li's army there were freemen as well as slaves who had been freed. After a victorious battle, rewards routinely would be conferred. The former slaves worried that they would not get the same rewards as the freemen, but Li Yuan distributed rewards equally according to their merits. That helped Li Yuan defeat others and establish the Tang Dynasty; Li's army had adopted such strategies to win the support of the people.

In AD 618, the situation was very severe for the Sui Dynasty. But Emperor Yang still led a life of dissipation. He had a great many concubines and female servants, almost a thousand. Every day one of the concubines would give a dinner party, taking turns, for the emperor and others. They all drank till they were very drunk. Once, patting his own head, the emperor said to his empress, "Who will come to cut off this nice head of mine?" (This sentence was really recorded in the history book.)

The capital of the Sui Dynasty was ChangAn City. But now Emperor Yang wanted to escape to the southern provinces beyond the Yangtze River, which was always deemed a natural defensive "moat." Some courtiers did not agree to the plan. They left the emperor and went to somewhere else with their followers. The emperor sent his troops to pursue them and killed some of them, which caused panic among the courtiers. Thus the emperor gradually lost support even among his courtiers. Anyway, he went to Yangchow (Yang here means Raise) City.

In the third moon of the same year, it was in Yangchow City that the emperor of the Sui Dynasty was strangled by his own general Yuwen (double surname) Huaji (?–AD 619). When Yuwen and other generals went into the palace to see the emperor, Emperor Yang knew that it was his last day in this world. He said to his generals, "An emperor has his own way to end his own life. You can't kill me with a sword. Give me the poison." Since he already knew that his dynasty was not going to last much longer, he always had some poison ready and let a eunuch carry it. But now the eunuch was nowhere to be found. The emperor had to accept another way to die. He used a muslin strap as girdle. Now he untied it and handed it to them. Thus he was strangled with his own girdle. One of his sons, twelve years old, happened to be with him and was killed right before his eyes. So the Chinese people maintain the saying that an emperor no longer in power is as weak as an ordinary person. When Yuwen Huaji had killed the emperor, he took the empress, called Empress Xiao in the history books and reputedly a beauty, away with him. Yuwen occupied a region including Yangchow City and became a warlord. At that time there were quite a few warlords here and there, supported either by the former troops of the Sui Dynasty or by the rebelling peasants.

In the fifth moon, Li Yuan declared himself the emperor of the Tang Dynasty since the Sui Dynasty had been overthrown. He conferred the title of princes to his sons and relatives. He made his eldest son the crown prince (AD 589–AD 626), his second son Prince Qin (AD 599–AD 649) and his third son Prince Qi (AD 603–AD 626). His fourth son, Li Yuanba, died early (AD 599–AD 614). However, the warlords all over the country should still be subdued if Li Yuan wanted to extend his reign nationwide. This was not an easy task and there was no guarantee of final victory.

In the first moon of AD 619, Prince HuaiAn, by the name of Li Shentong (?–AD 630), a cousin of the emperor of the Tang Dynasty, was sent to fight Yuwen Huaji in Wei (Wei here is the name of an ancient kingdom) Town. Yuwen could not resist the strong attack and fled east to Liao (Liao here means Meaningless) Town. Prince HuaiAn took Wei Town and slew two thousand of Yuwen's soldiers. Then he chased Yuwen to Liao Town and surrounded it. Being short of food, Yuwen wanted to surrender, but Prince HuaiAn would not accept it and continued to assail.

A warlord, Dou Jiande (AD 573–AD 621), came to attack Yuwen, too. Prince HuaiAn withdrew his troops and let Dou fight Yuwen. Dou was born into a peasant family and had been recruited in the Sui army to invade Korea. Later he joined a rebellious peasant army. When the leader died in a battle, he took the position as leader. Since he never killed innocent people, his army developed to the number of one hundred thousand strong because many poor people joined it. He became a warlord and called himself Prince Xia. He occupied most regions to the north of the Yellow River. He wanted

to expand south and so came to attack Yuwen Huaji. After a series of engage-
ments, Dou took the town and killed Yuwen. He let Empress Xiao go to the
Tujue Clan to live there because Princess Yicheng, the sister of Emperor Yang,
had been married to the khan of the Tujue Clan and now she sent her men
here to fetch her sister-in-law. Empress Xiao lived there for more than ten
years. In AD 630 when Tang army defeated the Tujue troops, she came with
Tang army to live in ChangAn City for the rest of her life. She died in AD 647
at the age of eighty or so. She was buried together with Emperor Yang.

In AD 621, Prince Qin, the second son of Li Yuan, reorganized his troops.
His soldiers were all clad in black and divided in two detachments. In every
battle, Prince Qin led his troops as a vanguard and conquered all he fought
with. Prince Qin went to attack Louyang (Lou here is the name of a river
and Yang here means South Side, because the river is on the south side of the
city) City that year. This city was later made the second capital of the Tang
Dynasty, called East Capital, and later still, Divine Capital.

Luoyang City was at the time occupied by the warlord Wang Shichong
(?–AD 621). Wang Shichong was a favorite courtier of the late Emperor Yang
of the Sui Dynasty. When Emperor Yang was killed, he supported Prince
Yue named Yang Tong, who was a grandson of the late Emperor Yang, to
be the emperor. They lived in Luoyang City and made it their capital. After
Wang Shichong defeated another warlord, Li Mi (AD 582–AD 619), he deposed the emperor Yang Tong and made himself emperor. As he was strict
and cruel to the people, many of them ran away from the city. Then he issued
an order: if anyone left the city, his whole family would be killed, and if any
family escaped from the city the immediate neighboring families would be
killed. But this defeated his purpose: the more he killed, the more people ran
off. Even some of his generals fled to Tang army. Once Wang Shichong sent
his son to Hulao (meaning Tiger Jail) Pass with several thousand soldiers
to get grain for his army. One the way back his son was ambushed by Tang
troops. The soldiers either were slain or fled and the grain were taken by the
Tang army. The son escaped alone.

When Prince Qin and his army approached the city, Wang Shichong
came out with twenty thousand soldiers to meet him. Wang's troops were
arranged in battle array, facing the Gu River, with the Tang army on the opposite side. Prince Qin stood on a high spot to look at the enemy's formation.
He said to those about him, "The rebels are at their wit's end. They bring all
their soldiers out to pin the hope on this battle. If we can defeat them today,
they won't come out to fight again." He ordered a general Qutu Tong to go
with five thousand men across the river to launch an attack. He told the
general that when they began to fight he must make a signal by sending up
a whiff of smoke.

Qutu Tong (AD 557–AD 628) was from a minority and lived in ChangAn City. He was an upright person and worked at first for Emperor Wen, the first emperor of the Sui Dynasty and the father of Emperor Yang. In the third moon of AD 597, he was sent by Emperor Wen to inspect the horse farm in Longxi (Long here is the name of a place and Xi here means West) in the northwest part of Sui territory. The farm belonged to the government. Qutu found that more than twenty thousand horses had not been reported to the government. It was a crime. Emperor Wen was angry and wanted to execute one hundred fifty persons involved. Qutu thought that it was not proper to kill so many officials over a bunch of horses. But Emperor Wen insisted. Then Qutu begged that His Majesty kill him and pardon the others. At last Emperor Wen pardoned them from the death sentence.

At the end of the Sui Dynasty, when Emperor Yang left ChangAn City for Yangchow City, he ordered Qutu Tong to stay in ChangAn City. Then the Tang army came to attack him, and after many battles, he was captured and sent to see Li Yuan, who released him and made him the minister of the Military Ministry, granted him the title of Duke of Jiangguo, and sent him to fight under Prince Qin, his second son.

When Prince Qin saw the smoke, he dashed with his troops into the battle to catch the enemy in a vise formation. Prince Qin went ahead with several dozen horsemen through the enemy's ranks. He killed many of the enemy and in the process was separated with his horsemen. Only one general, Qiu Xinggong, followed him. Wang Shichong came after them, with a few soldiers on horseback. A stray arrow hit the horse under Prince Qin, who had to jump from the falling horse. His general Qiu shot at the pursuers, and every arrow killed an enemy. The chasers stopped. The general let Prince Qin ride on his horse. He himself ran before the horse, wielding his long-handled sword. At last they both returned to their own side of the battlefield. The fighting went on hotly for almost another six hours. Wang Shichong withdrew into the city. Prince Qin approached the city walls and surrounded it.

As it was a big city and its walls were very strong, the soldiers of Prince Qin attacked the city day and night for more than ten days, but could not overcome it. However, food became scarce in the city and many people were starved to death.

As the assault was in vain, for so long, someone suggested that they should withdraw, but Prince Qin insisted on the continuation of the attack. He said, "If we withdraw now, the enemies inside the city will revive their fighting ability very soon. We can't let them have such a chance."

Wang Shichong had a follower called Zheng Ting who was not impressed with Wang Shichong's leadership and wanted to become a monk. To him, that meant that he would no longer have to be concerned with anything Wang Shichong did, good or bad. Wang Shichong thought that it meant that Zheng Ting thought he would fail this time and wanted to desert him by becoming a monk. So Wang Shichong did not give his permission. Zheng Ting became a monk anyway, without permission. Wang Shichong was enraged and had Zheng Ting killed. Generally, in such critical moments, a ruler should strive to make everyone working for him feel confident and happy with him. To kill a follower without any serious reason incites others to seek a chance to desert him. That was one of the reasons why Wang Shichong failed.

In the third moon of AD 621, Dou Jiande led his army to the rescue of Luoyang City at the request of Wang Shichong. Dou wrote a letter to Prince Qin, asking him to retreat and return to Wang all the area he had occupied thus far. That was the condition for a peace treaty, failing which Dou would attack the Tang army. As Dou had one hundred thousand soldiers, someone in the Tang army thought that they might be attacked from both sides; it was suggested that the Tang army should beat a retreat. Prince Qin did not go with the suggestion, but used another strategy. He divided his army into two detachments, one keeping pressure on the besieged city and the other marching to meet Dou's troops. Prince Qin had only three thousand five hundred soldiers with him against Dou's one hundred thousand soldiers. But the Tang detachment occupied Hulao Pass, which was at such a location geographically that it was easy to defend and hard to conquer.

Dou was blockaded by the Tang army at Hulao Pass and could not get to Luoyang City. Someone suggested to Dou to withdraw from here and maneuver to attack certain cities occupied by other Tang troops. Then, the Tang army surrounding Luoyang City would have to go to the rescue of these cities. Thus Luoyang City would be safe. One classic rule of war which is to avoid the strong and to attack the weak. Dou was about to take the advice when another officer said that if they retreated now, they would be deemed cowards, afraid of the Tang army. Therefore, Dou made the final decision to fight the Tang army to the last gasp.

A few days later, the combat between Dou and Tang armies began. Prince Qin led five hundred cavalrymen with four generals, who were Li Ji, Cheng Zhijie, Qin Shubao and Weichi Jingde, all being distinguished, brave generals at that time. On the approach to Dou's camp, Prince Qin left part of his cavalrymen under a general in an ambush somewhere. He did it three times so that he was left with only three cavalrymen and the general Weichi Jingde with him. He said to Weichi, "I have my bow and arrows. You have your lance. We can fight through even thousand of enemies." He added, "The enemies are lucky if they don't come to me." At three miles from Dou's camp, they met with some enemy patrolmen who thought that they were scouts for Prince Qin's army. But Prince Qin shouted, "I am Prince Qin." He shot at the enemies and killed an officer. Presently five or six thousand cavalrymen came out from Dou's camp. The three cavalrymen were frightened. Prince Qin said to them, "You go ahead. Weichi and I will bring up the rear." When the pursuers came nearer, one arrow from Prince Qin killed one of their cavalrymen and the rest stopped short, then came after Prince Qin again. But they did not dare to come to close, only following at a safe distance. Prince Qin lured them into his ambushes and defeated them in the first combat.

For months, both sides had several skirmishes and Dou's army could not gain any ground on the Tang army. Prince Qin sent some general to go round to the back of Dou's army and captured Dou's grain wagons. One of Dou's followers, called Ling Jing, suggested that they should take another route to attack other towns which had few Tang men-at-arms in defense. They could have three advantages: 1) they could easily march to their destination; 2) they could expand their territory and enhance their strength; 3) the Tang government would be shocked and the Tang army would have to retreat from Luoyang City. Dou was about to follow his advice when messengers after messengers arrived from Wang Shichong to require immediate rescue. And the messengers bribed some of the generals in Dou's army to urge Dou to fight his way to Luoyang City. Those generals said to Dou that Ling Jing was only a scholar and did not know anything about war, and they begged Dou not to listen to him. So Dou said to Ling Jing, "My generals want to fight. That's Heaven's blessing. Fighting under Heaven's blessing, I will win the victory. I can't take your advice." Ling Jing wanted to argue, but Dou told his men to drive him out. When his wife told Dou to take Ling's good advice, Dou said, "You, woman, don't know such things. I came to their rescue. Now they are practically being hung by their tails and will perish sooner or later. If I desert them at such a critical moment, I will be deemed a coward who fears the enemy, and deemed to have broken my promise. I won't do that."

A spy came to report to Prince Qin: "Dou's waiting for a chance that we use up our fodder and let our horses graze on the north side of the river, and then he will attack us." In the fifth moon, Prince Qin put a thousand or so horses to graze outside his camp region as a tactic to tempt Dou to attack. Accordingly Dou came with his troops, in a parade stretching for twenty miles. Many Tang generals were struck with dread at the number, which far surpassed theirs. Prince Qin led them to a high spot and said to them, "Those rogues rose up in Shandong Province and didn't meet with any strong enemies. They are without discipline when they make so much noise facing their enemies. They show contempt for us when they march up so close. If we don't go out to fight but just wait, their morale will ebb. When they have stayed there long enough, their soldiers will be hungry and they will withdraw. Then we can chase and fight them. The victory is surely ours. I promise you, when the sun passes its apex, we will subdue them."

A general from Dou's army rode a steed formerly belonging to Emperor Yang of the Sui Dynasty. He came out to show it off. Prince Qin said, "That is really a good steed." His brave general Weichi Jingde stepped forth to ask for permission to go and get it. Prince Qin said, "I can't risk losing a brave man for the sake of a horse." But Weichi did not care and rode out with other two generals into the enemy's formation. He captured the Dou general and pulled the steed along with him back to the Tang camp ground. No one in the Dou formation could stop him.

At noon, just as predicted by Prince Qin, Dou's soldiers were hungry and tired. They sat down and began to eat and drink. Prince Qin said, "It's time." He led his generals and army forward. Dou's army put up a hasty resistance but they were put to rout. Tang troops chased them for thirty miles, slew more than three thousand Dou soldiers and captured fifty thousand, who were sent away back to their respective homes. Dou Jiande himself was also captured. When he was taken into the presence of Prince Qin, Prince Qin said to him, "It has nothing to do with you when I'm attacking Luoyang City. Why do you come all the way to fight me?" Dou replied, "If I didn't come now, it would be inconvenient for you to come all the way to attack me in the future." (What he meant was that after Prince Qin conquered Luoyang City, he would just as well come to attack Dou sooner or later.)

When the news of Dou's army being defeated spread into the city, Wang felt hopeless and surrendered. The city fell into the hand of Prince Qin. All the captives were sent to the capital. Dou Jiande was killed. The emperor wanted to kill Wang Shichong as well, but Wang Shichong said to the emperor, "If we enumerate my wrongdoings, I do deserve death, but Prince Qin promised not to kill me." Therefore, he was pardoned and sent to live in Sichuan (Four Streams) Province, but when he reached Yongchow (Yong here means Harmony) and lodged in the local government post house, he was killed there by his personal enemy Dugu (double surname) Xiude, who was the magistrate of Dingchow (meaning Fix District). This was because when Wang Shichong had deposed Emperor Gong, whom he had originally supported, some scores of his followers plotted to kill him but they were all caught and killed by Wang Shichong, Dugu Ji, the father of Dugu Xiude, among them. To avenge his father's death, Dudu Xiude used a ruse to kill Wang Shichong. He pretended to have an edict from the emperor to announce to Wang. Wang had to come out and prostrate himself to listen, as tradition demanded it. Dugu seized the moment to draw out his sword and killed Wang. When the emperor heard of this, he deprived Dugu of his position as magistrate.

The failure of Dou and Wang could be attributed to their shortcomings of character. Dou was a rash and thoughtless person. He had poor judgment and developed poor strategies. He could not follow good advice and so his failure was certain from the beginning. As for Wang, he was cruel in character and could not restrain himself from trying to force people to serve him. He wanted others to obey him by means of killing. He did not know that this approach could only make people turn their backs on him. The loss of supporters was his downfall. Forbearance is essential to a successful leader.

Li Mi (AD 582–AD 619) was also a warlord. In 616, he joined a large rebellious army called the Wagang Army, a famous rebellious peasant army at that time, headed by Zhai Rang. Wagang was the name of a place used as their base. In the tenth moon of AD 616, they defeated the government army of the Sui Dynasty. Li Mi was a man of talent and had many supporters. In the second moon of 617, Li Mi killed Zhai Rang and hundreds of his followers and made himself the head. In the third moon of 618 when Yuwen Huaji killed the emperor of the Sui Dynasty, Li Mi had a battle with Yuwen and defeated him, but his own army was greatly weakened, having lost so many fighters. Therefore, he was defeated by Wang Shichong later. In the ninth moon, Li Mi surrendered himself to the Tang army. Some of his followers became generals of the Tang army, especially under Prince Qin. In the eleventh moon, Li Yuan, the emperor of the Tang Dynasty, sent Li Mi to gather his former followers in Shandong Province (in the eastern China facing the East Sea), but he betrayed the Tang government and was killed by a Tang general in 619.

Liu Wuzhou (?–622) was an ambitious man. He came from a rich family. When Emperor Yang of the Sui Dynasty invaded Korea (three times from 612 to 614), he joined the Sui Army and became an officer. In 617, he gathered ten thousand men and wanted to be a warlord. But when the Sui government army came to attack him, he surrendered himself to the Tujue Clan for support. So the Sui government army was conquered. Backed by the Tujue Clan, he announced himself an emperor. In the third moon of 619, he led twenty thousand soldiers, together with Tujue troops, to invade Tang territory. Prince Qi, the third son of Li Yuan, came to resist him but was defeated. Then Liu Wuzhou occupied quite a few towns belonging to the Tang government. In the eleventh moon, the emperor Li Yuan ordered his second son, Prince Qin, to go to fight Liu Wuzhou. Within two years, Prince Qin wiped out much of Liu's army. Liu himself fled to the Tujue Clan with five hundred men. Before long, they killed him for betrayal.

Liu Heita (?–AD 623) was a friend of Dou Jiande in youth. Later he joined the Wagang army under Li Mi. When Li Mi was defeated by Wang Shichong, he was captured by Wang, who made him a cavalry general. Before long, he escaped with his cavalrymen to join Dou Jiande. When Dou was captured by the Tang army, he returned to his home village to live a rural life. When Dou was killed by the Tang government in the seventh moon of 621, his former followers set out to avenge him. They asked Liu Heita to be their leader and formed an army. They subdued the Tang army headed by Prince HuaiAn, and in half a year reoccupied all Dou Jiande's former region. In 622, they had a battle with the Tang army led by Prince Qin, the second son of Li Yuan. Prince Qin had the dam of the Ming River broken and let the water flood the troops of Liu Heita, who escaped to the Tujue Clan. Before long, Liu Heita came back with Tujue troops. At the beginning of 623, the Tang army battled with him again and used a ruse to buy some of his followers over. Liu Heita was defeated again. He escaped with some hundreds of his men on horseback. On the fifth day of the first moon in 623, Liu Heita reached Raochow (Rao here means Abundant) and tried to enter the city to get some food. The magistrate of Raochow pretended to welcome him into the city, but ambushed him while he was going through the gateway of the city. Liu Heita was caught and killed.

From the above battles, one can see that good strategies and bravery are basic factors in victory. And a clever leader should also have many faithful, brave supporters to fight for him. Prince Qin had all these assets and so was always victorious.

MR. WU'S SPONSOR BECOMES THE SECOND EMPEROR OF THE TANG DYNASTY

Emperor Li Yuan owed the establishment of the Tang Dynasty to his second son, Li Shiming, known as Prince Qin, who had conquered so many warlords and expanded the territory of the Tang Dynasty. Li Yuan had already made his eldest son Li Jiancheng the crown prince, in accordance with tradition. Li Jiancheng was not a man of much ability and often indulged in wine, women and hunting. Li Yuan knew that the eldest son was not a suitable successor to the throne, and he decided that he should make his second son the crown prince.

The eldest son suspected something and consulted the third son, his brother, who was jealous of his second brother, too. Therefore, the eldest son and the third son formed a union against the second son.

Li Yuan had many concubines, and two of them, Concubine Chang and Concubine Yin, were his favorites. The first and third sons bribed both concubines, who in return often spoke well of the two sons before Li Yuan. They both also spoke ill of the second son as he never bribed them, nor even sweet-talked them.

The two concubines held a deep abhorrence against Prince Qin, the second son, because when Prince Qin took control of Luoyang City, he brought all the valuables back to the capital. The concubines asked him for some precious gems and the like, but Prince Qin told them that all the trophies had been handed in to the national treasury. Then when the concubines asked Prince Qin to confer official positions on their relatives, Prince Qin said that official positions were granted to those who had shown merit in war. And then, since the emperor permitted Prince Qin to handle things as he thought fit, Prince Qin granted Prince HuaiAn some ten acres of land as a reward for his valor in battle. But the father of Concubine Chang asked his daughter to beg the emperor to grant him some land, and the emperor gave him the same piece of land that Prince HuaiAn had already been given. Prince HuaiAn, of course, refused to give up the land. So Concubine Chang complained to the emperor that Prince Qin had taken the land away from her father and given it to Prince HuaiAn. The emperor sent for Prince Qin and reproached him for it.

The father of Concubine Yin was an ignoble person and bullied common people. Once an official working for Prince Qin rode past his magnificent residence, and his servants pulled him down from the horse and beat him till a little finger of his was broken. The father was afraid that Prince Qin would complain to the emperor and so he talked about it to his daughter, who complained to the emperor, lying that the officers under Prince Qin had bullied her father's servants. The emperor reproved his second son for it. When Prince Qin explained, the emperor would not believe him and began to distrust him. The concubines always said to the emperor that when the emperor died and if Prince Qin became the emperor, they would certainly be killed. They added that the crown prince was a kind person and only he would let them live. This all happened in 622.

In the sixth moon of 624, the emperor went to Renzhi (meaning Mercy-Wisdom) Palace for the summer with his second son, Prince Qin and his third son, Prince Qi. He left his eldest son, the crown prince, in the capital to manage routines.

The eldest son was always jealous of the second son, afraid that his brother would someday usurp the throne lawfully belonging to him. A courtier, Yang WenGan, had served the crown prince faithfully and had become his favorite. When Yang WenGan had been promoted to be the governor of Qingchow (Celebration District; Chow was often used in the name of a place), he had secretly recruited many brave men and trained them to be the bodyguards of the crown prince.

As his third brother went with the emperor and the second brother, the crown prince told him privately that he should look for a chance to kill the second brother. But someone reported his secret recruiting to the emperor, who immediately summoned his eldest son to the summer palace.

While the eldest son was preparing to go and see his father, he sent two messengers to the governor Yang WenGan in Qingchow and asked him to rise to arms.

When the crown prince reached the summer palace, he was confined by the emperor, who then sent for Governor Yang WenGan. This accelerated Yang's rebellion. The emperor consulted his second son and promised to make him the crown prince when the rebellion was quenched. So Prince Qin, the second son, led his army to fight the rebels.

As Prince Qin left the summer palace, the third son and the two concubines pleaded on behalf of the eldest son. The emperor always listened to his concubines and therefore pardoned his eldest son, who was freed from confinement and allowed to go back to the capital.

In the seventh moon of 624, Prince Qin defeated the rebellious army and Yang WenGan was killed by his subordinates. His head was conveyed to the capital. But the emperor never mentioned his promise to make his second son the crown prince.

To the north of China, there was a clan of nomads called the Tujue Clan, which frequently invaded the territory of the Tang Dynasty. Once a courtier suggested to the emperor, "Why does the Tujue Clan so often invade our territory? It is because we have a huge accumulation of treasure in ChangAn City. If we take all the treasure somewhere else and burn the city to ashes, we won't need to worry about any further invasion."

The emperor thought that the suggestion was a good one and so did the eldest son and the third son. The emperor thought he would go ahead, and was about to send someone out to find a site for the construction of a new capital when his second son opposed the idea. He said, "The nomads in the north have invaded China from time immemorial. And since the establishment of our new dynasty, we are always victorious. Why would we now desert the city and flee from the nomads? It is shameful. I will go to fight them. If I can't win, we can leave the city then."

The emperor said, "Good." But the eldest son and the concubines said to the emperor, behind the back of the second son, "The aggression of the nomadic Tujue Clan is no big problem. If we give them part of our treasure, they will be glad to leave our country alone. But if Prince Qin gets full control of the entire army, he will usurp the throne. That's his real purpose."

At this the emperor became infuriated. When he was about to send for his second son and scold him, there came the news that the Tujue Clan was in fact marching across the border. Therefore, the emperor went ahead and summoned his second son but instead of reprimanding him, ordered him to go with a large army to drive back the invaders. In the eighth moon of 624, Prince Qin did drive back the Tujue invaders.

In 626, things got serious. According to tradition, the eldest son was an-nounced to be the successor to the throne, but he was not a capable man and was really not fit to rule the country. The second son was a man more intel-ligent and capable. In fighting all the rebellious forces and warlords, he had been the one who conquered most of them and had provided good service in the establishment of the Tang Dynasty. Many courtiers and most of the peo-ple at large supported him to be the successor to the throne. Therefore, the eldest son was jealous of him. The third son was also an ambitious man. He knew that he was not so powerful as his other two brothers. He wanted to use his eldest brother to gain his aim and so formed an ally with him against the second brother.

Even though his second son was so talented that the emperor had once decided he would remove his eldest son from the position of crown prince, anytime the two sons had disputes, he always stood on the side of his eldest son. This made Number Two Son feel unhappy and insecure.

The eldest son was aware that Number Two was better qualified to suc-ceed the emperor when the time came, and he was afraid of him. The best way out, it seemed, was to kill the rival and be done with this question once and for all. So he and the third brother hatched a plot.

One evening, the eldest son invited his second brother for a dinner. The second brother rather incautiously presented himself at the residence of his eldest brother and ate and drank what he was served. He spat a lot of blood, but it seems that the poison in the wine was insufficient and he did not die.

The eldest son, the third son and the two concubines spoke ill of the sec-ond son whenever they got a chance to talk to the emperor, who believed them and would punish his second son. But finally a courtier said to the em-peror, "Prince Qin has done many things contributing to the establishment of the Tang Dynasty and is also a pillar of the country in fighting both the remaining warlords and the nomads in the north. Your Majesty should not punish him. If he falls ill, who will defend the nation when danger comes?" So the emperor changed his mind. Later, when his third son advised him secretly to kill his second son, he did not listen to him.

The supporters of the second son thought that it was the right time to settle the score between the three brothers. They advised him to take action. But Prince Qin wanted to wait till his brothers take action first so that no one would blame him for it.

The eldest son and the third son knew that their second brother had many brave men serving him. So they sent a cartful of gold and silver to one of the brave men by the name of Weichi (double surname) Jingde (AD 585–AD 658) and asked him to turn over to serve them, but the man rebuffed them. Then they made a false accusation against Weichi Jingde and put him into jail. They advised the emperor to kill him. Only when the second son begged his father hard to spare him was Weichi Jingde pardoned and released. When young, Weichi was known for his valor. He had joined the army of Liu Wuzhou (see above) and defeated the Tang army. But in 620 when he met with Prince Qin, Prince Qin defeated him and then sent someone to persuade Weichi to surrender himself to the Tang army. He became one of the faithful followers of Prince Qin.

Then the eldest son and the third son sought to drive off all the supporters of the second son by assigning them positions in other cities far from the capital, leaving the second brother unprotected. But Prince Qin and his supporters decided to take the initiative before his supporters were sent away.

On the fourth day of the sixth moon in 626, Prince Qin and his supporters laid an ambush at Xuanwu (Xuan here means Mystic and Wu here means Karate) Gate of the palace, where the other two brothers would pass through into the palace every day to pay their respects to their father, the emperor. The two brothers were slain and now Prince Qin was the sole successor. No one would be his rival for the crown anymore.

On the seventh day of the sixth moon, Prince Qin was made crown prince and started to take charge of all national affairs. His father was only the emperor in name.

On the eighth day of the eighth moon, his father abdicated and next day Prince Qin was crowned as the emperor. He was generally known as Emperor Taizong, or Tang Taizong. His good reign brought prosperity to the country, which was famous in Chinese history. In subsequent dynasties, his excellent reign was always mentioned as a good example of ruling the country for other emperors to learn from. But none of the emperors in the subsequent dynasties learned anything from him.

To gain more supporters, the new emperor began to give grants and promotions to those who had some influence in the court. One of those was Wu Shiyue, the father of Empress Wu. He was appointed the governor of Yuchow (meaning Happy District) in HeNan (He here means River and Nan here means South) Province).

In the third moon of 630, as Emperor Taizong had subdued all the minorities to the north and northwest of the Tang territory, he gained another title: Heavenly Khan, which meant that he could command all the Clans as their general khan.

In the seventh moon of 634, the emperor asked his father, the abdicated emperor, to live in Jiucheng (Jiu here means Nine and Cheng here means Completion) Palace for the summer. His father did not like it because Emperor Yang of the Sui Dynasty had died there. It was a nice enough place — Emperor Yang had lived there — yet who wanted to live in a place where someone had died? So in the tenth moon, the emperor ordered Daming (Da here means Big and Ming here means Bright) Palace to be built for his father to live in the summer. Before it was finished, his father was taken seriously ill. On the sixth day of the fifth moon in 635, the first emperor Li Yuan died.

On the twenty-seventh day of the tenth moon, the late emperor was buried in a tomb called Mausoleum Xian. (The tomb of every emperor or empress in old China had a name beginning with the word Mausoleum.)

EMPRESS CHANGSUN AND A FEW OF THE COURTIERS

When Emperor Taizong succeeded to the throne, he made his wife Empress Changsun (double surname). Empress Changsun (601–636) also came from a noble family. Her father had been a general in the Sui Dynasty. She was an educated and rational woman. She had been married to the emperor at the age of thirteen. She was thrifty by nature and always helpful to the emperor, who often discussed politics with her after levees. In the third moon of 627, Empress Changsun set an example when she took up breed silkworms herself and the wives of many courtiers followed suit. The example showed that even noble ladies should do productive work just like common people.

Once when the lady who took care of the crown prince asked the empress for more utensils, Empress Changsun refused to give more, saying, "As the crown prince, he should be given more moral education, not more utensils."

Emperor Taizong had a good wife and he also had some faithful courtiers. One, called Wei Zheng (580–643), had served the former crown prince. According to tradition, he should be considered as coming from the enemy's side, for which he would never be trusted, much less be given a high official position. But as he was an upright person, the present emperor liked him and appointed him as a prime minister (there were several prime ministers in the feudal Chinese cabinet). Wei Zheng often gave the emperor advice, steering him away from anything he thought improper. Generally the emperor was receptive to criticism. But once he was angry with Wei and said to Empress Changsun, "I will kill that peasant." Wei did come from a peasant family. But the empress congratulated him for having a courtier so loyal and upright. The emperor realized that she was right and was no longer angry with Wei.

In 634, Emperor Taizong and Empress Changsun went to Jiucheng Palace for the summer. The empress fell ill and soon got worse. It looked like a hopeless case, though the imperial doctors gave her all the medications they could think of. The crown prince, her eldest son, suggested that such measures should be taken as to issue an order for amnesty and to introduce, or rather induce, people to become monks or Taoists. In ancient times, an amnesty was deemed an act of mercy which would call down blessings from Heaven. And to persuade people to become monks or Taoists would please Buddha, who in return would bless the ill person and turn the illness for the better. Nevertheless, the empress did not agree because she thought that an amnesty was a serious national event and should not be used for the sake of personal recovery from illness. And to make people turn to be monks or Taoists was against the voluntary religious principle. So the crown prince had to give up his ideas.

On the twenty-first day of the sixth moon in 636, the empress died. In the eleventh moon, she was buried in her tomb. The tradition for imperial burial was to put many valuable things in the coffin with the body, but the last will of the empress was to exclude such things. She had said, while still alive, that the reason so many graves of nobles and rich people were dug open was because the grave-diggers coveted such things inside. The digging disturbed the rest of the dead. If there was nothing worth digging for, the dead would not be disturbed.

The emperor had quite a few helpful courtiers. Wei Zheng was one of them, actually the most helpful one. Wei Zheng lost his parents in his youth and he lived in poverty. But he loved to read. He had become a Taoist. In the last year of the Sui Dynasty, a vice magistrate of Wuyang (Wu here means Karate and Yang, the Sun) District appointed Wei Zheng as the secretary. When Li Mi's army came, the vice magistrate joined Li's army and took Wei Zheng along with him. Li Mi made him his literary advisor, but he really took charge of the documents, records and all that. When Li Mi failed and joined the Tang army with some of his followers, Wei Zheng was one of them. The emperor Li Yuan did not know that Wei was a capable man and did not give him any official position. Then the crown prince asked Wei to work for him. After the crown prince died, the current emperor Taizong gave Wei a position as a counselor, and gradually promoted him to be a prime minister.

Changsun Wuji (594–659) was the elder brother of Empress Changsun, the brother-in-law of the emperor, and he too was appointed as a prime minister. He was a learned man. When Li Yuan held up his own banner against the Sui Dynasty, Changsun Wuji, as a relative of Li family, went to see Li Yuan, who sent him to work with Prince Qin, his second son. He had followed Prince Qin ever since.

Another prime minister was Fang Xuanling (579–648), who had been a faithful follower for a long time. When he was eighteen years old, he passed the government test of the Sui Dynasty and received an official position. But when Li Yuan rose up against the Sui Dynasty, Fang went to join Prince Qin and became his counselor as well as secretary. Except for the upstanding Wei Zheng, the other courtiers often tried to do or say things just to please the emperor.

Once Empress Changsun heard that Courtier Zheng Renji had a daughter who was beautiful and learned, aged about sixteen or seventeen. No girls in the western part of the city could match her in beauty. She mentioned this to the emperor, who said, "Send someone there to fetch her; I want her to be my concubine." So a eunuch ran to get a messenger. When the messenger was about to leave with the imperial edict from the emperor, Wei Zheng came in. He blocked the messenger's way and said to the emperor, "Your Majesty can't do this. I have been told that the girl has already been engaged to a young man called Lu Shuang. People will criticize Your Majesty if Your Majesty makes her a concubine." The emperor said, "Don't worry. I will find the man another girl for his wife." Wei said, "Your Majesty already has over ten thousand girls in your palace. Why would Your Majesty want a betrothed girl? It's against tradition." The emperor argued, "I'm the emperor. I can do whatever I like." Wei stood firm: "Your Majesty can kill me before doing something immoral." Then Fang Xuanling suggested that His Majesty should summon the young man to his presence to ask him if he was indeed already engaged to the girl. The emperor sent for the young man, who knelt down, shivering all over. Fang Xuanling asked him, in behalf of the emperor, "Tell me, young man, if you are engaged to the daughter of Zheng Renji." The young man stammered, "No...no." When the young man left the palace, the emperor said to Wei, "Did you hear it? There's no such thing as the engagement." Wei retorted, "The people would have to lie about their betrothal. The young man was so frightened. He thought that Your Majesty might find fault with him under some other pretext. How could he tell the truth?" As a result, the emperor gave in.

As the emperor often thought of his deceased wife, he had a tower built so that he stand high above the ground to look at her tomb whenever he was thinking of her. Once he went with Wei Zheng on the tower. He asked Wei if he saw the tomb. Wei pretended to look and said, "Your servant has poor eyesight and can't see it." The emperor said, pointing to the direction of his wife's tomb, "There, in the northwest." Wei said, "Your servant thought Your Majesty wanted your servant to look at the late emperor's tomb (he meant the tomb of the late father of the present emperor). As for the tomb of Her Majesty, your servant always sees it in the heart. Why would he need to climb a tower to look at it?" The emperor thought he had a good point and ordered the tower pulled down.

Although Wei Zheng always criticized the emperor and even interfered with some of the emperor's decisions, the emperor was good enough to appreciate his straightforwardness. According to the record, Wei Zheng criticized the emperor more than two hundred times. When Wei died, Emperor Taizong said, "Using bronze as a mirror, one can straighten his hat and clothes; using history as a mirror, one can know the fall and rise of the dynasties; using another person as a mirror, one can know his own right and wrong. I keep these three mirrors to prevent myself from making mistakes. Now Wei Zheng has died. I lost one of the mirrors."

In the first moon of 638, a new book "Record of Pedigree" was finished. The old record of pedigree did not have the names of all the newly rising courtiers in it. So the emperor ordered a new record of pedigree compiled to reflect the changed conditions of the social classes. The imperial family belonged to the first class. The imperial in-law families were arranged in the second class.

In the second moon of 638, the emperor traveled to Puchow (Pu here means the plant Cattail). The magistrate there wanted people to dress in yellow cloth to welcome the emperor. He also had people's houses decorated and got ready hundreds of sheep and fish to treat all the noblemen accompanying the emperor. The emperor scolded him and said, "When I am traveling, I should be supplied from the local government storage. What you are doing is just what the corrupt emperor of the Sui Dynasty did."

In the third moon, a courtier requested to collect all the articles written by the emperor and to publish them. The emperor did not agree, saying, "All my words or writings, if beneficial to the people and nation, have already been written down in the history record. (In feudal China, everything the emperor said or did would be written down to make part of history.) If it was not beneficial to the people and nation, what's the use to publish it? Some other emperors, like the emperor of the Sui Dynasty, have their books in circulation, but that did not prevent their dynasties from crumbling. An emperor should care about having good policies. Why care about his publications?"

In the first moon of 639, Fang Xuanling had been in the position of a prime minister for fifteen years. His son Fang YiAi married Princess Gaoyang, the daughter of the emperor, and his daughter was married to Prince Han. He thought that he was now at the peak of his career and his family had enjoyed great blessings. A Chinese philosophical concept was that everything, when it reached the apex, would begin to go down the slope. Therefore he handed in his resignation, but the emperor did not accept it.

Wang Gui, the minister of the Etiquette Ministry and Duke of Yan, was a generous person, but was very self-disciplined and thrifty by character. At that time, all the courtiers had family temples built to worship their ancestors. Wang Gui did not build a family temple and worshipped his ancestors in a special room at home. This was deemed indecent and someone in the Judicial Ministry complained to the emperor. The emperor did not make any comment on it, but ordered a family temple built for him at the expense of the government.

In the second moon, a general Weichi (double surname) Jingde (585–658) was appointed governor of Fuchow (Fu here is the name of a town). Before he left, the emperor said to him, "I was told that you had a rebellion in mind. Why?" The general replied, "Your servant followed Your Majesty in the conquest of all the warlords and riotous forces. Your servant went through so many battles and survived with so many wounds on my body. Now there were no more wars anywhere. Why, if I rebel then, in the chaos, would I rebel now in peace?" He took off his clothes and showed his wounds to the emperor, who was greatly touched. The emperor said, "I didn't really suspect you, or I would not have asked the question." (He implied that if he had actually suspected him, the general would have heard about it on the way to prison, not in the palace.)

Weichi had joined the army of another warlord and had defeated the Tang troops. In 620, he was surrounded by the army of Prince Qin, the present Emperor Taizong, who liked him for his bravery in fighting. So after Weichi surrendered to him, Weichi became a faithful follower of Prince Qin and achieved many merits in conquering other warlords such as Dou Jiande and Wang Shichong in attacking Luoyang City.

Li Jing (571–649) was a celebrated strategist and was given a title of Duke of Weiguo in the Sui Dynasty. In the last years of the Sui Dynasty, Emperor Yang sent him to work under Li Yuan to resist the invasions of the Tujue Clan. When Li Yuan rose against the Sui Dynasty, Li Jing disguised himself and went to report to Emperor Yang, but he was hindered in ChangAn City in the crowds. When Li Yuan conquered ChangAn City, he captured Li Jing and wanted to execute him. Right on the execution grounds, Li Jing shouted, "Your Majesty took up arms to bring the country into peace. Has Your Majesty now abandoned that goal, to kill a useful man for personal hatred?" Prince Qin persuaded the emperor to pardon Li Jing and accepted him to be one of his generals. Li Jing helped the Tang government militarily.

In 621, he designed stratagems for the emperor to beat the warlord Xiao Xian. The emperor accepted his stratagems, ordered General Li Xiaogong (591–640) to attack Xiao Xian, and ordered Li Jing to help him. They built warships and trained soldiers to fight on the water. Then Li Xiaogong and Li Jing commanded two thousand warships and brought them down the river. Wen Shihong. Xiao Xian's general, camped at the mouth of the Clear River, which emptied into the Yangtze River. Li Xiaogong went to attack Wen Shihong with part of the Tang army, but was defeated. Wen Shihong let his soldiers pillage the villagers wherever they chased Li Xiaogong. So every soldier was burdened with something as a trophy. Li Jing led his part of the Tang army to assault Wen's soldiers and put them to rout. Li Jing captured four hundred warships that belonged to Wen Shihong. Ten thousand of Wen's soldiers were either slain or drowned. Li Jing let some ships float on the water to confuse Xiao Xian and then marched to beat Xiao Xian's army. Xiao

Xian surrendered. In 627, Li Jing was appointed the minister of the Judicial Ministry and in 629 he was made the head of the Military Ministry.

Emperor Taizong and his late father always paid special attention to the education of the younger generation and to the selection of the government officials as well. In the second moon of 624, the late emperor, the father of the present emperor, had issued an edict that public schools should be set up in villages, towns and cities. Then the late emperor attended the school opening ceremony in the capital and ordered all the children of the princes and courtiers to go there for lessons.

Prior to the Tang Dynasty, the selection of officials was based on the recommendations of courtiers. This method ruled out a wide selection of more talented people to serve the government. The Sui Dynasty had adopted a new system to choose officials. It was to hold government tests so that everyone having such a desire could come to try out and be selected to be officials. But as the Sui Dynasty was short lived, the system had not been carried out long. As a matter of fact, Emperor Taizong was the one who actually gave the government tests as a routine. He said, when he saw so many educated people come for the tests, "Now all the scholars under Heaven fall into my 'trap'."

In 640, the territory of the Tang Dynasty was about 8490 kilometers from north to south and 4755 kilometers from east to west. There were several different ethnic groups to the west and north of the Tang Dynasty. Some of them often trespassed into Tang territory and the Tang government had to counterattack and drive them further west or north. The newly conquered land was put under Tang control. Thus Tang territory was expanded under Emperor Taizong.

To successfully establish a new dynasty from the chaos of the old dynasty, three conditions had to be satisfied. They needed a talented leader or commander; they needed the support of the people and many faithful followers; they needed strong forces and better stratagems. The Li family had all these and so they could conquer all the rivaling parties and form the new dynasty.

In feudal China, fighting between imperial brothers for the throne was a constant event. Whoever got stronger support would win the crown. In our story, the second brother had many wise and brave supporters and had the command of the army. The eldest brother and the third brother had only two concubines to support them, although the concubines were the favorites of the emperor, their father. However, sometimes, even a father cannot make a son listen to him, especially when the son has strong support. That was why Li Yuan had to abdicate and give the throne to his second son.

CHAPTER 2. MISS WU BECOMES AN IMPERIAL CONCUBINE

In 637, the bereaved wife of Wu Shiyue left Wenshui Town in Bingchow with her two daughters for ChangAn City, the capital. She wanted to live with her relatives there, because her two step-sons had treated them badly. When they reached the capital, former colleagues of Wu Shiyue came to visit them and consoled them, expressing their hearty condolences. They all saw that the younger daughter Wu had grown into a young beauty. (The standards of beauty are very different in different times and to different people. In the Tang Dynasty, the typical beauty should be a little chubby, certainly not thin, as can be seen from paintings handed down from that time.)

When Emperor Taizong heard that the young girl was beautiful and accomplished in many ways, he summoned her to the palace to be one of his concubines. At that time she was only thirteen. In the palace of feudal China, imperial concubines had different ranks, too, just like the courtiers; there were eight ranks in all, under the empress, the wife of the emperor. When Wu first entered the palace, she was low in rank. There would be a long way for her to go if she had set her sights on the position of empress.

On the day when the future Empress Wu left her home for the palace, her mother cried bitterly because she was worried about the fate that would be waiting for her daughter and wondered when she could see her daughter again. But her daughter comforted her, saying, "Don't cry, Mother. Maybe, our fortune will turn."

When Emperor Taizong saw her, he was so charmed with her great beauty that he called her Meiniang, Charming Girl. She never had a given name recorded in the history book. Now her full name, Wu Meiniang, given by the emperor, is in Chinese history book. But for convenience we will stick with

Charming Girl Wu. Everyone now called her Charming Girl, the name given by the emperor.

Her assigned duties were to record the activities of other concubines, including their daily activities as well as their productive actions such as silkworm breeding, and report to the emperor. This post was an honor, signifying that the emperor looked upon her as someone of importance since she was the daughter of his favorite courtier. Besides, many concubines were not as learned as she.

Anyway, sometimes, exceptions did happen. In the second moon of 623, Princess Zhao died. She was the daughter of the first emperor of the Tang Dynasty, Li Yuan, and the sister of Prince Qin. That year Li Yuan was still on the throne. At her funeral, her father ordered the drums and trumpets to be played in the funeral procession. When a courtier protested that it was against etiquette rules to play music at the funeral of a female, the emperor said, "Drums and trumpets are military music. Since the princess beat the drum herself for the battles, she was not an ordinary female and deserved the accompaniment of drums and trumpets at her funeral." (Thus, in the Tang Dynasty some rules could be broken under certain circumstances for a female.)

Since Charming Girl Wu was to report to the emperor what other concubines did during the day, she saw him very often. Like every other concubine, she also wanted to show herself off before the emperor. Once the emperor took some concubines, Charming Girl Wu among them, to look at a blood horse that had been sent to him from what the Chinese history book calls Western Area, in the present Xinjiang (meaning New Territory) Autonomous Region. The horse had a name: Lion Steed. It was so huge and wild that no one could tame it. Charming Girl Wu stepped forward and said to the emperor, "I can tame it, but first I need three things: an iron stick, an iron hammer, and a dagger. I will hit it with the iron stick first. If it remains wild, I will hit its head with the iron hammer. If it still can't be tamed, I will cut its throat with the dagger." The emperor praised her for her courage.

Anyway, she did not become Emperor Taizong's favorite or her destiny would have been totally different. It might be that the emperor preferred gentle females and Charming Girl Wu was certainly not the type. She did not bear any child for the emperor and spent more than ten years in the palace without any promotion, while some other concubines moved ahead. But her knowledge was broadened during her tedious life there. She had learned about politics, and about each figure's relationship in the palace and even throughout officialdom. Most of all, she learned from the emperor about how to rule the country well.

The wife of the emperor died early and the emperor did not name any concubine to be the new empress. This was favorable for Charming Girl Wu, because if she did anything improper, no one could punish her except for the emperor himself.

THE SONS VIE FOR THE SUCCESSION

According to tradition the first son should be the successor to the throne, and so was it. But Li Chengqian (619–645), the first son of Emperor Taizong, was a hypocrite. He was small, and lame in one leg. He was ashamed of himself for the lameness. He thought that a crown prince should not have bodily defects. He developed a feeling of self-spitefulness. However, he acted like a gentleman before his father, but led a dissipated life behind his back. Although he had a wife and some concubines, he really did not like women. He was fond of a boy of thirteen who played some musical instrument. He played with the boy in the daytime and slept with him at night. (At that time, and in that place, such preferences were not considered remotely normal.) As a crown prince, he had to learn palace etiquette and how to rule the country, but he preferred the lifestyle of a nomad. He often attired himself as a chieftain of the Tujue Clan, an indigenous people to the north of the Tang Dynasty. He let his men don the uniforms of Tujue warriors and lived in a tent in the back garden of his residence. He and his men often slipped out of the palace to steal sheep or cattle from the common people, and roasted the stolen animals over a campfire. They ate and drank like savages.

A courtier by the name of Yu Zhining, serving the crown prince as a counselor, once advised him not to do such improper things. The crown prince was enraged and sent two assassins to kill him. When the two assassins reached Yu's house, they saw that Yu lived like a common man. They knew that Yu was a good courtier and they forbore to kill him.

Yu Zhining (588–665) had been a courtier in the Sui Dynasty and later had been appointed the mayor of Koushi (Kou here is a surname and Shi here means Surname) Town. When at the end of the Sui Dynasty there were rebellions everywhere, he resigned and took his family and relatives to live in a secluded village. In the eleventh moon of 618 when Li Yuan declared himself the emperor of the Tang Dynasty, Yu Zhining went to see him and was given an official position. Then he worked with Prince Qin. When Prince Qin became the emperor, he was given promotion and was made a counselor to the crown prince.

A crown prince had a high-ranked courtier who was also a great scholar as his tutor. The crown prince did not like to study, and so was often taken to task by the tutor. Once when he said that he did not wish to be emperor or would not be one in the future, and that he loved the life of a nomad, the tutor was really disappointed in and angry with him. He threatened to tell the emperor. The crown prince told his men to beat the tutor and they did, until the emperor was informed of the event and hurried to his rescue. The crown prince and his men had already fled to his residence. The emperor was so disappointed in the crown prince that he had half a mind to depose him from the position. He began to pin his hopes on his second son.

The second son Li Tai (618–652) was a man of ambition, titled Prince Wei. He was able in writing and calligraphy. He organized a group of scholars to put together a book of geography, divided into five hundred fifty volumes. When he learned that the emperor had a preference for him, he started to aspire after the position of crown prince. The two brothers thereafter plotted against each other. The first son felt some danger and wanted to become emperor as soon as possible.

In the first moon of 642, the second son, Prince Wei, finished the geography book with the assistance of his scholars. When he presented the book to the emperor, his father praised him and granted him with ten thousand scrolls of brocade. Then the emperor decided to make this son the crown prince. But a courtier said to the emperor that according to tradition, the crown prince should be designated based on seniority, and besides, the present crown prince had no serious fault that meant he should be deposed.

Since the death of the empress, his mother, the crown prince had made endless demands for almost everything. The record showed that the crown prince requisitioned more than seventy thousand various items in just less than sixty days.

The crown prince's preference for the lifestyle of the Tujue clan of nomads, who lived in tents and ate roast sheep, was deemed a betrayal to the national tradition at that time. Especially in a crown prince this lack of loyalty to one's own kind was a serious defect in his character. Other two counselors assigned to him by the emperor advised him to stop the misconduct. But he would not listen, and on the contrary, he secretly sent someone to assassinate them, but also in vain.

Prince Han, the seventh son of the first emperor Li Yuan and the stepbrother of the present emperor, was also known to do unlawful things and was scolded by Emperor Taizong. He befriended the crown prince. They often divided their men into two groups and fought with each as if in a real conflict. The game caused bleeding or even death. Anyone who disobeyed would get a severe beating. The crown prince once said, "When I become the emperor, if anyone gives me advice, I will kill him. When I kill hundreds of them, until no one dares to advise me anymore."

Prince Wei, the second brother of the crown prince, disdained his brother who was lame in so many senses. So Prince Wei developed an ambition to usurp the position of crown prince. Both brothers wanted to get support among the courtiers. Some of the courtiers spoke ill of Prince Wei before the emperor, while others said that the present crown prince was not suitable to be the successor and only Prince Wei was the right one for it.

The emperor ordered the crown prince's favorite young musician arrested and executed. The crown prince took the body and buried it in his garden, with a gravestone set up with a false official title inscribed on it. When the emperor learned of this, he was indignant. And the crown prince, knowing that his father was angry with him, he avoided meeting his father as often as possible. He thought that it must be his rival brother who had told his father on him. He hated his brother all the more and started planning to kill him.

Helan (double surname) Chushi, the son-in-law of Hou Junji (?–643), who was the chief of the Official Ministry, was working for the crown prince. Hou Junji often went to see the crown prince, too. When the crown prince asked Hou Junji how to avoid further disaster, Hou hinted to him to rebel. If he could usurp the throne from his father, he would be the emperor and no one could do anything against his will anymore.

Hou Junji had been a brave general under Prince Qin, the present Emperor Taizong. He had gone through many battles victoriously. Therefore, in the ninth moon of 626, after Prince Qin had become Emperor Taizong, the emperor granted him with the title of Duke Luguo. In the eleventh moon of 630, he was made the minister of Military Ministry. In 637, his title was changed to Duke of Chengguo. In 638, he was made the minister of Official Ministry. But Hou thought that he was such a brave and talented man, he should have been appointed a prime minister. Once when he had been sent to fight some tribal peoples in the west, he defeated them but took many trophies for himself. And his subordinate generals followed suit. This was deemed embezzlement. He was put into jail. Only when a courtier reasoned with the emperor that Hou's merits could offset this crime was he released. But he was now full of hatred and still thought that he should have been rewarded for the victory he had won. This was the reason that he wanted to instigate the crown prince to rebel. If the crown prince was successful, he would be appointed a prime minister.

Prince Han also suggested to the crown prince to rebel. Tu He, the husband of Princess Chengyang, joined in the conspiracy. All of them bound themselves by a ritual vow. Their plan was that the crown prince would pretend to be ill and when the emperor came to see him, they would kill the emperor.

In the ninth moon of 642, Emperor Taizong asked Wei Zheng to be a counselor to the crown prince in hopes that he could help the crown prince to correct his bad behavior. But Wei refused to accept the assignment. The emperor persisted and he had to accept; however, since he was ill in bed, he could not go to see the crown prince.

In the fourth moon of 643, supported by Prince Han and Hou Junji and others, the crown prince changed his plan and decided to attack Taiji (meaning Extreme Pole) Chamber where the emperor lived. When the emperor learned of the conspiracy, he imprisoned his first son and killed all the others, including Prince Han and the minister Hou Junji. At first the emperor wanted to pardon Prince Han because he was his stepbrother, but at the insistence of some senior courtiers on equality under the law, the emperor had to order Prince Han to end his own life at home.

Once the emperor sent Hou Junji to a famous general, Li Jing, to learn the art of war. But Hou reported to the emperor, "Li Jing is going to rebel." Surprised, the emperor asked what made him think so. The reply was, "Because Li Jing only taught me the general idea of the strategies. He keeps the essence of it as a secret from me. That's why I draw the conclusion." When the emperor asked Li Jing about it, Li answered, "Well, that actually shows that Junji is going to rebel. In this peaceful time, what I teach him is enough to enable him to fight off any invasions. He wants to learn all I know; what else can it mean except that he wants to learn aggressive strategies he can use in a rebellion?"

And once Li Daozong, Prince Jiangxia, had said to the emperor, "Junji has great ambition, but not great wisdom. He feels it is a shame to be under Fang Xuanling and Li Jing. He's not satisfied to be the minister of Official Ministry. In my opinion, he will lead a rebellion." The emperor said, "Don't judge him like that. Don't be so suspicious." Now, as Hou rebelled and was executed, the emperor apologized to Prince Jiangxia and sighed, "Just as you prophesied."

SELECTING THE CROWN PRINCE

The ninth son of Emperor Taizong, Li Zhi (628–683; on the throne 649–683), was born back on the fifteenth day of the sixth moon in 628 when Empress Wu was four years old. He would eventually be the second husband of Empress Wu, despite the four years age difference. In the second moon of 631, Li Zhi gained the title of Prince Jin.

In 643, perceiving an opportunity since his eldest brother was no longer the crown prince, and supported by the courtier Cen Wenben and others, the second son made sure to make a good impression on his father, who then promised to make him the crown prince. Cen Wenben (596–645) was a prudent man. He supported the second son from the standpoint of seniority.

Cen Wenben's father was the mayor of Handan Town. When he was falsely accused of some crime and put in prison, Cen Wenben, at the age of fourteen, came forth to plead for his father. He was so eloquent and reasonable that his father was released as not guilty. When he was asked to write an essay on the "Water Lily", he finished it in no time, on the spot, and was deemed a boy prodigy. When he grew up, the warlord Xiao Xian (583–621) in Jingchow (Bramble District) sent for him, and he worked for Xiao Xian, who was the nephew of Empress Xiao of Emperor Yang of the Sui Dynasty. Xiao Xian was appointed mayor of Lu (a surname here) Town. After the overthrow of the Sui Dynasty, Xiao gathered some men and became a warlord. When the Tang army came to attack, Xiao Xian fought back but was defeated in all the battles. When he was surrounded by the Tang army, Cen Wenben persuaded him to surrender so that no more people would die. Xiao Xian was sent to ChangAn City, the capital of the Tang Dynasty and was killed there. Cen Wenben joined the Tang army and was given various official positions until he was promoted to be a prime minister.

In the eighth moon of 644, when Cen Wenben was made a prime minister, he was sad and afraid. At home, when his mother asked him why, he said, "The higher my position, the heavier my responsibilities. I am not sure I can perform my duties well." When relatives and friends came to congratulate him for the promotion, he said, "You'd better mourn for me, not congratulate me."

His brother Wenzhao loved to entertain friends and host feasts. The emperor did not like this and once said to Wenben, "What your brother's doing may bring you trouble. What if I send him out of the capital to be an official in some other town?" Wenben said, sobbing, "My mother specially loves my brother, who has never stayed away from home for a day. If he is sent somewhere else, my mother will be sad and pine away. So if my brother's sent away, my mother will be gone soon." He cried. The emperor had pity on him and changed his mind. And the brother Wenzhao did not bring any trouble to Wenben all his life.

But Changsun (double surname) Wuji, the brother of the emperor's deceased wife, strongly objected to making the second son the crown prince. He begged the emperor to make his ninth son, Prince Jin, the crown prince.

When the second son heard about that, he threatened the ninth son, saying, "You were a friend of Prince Han. Are you afraid that something will happen to you since he's died?" He implied that if the ninth brother wanted to be safe, he should not vie with him for the position of the crown prince. The ninth son was so fearful that it showed on his face. When the emperor detected it, he insisted on knowing the reason. So the ninth son had to tell his father about the threat. Then the emperor realized that if he made the second son the crown prince, his first son and the ninth son would be in danger whereas if he made the ninth son the crown prince, the first son and the second son would be safe. So the emperor made his final decision to name the ninth son as the crown prince.

To win the support of the chief courtiers, the emperor played a little trick. One day, when he dismissed court, he told Changsun Wuji, Fang Xuanling, Li Ji and Chu Suiliang to stay behind. He said, "I'm disappointed in my cousin Prince Han and my first son." Just finishing the words, he fell back as if in a swoon. The four courtiers were in panic and hurried to help him. When the emperor was assisted to sit up, he drew his sword as if he would kill himself. Chu Suiliang then took the sword from the emperor and handed it to the ninth son, who was present. The four courtiers asked the emperor what was wrong with him. The emperor said, "I want to make Li Zhi the crown prince." The four courtiers had no objection. That day, the second son, Prince Wei, was put in confinement for the safety of the ninth son. Thus, on the seventh day of the fourth moon, the ninth son was announced to be the crown prince.

In the seventh moon, his first son was sent to live in Qianchow (meaning Black District) in confinement, where he died in the twelfth moon of 644. His second son was sent to live in Junchow (meaning Equal District), also in confinement.

From the lesson he had learned through the downfall of his first son, Emperor Taizong seized every chance to educate his ninth son. When they were eating rice, the emperor would say, "If you know how hard it is to grow and reap rice, then you won't lack rice." (This is literally translated from the traditional text so that the readers can know what exactly the emperor said.) When the son was riding a horse, the emperor would say, "If you know how to let the horse work and rest alternately and never use up its energy, you will always have a horse to ride." When he saw his son in a boat, the emperor would say, "Water can float a boat, but can also capsize it. People are like water and the sovereign is like a boat." (This is always quoted in the time to come.) Whenever the emperor held court, he bade his son to stay at his side to learn how he managed state affairs. Besides, the emperor also wrote a book for him, titled "Rules For An Emperor To Follow." He even went so far as to encourage the son to make decisions about important issues.

INTRODUCTION TO THE CROWN PRINCE

Emperor Taizong had a pious belief in Buddhism. In 627, the famous monk Xuanzhuang (602–664) headed off alone to India, where Buddhism originated. He stayed there for more than ten years and studied the Buddhist sutras. He even gave lectures to and had debates with Indian monks. In 643, he set out on the return journey, bringing back 657 copies of Buddhist sutras. In the second moon of 646, the monk Xuanzhuang arrived in ChangAn City to the welcome of the emperor. The monk Xuanzhuang built the five-storied Big Wild Goose Pagoda in the Temple of Big Mercy–Benevolence (the Temple had been ordered to be built in the capital by the crown prince in memory of his mother, the late empress of Emperor Taizong) in ChangAn City (now XiAn City). Travelers can still see the pagoda there nowadays. The monk Xuanzhuang spent more than ten years translating one thousand three hundred and thirty volumes of the sutras from Sanskrit into Chinese. Later these sutras spread to Korea and Japan. He dictated a book about the Asian countries he had journeyed through. (The monk's alleged adventures were described in the world-renowned novel titled "A Journey to West" by Wu ChengEn (1504–1582) in the Ming Dynasty (1368–1644). The hero in that novel is the well-known Monkey King or Golden Monkey.)

In the late years of his life, Emperor Taizong became suspicious of his courtiers. He commanded a prime minister named Liu Ji (?–645) to kill himself at home. Liu was really a learned and upright person. At the end of the Sui Dynasty, Liu Ji worked for Xiao Xian (see above). When he went to work with the Tang government, he was appointed the administrator of the governor's *yamen* or headquarters in Nankangchow (meaning South Health District). During the reign of Emperor Taizong, he was gradually promoted to be a prime minister. In 645 when the emperor left for the Korean war, he let the crown prince take on the administration of the nation and ordered Liu Ji to assist his son. Liu said, "Be at rest, Your Majesty. If any courtier is guilty, he will be executed." As the emperor was ill, Liu said to other courtiers, "His Majesty's illness is so serious. I'm worried." But a courtier named Zhu Suiliang reported to the emperor that Liu said that he would act as the regent to the crown prince when His Majesty died. He would kill anyone who disagreed with him. So the emperor suspected Liu of harboring ambitions for power and ordered him to kill himself by his own hand. (But Zhu Suiliang was also a good courtier. No one could understand why Zhu would say something falsely to the emperor and cause his death. The history book just lists the fact.) After the death of Emperor Taizong, the son of Liu Ji wrote a memorial or memorial to the succeeding emperor to alert him to Zhu Suiliang's false report. The emperor ignored it because Zhu Suiliang was a favorite courtier at that time. Only when Empress Wu was on the throne was the false accusation of Liu Ji cleared.

In the first moon of 643, a secret report came that Liu Lancheng, the governor of Daichow (Dai here means Substitute) was planning a revolt. So Liu Lancheng was executed. General Qiu Xinggong took the liver and heart of the executed governor, cooked and ate them. When the emperor heard of it, he scolded the general. "When Lancheng rebelled, the government has the law to punish him. You didn't need to do such a thing. If doing this was

supposed to be a show of loyalty, the princes should do it before you did."
General Qiu felt ashamed of himself.

In the fifth moon, Emperor Taizong asked Fang Xuanling, "Why did the
historiographers in the previous dynasties never show the historical records
to the emperors?" Fang answered, "Because the historiographers always
wrote down the exact facts, bad or good. If the emperors read the records
of their bad behavior or deeds, they would probably get angry and kill those
historiographers." The emperor said, "I'm different from the previous emperors. I want to read the records to know my earlier mistakes and avoid them
afterwards. You can compile some excerpts and let me read it." Another
courtier said, "Your Majesty does things correctly and records show nothing
bad. It makes no difference whether Your Majesty reads them or not. But if
subsequent emperors are not as clear-minded as Your Majesty, the historiographers cannot elude execution. If they want to avoid danger, they will write
down what the emperors like. Then how can the records be credible?" At the
insistence of the emperor, Fang Xuanling had to choose a period of records,
after some deletion and change, and presented it to the emperor. When the
emperor read the record for the event on the fourth day of the sixth moon
(denoting the event to kill the two brothers of the emperor), he found the
narration was ambiguous. The emperor ordered to write the facts as they
were.

In the second moon of 646, Emperor Taizong was ill in bed and tradition
demanded that the crown prince should come to stay with him and take
care of the medicine and food the emperor needed. The concubines came to
visit the emperor by turns. Charming Girl Wu also came and started to get
to know the crown prince personally. The crown prince was charmed by her
beauty. As Charming Girl Wu had been neglected for so many years, she was
yearning for love. She and the crown prince fell in love with each other at first
sight. Although Charming Girl Wu was the concubine of the father in name
and should not love the son of her husband, and the son should not love the
concubine of his father, yet such things did happen occasionally in Chinese
history. Later, when the son succeeded to the throne, in one of his imperial
edicts he wrote as an explanation of this affair, "When I was still the crown
prince and had the chance to be often at the side of my late father, I behaved
myself and never even glanced at any females there. My father knew it and
praised me, and gave me Charming Girl Wu."

In ancient China, it did happen that a man might give away his concubine to someone else in order to promote their relationship, but there is some
doubt that a father would give his concubine to his son, especially when the
father was an emperor.

In the third moon, the emperor got better. A courtier reported to the emperor that Zhang Liang, the minister of Judicial Ministry, had adopted five hundred sons and that Zhang Liang had once asked a fortune-teller, "I have some dragon scales on my arm. (The ancient Chinese people thought of the emperor as the impersonation of the dragon.) If I want to rebel, is it okay?" So the emperor had Zhang Liang arrested. When Zhang Liang pleaded for himself, the emperor said, "If you don't want to rebel, why do you adopt five hundred sons?" Then he had all the courtiers discuss the case. Almost all the courtiers found Zhang Liang guilty and thought he deserved the death sentence. One courtier by the name of Li Daoyu noted that Zhang had really committed no action of rebellion and did not deserve a death sentence even if he was guilty. But Zhang Liang was executed for treason.

Soon the position of a vice minister in the Judicial Ministry became vacant. The emperor wanted the prime ministers to choose someone to fill it. They nominated some candidates, but none met the requirements of the emperor. Suddenly the emperor said, "I've found someone. When Li Daoyu said that Zhang Liang had really committed no action of rebellion, he was right. Although I didn't listen to him at that time, I have regretted it ever since." Then the emperor had Li Daoyu fill the vacancy.

On the twenty-second day of the twelfth moon, it was the birthday of the emperor. The emperor said to the courtiers, "Today is my birthday. People always enjoy the day in merry-making, but I feel cheerless. As an old poem had it: How distressful are the parents, when it is the hard labor to bear me, and how can we feast on the mother's hard labor day?" Thus speaking, his tears rolled down his cheeks. The courtiers wept, too.

In the first moon of 647, all the minorities in the north and west pledged obedience to the Tang government. The emperor gave their chieftains respectively the titles of governors or magistrates to rule over their own regions. The chieftains prostrated and cheered the emperor.

In the third moon, Emperor Taizong was ill again. He hated the weather in the capital.

In the fourth moon, the emperor ordered to rebuild Emerald Palace on the site of the ruined Taihe Palace on Mount Zhongnan. The Emerald Palace was finished very soon.

In the fifth moon, the emperor went to live in Emerald Palace and let the crown prince handle the national affairs. One day the emperor asked the courtiers why he could make all the minorities obey him while the previous emperors could not do it. The courtiers all said, "Your Majesty's merits are great like Heaven and Earth." The emperor said, "No. I can achieve it because of five things. The previous emperors were generally jealous of those with abilities surpassing their own; but when I see the abilities in others, I deem it as I have them. The previous emperors couldn't see that everyone had only certain abilities, not all the abilities, but I only use the abilities a person has and avoid his shortcomings. The previous emperors, when seeing good men, wanted to favor them, and when seeing bad men, wanted to push them into an abyss; but I, when seeing good men, respect them, and when seeing bad men, pity them. The previous emperors hated upright men and killed them openly or secretly; but since I inherited the throne, so many upright men have been in my court. Since ancient time, other emperors always thought their own race superior and the minorities inferior; but I love the minorities and treat them fairly so that they look upon me as their parent. That's why I achieved the present merit." All the courtiers eulogized the emperor.

In the sixth moon, the emperor appointed Li Wei as the minister of the Household Ministry, which was in charge of the things concerning all the people and their families nationwide. At that time Fang Xuanling, always a faithful follower since the emperor had still been Prince Qin, stayed in the capital to aid the crown prince for the administration. Someone came from the capital. The emperor asked him what Fang had said about the appointment of Li Wei. The answer was that Fang only said that Li had a beautiful beard, which implied that Li was not a man of talent. So the emperor re-appointed him as the magistrate of Luochow (Luo here is the name of a river).

In the first moon of 648, from his experience as a ruler, the emperor wrote a book in twelve chapters, titled "Paragons for the Emperor." He gave it to the crown prince Li Zhi and added, "You must also learn from the examples of some good emperors in the previous dynasties. It is said that if one learns from superior examples, he may only get moderate results; and if one learns from moderate examples, he will get inferior results. (Ancient Chinese people divided everything into three levels: superior, moderate and inferior.) Since I sat on the throne, I have done many improper things, like always having brocade, pearls and jade for decoration, often building palaces and pavilions, obtaining dogs, horses and hawks from distant places, and my travels involving unnecessary supplies. Those are my shortcomings. You can't learn these things from me. As I saved many people and expanded the territory, my merits surpass my demerits. So people are not complaining and the dynasty is still standing. But comparing with the ideal of perfection, I should feel ashamed of myself. You don't have my merits, but will inherit my empire. If you perform your best to do all the good things, you may keep the nation in safety. If you become haughty, lazy and dissipated, you can't even keep yourself safe. A new dynasty is slow to establish but quick to collapse. The throne is difficult to get, but easy to lose. You must be careful, very careful."

In the sixth moon, the emperor married his daughter, Princess Xiangcheng, to the son of a courtier, Xiao Yu. He wanted to build a special residence for her, but the princess demurred, saying, "As a daughter-in-law, I must wait on my parents-in-law day and night. If I live in another residence, how can I perform my filial duties?" Xiao Yu (575–648) received the title of Prince of XinAn at the age of nine. His elder sister was Empress Xiao, the wife of Emperor Yang of the Sui Dynasty. When Li Yuan took ChangAn City, he sent for Xiao Yu and made him the minister of the Etiquette Ministry. Then he was promoted to be a prime minister.

The prime minister Fang Xuanling was seriously ill and sent in a memorial advising the emperor to stop invading Korea unless it entered Tang territory. His son Fang YiAi had married Princess Gaoyang, the daughter of the emperor. When Fang Xuanling died, the emperor shed sorrowful tears.

In the third moon of 649, the illness of the emperor got worse. The crown prince waited on his father at the bedside.

On the twenty-fifth day of the fourth moon, the emperor was moved to live in the Emerald Palace. The crown prince accompanied him there. The emperor said to his son, "General Li Ji (594–669) is a man of talent. As you haven't done any favor to him; he may not serve you faithfully when I am gone. Now I will order him to leave the capital. If he leaves immediately, you can let him return after my death and make him a prime minister. This favor will make him serve you loyally. If he hesitates to go, I will kill him for your future safety."

On the fifteenth day of the fifth moon, Li Ji was accordingly demoted to governor of Diechow (meaning Pile-up District). He left the capital right away and directly from the palace, without even returning to home to bid his family farewell.

On the twenty-sixth day of the fifth moon, Emperor Taizong left this world for Heaven. Before his death he summoned Changsun and Zhu Suiliang, his two trustworthy senior courtiers, to his presence and wanted them to support and help the crown prince in his administration of the country. He said to them, "I entrust my good son and good daughter-in-law to you." Zhu Suiliang (596–658) was a renowned calligrapher. He had been recommended to Emperor Taozong by Wei Zheng for his great skills in calligraphy. Later he became one of the favorite courtiers of Emperor Taizong. As he was so bold as to speak out his opinions without the consideration of offending the emperor or not, Emperor Taizong trusted him and so made him and Changsun the counselors to the crown prince when he was dying.

When the sad news of the death of Emperor Taizong spread nationwide, all the princes staying away from the capital returned to pay their last respect to the deceased emperor. Hundreds of people from all different ethnic groupings staying in the capital wailed hard. Some pricked their faces and ears till they bled, and some cut off their hair; all these done to the customs of their own tribes on such an occasion. Charming Girl Wu was twenty-five that year.

On the first day of the sixth moon, his ninth son, Li Zhi, was crowned as Emperor Gaozong at the age of twenty-two. Emperor Gaozong summoned General Li Ji back to the capital and made him a prime minister. On the twenty-eighth day of the eighth moon, Emperor Taizong was buried in Mausoleum Zhao.

Generally speaking, Emperor Taizong was one of the greatest emperors in Chinese history. He was not only talented militarily and politically, but also was good in character. He was modest and often accepted criticism and corrected his mistakes. His reign was deemed the best one in Chinese history. In subsequent dynasties it was often said that a ruler should learn from the example of Emperor Taizong; but none really tried to attain the aim.

SENT TO A NUNNERY

According to tradition, those concubines of the deceased emperor who had born children would be confined in their own chambers and those who had not borne any children would all go to a nunnery to be nuns. Charming Girl Wu, twenty-five years old that year, was included in the second group, of course.

Compared with living in the palace, life at the Ganye Temple nunnery was tedious and hard. Besides shaving off their hair, nuns must observe ten disciplines: 1) no killing of any living creatures (nuns and monks are all vegetarians); 2) no stealing, no desire for money and luxurious clothes; 3) no marriage, keeping away from males and no sexual thoughts; 4) no gossiping, no name-calling and never being a witness to any crimes (nuns and monks should be indifferent to worldly affairs); 5) no alcohol and no going to a wine house; 6) no eating meat and no riding on a horse or in a coach; 7) no looking at mirrors, no make-up on faces, no loud speaking, no laughing while talking, no playing any musical instruments, no dancing and no looking round while walking; 8) no learning witchcraft, no divining, no idle chatting and no commenting on political affairs; 9) no wearing clothes in the same color as those of males, no sitting together with males and no correspondence with the outside world; 10) no curse words, no speaking ill of anyone, no flirting, no strutting and no crossing legs while sitting.

Generally, a novice nun should get up earlier than the senior nuns and should labor hard. But these newly-arrived nuns could not really be classified as novice nuns. They were widows of the late emperor. So the head nun and senior nuns could not ask them to do anything against their will. Only they should abide by all the disciplines. Charming Girl Wu could not bear to live such a life. She often thought of Emperor Gaozong, but she was not sure when she might see him again, or ever again.

The twenty-sixth day of the fifth moon in 650 was the anniversary of the death of the late emperor. Emperor Gaozong came to the temple nunnery to have a memorial ceremony performed for his father. After the ritual, the emperor went to find Charming Girl Wu, who sobbed without saying anything and the emperor sobbed, too, thinking of the love between them.

Thereafter, Emperor Gaozong came to visit her frequently. As she was now a nun, the emperor would have to find a pretext to get her back into the palace. But at present he did not have anything in mind. Therefore, he had to leave her in the nunnery for the time being.

As the emperor could not always come, she thought of him and wrote a poem about it. The poem goes as follows:

> I look upon red as if it's green when I think of you; (meaning she could not even tell colors apart when she was thinking of the emperor)
>
> I grow languid and bone-thin, missing you.
>
> If you don't believe my tears running down often,
>
> You can open my trunk to check my skirt with pomegranate pattern (meaning that the trace of her tears could be seen on the skirt).

THE NEW EMPEROR REIGNS

In the tenth moon of 649, the new emperor asked Tang Lin, the head judge of the Supreme Court, how many prisoners he had now. The reply was "Over fifty, and two of them were sentenced to death." The emperor was satisfied, because the fewer the prisoners were, the better the rule of the country was. Then he learned that the prisoners under the ex-head judge always complained that they had been falsely accused, but no prisoners made any complaints now. The emperor wondered about that and once asked a prisoner his view; he said that since all the cases were justly judged, the prisoners had no grounds for complaints. The emperor pondered awhile and exclaimed, "That sounds like the way a case should be judged, alright."

Tang Lin had been the vice mayor of Wanquan (meaning Myriad Waterfall) Town in the Sui Dynasty. There were over ten prisoners of minor offense in the yamen. It was a good time for plowing and sowing when it was raining in spring. Tang Lin asked permission of the mayor to let those prisoners out temporarily, but the mayor did not agree. Tang Lin said, "If you are not confident, I will take responsibility for it." So the mayor took a vacation. (When the mayor was away, the vice mayor was responsible for everything in the yamen.) Tang Lin let those prisoners go home for the field work. He had an agreement with them that they would return to the prison before the mayor came back from vacation. The prisoners were grateful and returned in time. Tang Lin became famous for that. He also cleared three thousand prisoners of false charges. Therefore, when he worked for the Tang government, he was promoted to the position of the minister of Judicial Ministry.

He was thrifty and lived a simple life. He could always forgive people for trifling mistakes. Once when he went to attend a funeral, he forgot to bring white clothes with him. White color was traditionally used for mourning in China. So he told his page to go back to fetch him a white gown. The page mistakenly took another gown that was not white. He did not dare to give it to his master. Tang Lin guessed what happened and said that he suddenly felt short of breath and was not fit to cry for the diseased. He did not need the white gown anymore. Another time he had someone boil medical herbs for him, but something went wrong with it. When he learned the situation, he said to the man that since the weather was cloudy, not fine, it was not fit for him to take the medicine. He told the man just to throw it away. These two examples show that he was a man considerate of the awkward conditions of other people rather than the need of his own.

In the twelfth moon, Emperor Gaozong freed Prince Pu, his second brother, from confinement; he died in the eleventh moon of 652.

On the sixth day of the first moon of 650, the new emperor made his wife the empress, née Wang, and so the history book records her as Empress Wang (628–655). Her father was granted the title of Duke of Weiguo, but he died soon. Why didn't the new emperor declare his wife empress first thing after he had been crowned, but postponed it to the next year? By tradition, the coronation of an empress must be done at the beginning of a new year. The grand-aunt of Empress Wang was Princess TongAn, the sister of Li Yuan, the first emperor of the Tang Dynasty. When the second emperor had still been Prince Jin, Princess TongAn had said to Emperor Taizong, the father of the present emperor, that she had a grandniece, who was a nice, gentle, pretty lady. Emperor Taizong asked for the hand of the girl to be the wife of his ninth son, Prince Jin. When Prince Jin was made the crown prince, her father was promoted to be the magistrate of Chenchow (Chen here is a surname).

In the autumn that year, Princess Hengshan, a daughter of the late emperor and a sister of the present emperor, was to be married to someone in Changsun family and the wedding was planned to be held then. However, the courtier Yu Zhining said that rules prohibited a wedding for three years after the death of a parent. So the wedding was put off. Things concerning a parent were always observed to the traditional standards lest people would criticize them as unfilial sons and daughters.

One day the emperor went hunting and was caught by a heavy shower. Although he was clad in oilcloth, it was leaking and he got somewhat wet inside. He asked a courtier beside him, "How can I make the oilcloth stop leaking?" The reply was, "If it were made of tiles, it definitely wouldn't leak." The emperor was pleased at the humorous answer and quit hunting. (Only houses are covered with tiles. The courtier was hinting that the emperor should stay under a roof, not go out hunting.) This event showed that Emperor Gaozong was also ready to accept criticism, like his late father.

On the eleventh day of the first moon in 651, the emperor made Liu Shi, the maternal uncle of Empress Wang, a prime minister.

Prince Teng was the magistrate of Jinchow (meaning Gold District). He was a man of no mercy. At night he often went out of the city to disturb people in the villages. He liked to shoot people at random with his bow and pellets or bury someone in snow for fun. When the emperor was told about his behavior, he wrote to reprimand him, saying, "There are many ways to have fun. As you are my relative, I don't want to enforce law on you. So I just write to you in hopes that you will feel ashamed of yourself."

Prince Teng and Prince Jiang both were fond of accumulating wealth and led a life of self-indulgence. When Emperor Gaozong came to know it, he wrote to reproach them. Once when the emperor gave something to all the princes, he left out these two princes. He told them that as they could make fortune by themselves, he did not need to give them anything. Then he gave them each a cart of hemp cord so that they could put coins on it. (The bronze or brass coins used in the old China had square holes in the middle so that people could put them on a cord.) The two princes were ashamed of themselves.

In the ninth moon, the emperor said to the prime ministers, "I heard that the courtiers bear with one another for wrongdoings. How can they do justice to everything?" Changsun (double surname) Wuji, a prime minister and the maternal uncle of the emperor, said, "I can't say that there're no such thing. But no one dares to twist law on purpose. As for taking some trifling gifts, even Your Majesty can't avoid it." The emperor had nothing more to say as Changsun was his uncle and main supporter.

In the eleventh moon of 652, the emperor issued an edict, "From now on, anyone sending hawks, horses or dogs to the palace will be deemed guilty of a crime." He set foot down, determined not to go hunting anymore.

In the same moon, Princess Gaoyang, daughter of the late emperor, made Fang YiAi, her husband, sue his brother Fang Yizhi for the division of the family property. They were the sons of Fang Xuanling, a prime minister and a favorite courtier of the late emperor. Ever since the death of her father-in-law, she had always been wishing to divide the family property. It had been her idea, but on the contrary she had accused the brother-in-law of putting up the idea. So the brother-in-law had complained to the late emperor, which had caused the princess to lose the favor of her father. The princess was not happy. At that time, a thief had been caught stealing a jade pillow set with precious gems and pearls from the bedroom of a monk. When the monk was asked where he had received the precious jade pillow, he had said that it had been given to him by Princess Gaoyang. This revealed that the princess and the monk had been involved in adultery. The late emperor was infuriated and had executed the monk and confined the princess in her own residence. The princess had begun to hate her father. When her father had died, she had not even shown any sorrow on her face.

The case to divide family property was against the moral tradition of the old Chinese society. So the present emperor demoted Fang YiAi to be the magistrate of Fangchow (meaning House District) and Fang Yizhi to be the magistrate of Xichow (Xi here means Low Damp Place).

Xue Wanche (?-653), after joining the Tang army, had served Li Ji-ancheng, the first son of Li Yuan. When the first son and the third had been killed by the second son in 626, he had led palace guardsmen to attack the second son. Only when he had been shown the head of the first son did he go into hiding in the South Mountain. He came out after Emperor Taizong, the second son, sent someone several times to summon him to the capital. He helped General Li Jing and General Li Ji to fight invaders from the north and west and fought the Koreans, too. To reward his merits, Emperor Taizong married Princess Danyang to him. Princess Danyang was the daughter of Li Yuan, the sister of Emperor Taizong and the aunt of the present emperor Gaozong. Xue was a haughty man and was demoted to be the magistrate of Ningchow (meaning Quiet District) for some wrongdoings. When he was back to the capital, he befriended Fang YiAi. He often complained to YiAi about his demotion. Once he said to YiAi, "If the country gets into a tumult, we must support Prince Jing to be the emperor." Prince Jing was also familiar with YiAi, because his daughter had married YiAi's younger brother Fang Yize. Prince Jing (?-653), the sixth son of emperor Li Yuan, once said that he had a dream in which he took the sun and the moon in his hands, a sign to show that he was entitled to be a future emperor. Chai Lingwu was the son of Chai Shao who had married to Princess Pingyang, a daughter of Li Yuan and the sister of Emperor Taizong. At that time, both of his parents died. He was married to Princess Baling, a daughter of Emperor Taizong and a sister of the present emperor.

Princess Gaoyang tried to drive away her brother-in-law and deprive him of his inherited family title by falsely accusing him of harassing her. There-fore, the brother-in-law accused Princess Gaoyang and his brother of guilt in seeking to divide the family property. Emperor Gaozong let Changsun inter-rogate them, which exposed their plot of treachery. Those who participated in the plot were either executed (Fang YiAn, Xue Wanche and Chai Lingwu, all were sons-in-law of the late emperor Taizong and brothers-in-law of Emperor Gaozong) or forced to commit suicide (Prince Jing, Princess Gaoyang, Princess Danyang and Princess Baling).

Prince Wu was the third son of the late emperor Taizong and was appointed the governor of Anchow (meaning Safety District). His mother was the daughter of Emperor Yang of the Sui Dynasty. Prince Wu was talented like his father, Emperor Taizong, who had once wanted to make him the crown prince, but at the strong opposition of Changsun, Emperor Taizong had had to give up the idea and had made the present emperor the crown prince.

Changsun always looked upon Prince Wu as a future threat to the present emperor, his nephew. Now he seized the opportunity to make Fang YiAn put Prince Wu on the list of his conspirators. Then he reported to the emperor that Prince Wu was likewise involved in the plot. He put Prince Wu into prison and was about to execute him. The emperor was a kind person. He did not want to kill his step-brother. But Changsun had Prince Wu executed without letting the emperor know it. After the execution, he reported to the emperor that he had had to kill his step-brother for his future safety.

The reason behind the revolt was simple: Prince Jing wanted to be the emperor. Fang YiAn and Chai Lingwu had been the friends of Prince Tai, the second son of Emperor Taizong, the brother of the present emperor. If Prince Tai had been made the crown prince and become the emperor by now, they would have had higher positions than now. So both harbored enmity for the present emperor Gaozong. Xue Wanche hated the present emperor for the demotion he thought he did not deserve. Their spouses were involved involuntarily by law. Prince Wu was falsely accused.

In the tenth moon of 654, forty-one thousand people were hired to build the outside walls of ChangAn City to strengthen it so that it could resist any invasion. The work was finished in thirty days. A courtier sent in a memorial, saying, "Emperor Wei of Han Dynasty (206 BC–220) fixed the walls of ChangAn City and soon died. Now the city walls were fixed again. I'm afraid that something serious will happen." Yu Zhining begged the emperor to execute him for cursing the emperor. But Emperor Gaozong said, "Although what he said is like a curse, if I execute him, no one will express his opinions to me anymore." So he pardoned the courtier.

EMPRESS WANG BRINGS WU BACK TO THE PALACE

Empress Wang was the great granddaughter of a high-ranking general of West Wei Dynasty (535–557). Her maternal family had blood ties with the emperor's family. Her grandaunt, Princess TongAn, was a stepsister of Li Yuan, the grandfather of the present emperor. Therefore, Empress Wang had been chosen to be the wife of the present emperor Gaozong. But the emperor did not love the empress because she had been forced on him by his late father. Since she was his wife, he had to crown her as his empress.

Emperor Gaozong had many concubines, including Concubine Xiao. She came from a scholar's family in a southern province. Among all the concubines, the emperor liked her best as she was very pretty. Since Empress Wang did not bear any son for the emperor, and Concubine Xiao had a son and two daughters, Empress Wang felt a threat to her position as the empress.

Her maternal uncle Liu Shi advised her to adopt the eldest son of the emperor since the boy's own mother held low position in the palace and was not even a concubine. The emperor had merely had an affair with her and she had gotten pregnant. Although she bore a son for the emperor, he had never given her any title. Such things happened in the palace of old China.

If the emperor could make that foster son the crown prince, her position as empress would never be shaken by any other concubines. Concubine Xiao also begged the emperor to make her son the crown prince. But the emperor did not agree to the request of either of them. Empress Wang felt all the more urgent to have her foster son officially announced to be the crown prince. Therefore, she put her idea through her mother to her uncle, a prime minister, who befriended other prime ministers. Next day they suggested to the emperor that it was time for His Majesty to decide on who would be the crown prince. In feudal China, the successor to the throne was chosen by this order: first consideration would be given to the son of the empress and if the empress had no sons, then the eldest son would be the next. Although that was the tradition, yet the emperor had the final say in deciding which of his sons should be the crown prince. If Concubine Xiao's son could be made the crown prince, she would be the empress dowager when her son became the emperor after the death of the present emperor. But the courtiers wrote a memorial to the emperor suggesting that his eldest son should be made the crown prince.

On the second day of the seventh moon, at the insistence of the senior courtiers, the emperor had to make his eldest son the crown prince. So the hope of Concubine Xiao was shattered. She hated Empress Wang all the more and spoke ill of the empress to the emperor when they lay in bed side by side at night. Pillow whispers are always effective.

Charming Girl Wu knew that it would be very difficult to get back to the palace though the emperor came to see her whenever he had the chance to steal out of the palace. They even had sexual relations when they met in her room in the nunnery. Before long, something happened that changed her fortune.

At the beginning of the winter, Charming Girl Wu gave birth to a boy, another son of Emperor Gaozong, named Li Hong (652-675). This was an important event to the imperial family. At the same time another event took place. The conflict between Empress Wang and Concubine Xiao was coming to a head as they vied for the preference of the emperor.

In the spring of 653, the strained relationship between Empress Wang and Concubine Xiao reached its climax. Empress Wang spoke ill of Concubine Xiao to the emperor whenever she had the chance, but the emperor would not listen to her. Then she thought of Charming Girl Wu. She knew that the emperor loved Charming Girl Wu very much. If she could get Charming Girl Wu back to the palace, the emperor would give his preference to Charming Girl Wu and Concubine Xiao would be alienated. So she sent a messenger to the nunnery to tell Charming Girl Wu to let her hair grow back in.

On the twenty-sixth day of the fifth moon, it was the fourth anniversary of the death of the late emperor. Emperor Gaozong went to the nunnery to have some kind of memorial service. When he met Charming Girl Wu, she wept bitterly. He promised to get her back to the palace as soon as possible. The chance came even sooner. One day Empress Wang told the emperor her idea of getting Charming Girl Wu back to the palace. The emperor was glad to seize the opportunity and sent a carriage to bring Charming Girl Wu back. Charming Girl Wu was delighted to leave the nunnery at last after four years of de facto captivity there. When she was back in the palace, she was promoted to the second rank among the concubines because she had borne a son to the emperor. So she became Concubine Wu.

Not long after Concubine Wu came back, her son Li Hong was made Prince Dai, which strengthened her position in the palace. But she was all the more polite and amiable to everyone, and particularly showed her homage and obedience to the empress, who liked Concubine Wu very much and thought that she had made a right decision. She often threw in a few good words for her to the emperor, which was really unnecessary, but was welcome just the same.

EMPRESS WANG AND CONCUBINE XIAO UNITE AGAINST CONCUBINE WU

Once Concubine Wu had returned, the emperor began to withdraw from Concubine Xiao. Empress Wang was happy for that. But if she could have foreseen the turns of the events, she would never have made such a decision.

Although Concubine Xiao lost the emperor's favor, the next one he turned to with his love was not the empress herself but Concubine Wu. Then she understood how foolish she had been. She had driven out a wolf but brought in a tiger, as a Chinese saying goes. Out of jealousy, she began to hate Concubine Wu, which was another mistake for her. She should not have made an enemy, a terrible enemy, of Concubine Wu. If she had always been nice to Concubine Wu and never made her feel her life was in danger, Concubine Wu might not have sought every possible means to have Empress Wang deposed.

Concubine Xiao did not know that it was Empress Wang's notion to get Concubine Wu back in order to set her aside. She only knew that Concubine Wu did come back and that as a result the emperor was ignoring her. She was surprised that Concubine Wu could so easily occupy her former position as a favorite with the emperor, and so she began to abhor Concubine Wu, too.

Now Empress Wang and Concubine Xiao had to form a union to deal with Concubine Wu. They set their minds to getting rid of Concubine Wu, who was now like a thorn in their flesh. Concubine Wu could guess what they were planning against her. From the general situation in the palace, she knew that she could not give any ground; it would only make her own life miserable. She had to fight to win the victory. She began to give money generously to eunuchs and palace maids, who liked her better and would report to her whatever they knew that happened in the palace.

This was not merely a matter of jealousy and contention for the favor of the emperor among the three women. This situation involved almost all the courtiers, because each of them had her own supporters among the courtiers and each of them represented benefits of some of the courtiers. And each of them had her advantages and disadvantages.

Empress Wang was the wife of the emperor and had many established senior courtiers at her back. But the emperor did not even like her and she had not borne him any children. Besides, she was arrogant and treated the eunuchs and maids so badly that they disliked her.

Concubine Xiao was so pretty that the emperor had preferred her. They should still have had some feelings towards each other. Besides, she had borne a son and two daughters for the emperor. But she had few supporters either among the courtiers or among the eunuchs and maids in the palace.

Concubine Wu was beautiful and clever, and deeply loved by the emperor, for whom she had already borne a son by this time. She had some supporters among the courtiers and as she treated the eunuchs and maids well, she had their support, too. Some of them served as her spies on Empress Wang and Concubine Xiao. Only she had been a concubine of the late emperor — and the senior courtiers opposed her for that reason.

Empress Wang and Concubine Xiao were hateful of Concubine Wu and often said nasty things about her to the emperor, but he could not see any truth in them, because Concubine Wu behaved very carefully. When Concubine Wu heard any information about any improper conduct on the part of the two women, through her spies, and told it to the emperor, he believed it because the tips were always true. So the emperor had half a mind to remove Empress Wang from her present position, which Concubine Wu was aiming at, but he had not made up his mind yet. Concubine Wu was aware that if the emperor died before her (since his health was not good), Empress Wang would certainly treat her very badly or even have her killed. For her own security, she had to do something to have the empress deposed from her position and herself to occupy it.

The emperor was not happy as the empress and the other concubines were jealous of Concubine Wu and their relationship was a little tense. One evening when he was in Concubine Wu's chamber, he summoned the empress and all other concubines there to have a dinner party in hopes that he could persuade them to be nice to Concubine Wu. When Concubine Wu proposed a toast to everybody's health, no one lifted her cup. Then the emperor asked the empress to drink first. The empress could not refuse the demand of the emperor and lifted her cup. The other concubines followed suit. At the end of the party the concubines begged the emperor to divide his evening time equally among the concubines. The emperor promised, but he never kept his promise, because he was so fond of Concubine Wu and always listened to her.

Concubine Wu Fights Back

In the sixth moon of 654, Concubine Wu hinted to Dugu (double surname) Ji, the head eunuch of the emperor, to go to see Liu Shi, the uncle of Empress Wang, and to advise him to resign from the position of a prime minister. Dugu went and gave Liu the advice. He added to Liu that it was the idea of the emperor. The emperor did not want to remove him openly, and rather than lose face it would be better for him to resign. Since Empress Wang, his niece, had lost the favor of the emperor, Liu felt that the emperor had become a little cold to him. So he took the advice of the head eunuch and handed in his resignation to the emperor next day. The emperor accepted his resignation and appointed him the minister of the Official Ministry.

On the seventeenth day of the twelfth moon, the emperor started on a trip to visit the grave of his late father. He took Concubine Wu with him and she gave birth to her second son on the way; he was named Li Xian (Xian here means Sage.)

Concubine Wu knew that if she wanted Empress Wang to be deposed she must take some drastic steps. When she gave birth to a girl, the emperor loved it like the apple of his eye. As the empress did not have any children of her own, she liked it, too, or maybe gave that appearance just to please the emperor. One day, Empress Wang came alone to see the baby, just a couple of months old. At that particular moment, no one was in the baby's room. When Empress Wang left, Concubine Wu came back and learned that the empress had come to see the baby. She went in and strangled the baby to death, and covered it with the quilt as if nothing had happened. (This was only one version of the story. Another version holds that the empress asked a witch to use witchcraft on Concubine Wu to claim her life, which was very much against the palace rules and which was stated in later paragraphs of the traditional history. There was also a third version.)

After a while the emperor came and Concubine Wu stepped forth to meet him with a smile. By habit, he went into the baby's room. Once inside, Concubine Wu pulled aside the quilt and was about to pick up the baby as usual. Suddenly she cried out, as if she did not know what to do. The emperor was shocked. When he learned that the baby was dead, he fell into a great wrath. He wanted to know how such a thing could happen and then was told that Empress Wang had been in to visit a while ago. He cried, "It must be she who did it." Taking this chance Concubine Wu hinted that the empress was not qualified to hold her position any longer.

After the death of her daughter, Concubine Wu would no longer live in this chamber. So she moved to the Longevity Chamber (every chamber in the palace had a special name), where the emperor lived. (In ancient China the emperor had a chamber of his own. If he wanted to sleep with any concubine on a certain night, he would go to her chamber. He could also sleep alone in his own chamber.) The emperor allowed Concubine Wu to always live with him.

The Courtiers Take Sides

All the courtiers divided into those who were for and those who were against the removal of Empress Wang from her position. It was obvious that Concubine Wu would fill the vacancy when Empress Wang was deposed. Those who opposed the change were the old courtiers including prime ministers as Changsun Wuji, the maternal uncle of the emperor, Zhu Suiliang, a famous calligrapher, Liu Shi, uncle of Empress Wang, etc. They all came from noble families. Those in favor were those coming from common families. They were Li Ji, Xu Jingzong, Li Yifu, etc.

Li Ji (594–669) had been in a rebellious army against the Sui Dynasty. After the Sui Dynasty was overthrown, he had joined the troops of the Dynasty and received a series of promotions until he attained a duke's title. As he had not been an original follower of the late emperor, the late emperor had not trusted in him.

When the late emperor had been seriously ill in the fourth moon of 649, he had told his son, the present emperor, "Li Ji is a man of great talent. You may not be able to control him as you have not shown any favor to him. I will demote him now and send him to a remote place. If he leaves right away, you can summon him back and promote him to be a prime minister after my death. For this favor, he will become your faithful follower. If he hesitates to go, I will execute him so as to get rid of a potential threat to you." Thus, on the fifteenth day of the fifth moon in 649, Li Ji had been demoted without any fault on his part to be the governor of Diechow (Die here means Pile-up) in the present Gansu (meaning Sweet Respect) Province, about a thousand miles away from the capital. He had guessed what the late emperor Taizong had been thinking. Therefore, he had set out immediately when he had received the order from Emperor Taizong. Accordingly the present emperor had sent for him to the capital and promoted him to the position of a prime minister. But since Changsun Wuji and other prime ministers stayed in power so long, he had only the empty title. He was of course on the opposite side against them. Naturally he supported Concubine Wu.

Xu Jingzong (592–672) came from an official's family originally living in Hangchow (name of a city, where the famous West Lake is located). His father had been the vice minister of the Etiquette Ministry in the Sui Dynasty. He was a learned man and when he had passed the government tests in the Sui Dynasty, he had become a mid-rank official. When the powerful general Yuwen (double surname) Huaji had killed his father, he had wanted to kill him, too. Xu Jingzong begged hard on his knees to spare his life. So General Yuwen had spared him. For that he had been deemed a coward and despised on ever since. When once General Yuwen had been defeated in a battle by a rebellious peasant army, Xu had escaped in the chaos to join the largest peasant army, called Wagang Army. When the Tang army conquered others, Xu had joined the Tang army. He was thought to belong to the eighteen scholars serving the late emperor when the late emperor had still been Prince Qin. When Prince Qin had become the emperor, Xu had been given the task in 634 to write the history books with some other scholars. In 636 when the empress of Emperor Taizong had died, Xu had once joked with another courtier, saying that he looked like a monkey. He had chosen the wrong time and wrong place to make the joke. It was a violation of the etiquette rules and he had been demoted to be an official under the governor of Hongchow (meaning Flood District). Later he had bribed someone to throw in some good words for him to the emperor. He had been summoned back to the capital. In 645 when Emperor Taizong had gone to fight Korea, he had been ordered to write an imperial edict for the emperor. He had written it on the saddle of the horse for more than thousand words. The emperor had greatly appreciated his beautiful wording. It had become a popular story ever since. When the present emperor succeeded to the throne, he was appointed the minister of the Etiquette Ministry. In 650, since a tribal chieftain had offered him many precious things as a wedding deposit. (It was the tradition in ancient China that when anyone wanted to have the hand of someone else's daughter for himself or his son, he must send a matchmaker with a wedding deposit, which was generally silver, gold, scrolls of silk and brocade, and other precious things.) As Xu coveted riches, he had assented to the request of marriage. But other courtiers thought that it was inappropriate for a courtier to marry his daughter to a chieftain's son, and so did the emperor. And furthermore, as he had accepted bribes, he had been demoted to be a magistrate in the city of Zhengchow (Zheng is a surname). Two years later he was back to the capital through bribery. No doubt, these senior courtiers looked down upon him. So he would of course stand on the side of Concubine Wu.

Li Yifu (614–666) was born in Raoyang (Rao here means Abundance and Yang here means the Sun) Town in the present Hebei (meaning River North, to the north of the Yellow River) Province. His grandfather had been the deputy mayor of Shehong (meaning Shooting Flood) Town in Zichow (Zi here is the name of a tree) in the present Sichuan Province. Li grew up there. When he was still young, he had already a reputation for literary talent. At the age of twenty-one, he had been recommended to take part in government tests. He had passed the tests and received an official position. Since the death of the late emperor, he had not been promoted though he had used every possible means such as bribery and flattery, for which he had been scorned by those upright old courtiers like Changsun. Therefore, he had a fear that Changsun would demote him and send him to a remote place. He would naturally side with Concubine Wu.

The real reason for the opposition to the removal of Empress Wang was that they were sure that the emperor would make Concubine Wu the new empress, and then their interests would be greatly affected. But the reason they stated to the emperor was that Concubine Wu had been a concubine of the late emperor. Therefore, she was not fit to be the empress of the present emperor.

The supporters of Concubine Wu wanted her to be the empress because they wanted to redistribute the power since they had been kept out of the center that actually controlled the political power. They figured that as the emperor loved Concubine Wu so deeply, when she became empress she would use her influence with the emperor to bring them into the power center.

The event developed like this. At the beginning of 655, the emperor and Concubine Wu thought that Uncle Changsun would be the decisive factor. If he agreed to remove Empress Wang, the major obstacle would be cleared. So they went to visit him in his residence. They brought him a cartful of things made of gold and silver for family use and ten cartfuls of silk and brocade; moreover, the emperor promoted his son, in order to see what his reaction was. When it seemed that Uncle Changsun was delighted, the emperor said with a sigh, "I am sorry to say that the empress has not borne me a son." He hinted that Empress Wang should be removed. In any family, even a peasant family, if the wife did not have a son to carry on the family name and estate, the husband could divorce her just for that reason.

Uncle Changsun understood what the emperor meant, but he intentionally ignored him and digressed from what the emperor expected him to say. The emperor and Concubine Wu felt frustrated and went back to the palace. However, they still hoped to persuade him.

Concubine Wu's mother, Lady Wu, had known Uncle Changsun when they both were younger because her husband and Changsun had worked together. She came to visit her daughter and lodged in the palace. When she learned of the situation, she offered to go to see Uncle Changsun and try to persuade him. However, though Uncle Changsun was kind and polite to her, he declined her request and sent her away with her cartful of gifts. Then she went to see Xu Jingzong, whom she had also known years ago, as planned with her daughter before she left the palace. She gave the cartful of presents to Xu and asked him to try to make Changsun listen to him. Accordingly, Xu went to see Changsun, but received a flat refusal.

Emperor Gaozong resented the obstinacy of Uncle Changsun, but as he was his maternal uncle and had many supporters and followers, the emperor had to put up with him. Concubine Wu, nevertheless, kept out her antennae and was waiting for a chance.

Empress Wang and Her Supporters Take a Mis-Step

Empress Wang was envious and indignant with Concubine Wu, who was occupying the sole attention of the emperor. Now the emperor spent every night with Concubine Wu. He treated the empress and the other concubines as if they were nonexistent. As a legend has it, one day in the sixth moon, a wonderful idea struck Empress Wang (at least she thought it a wonderful idea) to get rid of Concubine Wu. She told her mother, who often visited her, to find someone who could exercise a special black art. Her mother went to a temple to worship Buddha. Since she had donated a great deal of money to the temple, the head monk always treated her with a rich dinner of vegetables. At dinner, she asked the head monk if he knew some sorcerer or sorceress. So he recommended to her a sorceress who lived behind the temple. She made a cloth doll and wrote on it the name of Concubine Wu and her birthday. Then she put some needles into it, in the heart and in the head, and chanted some magic words. This was to create a curse that would make Concubine Wu die from headache and heartache. No trace of murder could be found on the body. The mother took the cloth doll into the palace and gave it to the empress, telling her to chant the magic words every day at the doll.

Concubine Wu had a spy working even in the chamber of Empress Wang. Her eunuch saw the empress often going into a special room where the empress stored the cloth doll. He reported it to Concubine Wu, who told it to the emperor, saying, "This is a great crime of the empress, to curse the emperor, a crime deserving death." The emperor flared up and sent his eunuchs to search the chamber of the empress and they found the cloth doll. Though it was not the emperor's name on it, still it was a violation of the palace rules. So he gave orders to forbid the empress to leave her chamber and her mother to enter the palace again.

On the tenth day of the seventh moon, the emperor demoted Liu Shi, the uncle of the empress, from the position of the minister of Official Ministry to be the magistrate of Suichow (meaning Favorable District).

The emperor was all the more determined to get rid of Empress Wang and make Concubine Wu the empress. Uncle Changsun and his fellow supporters of Empress Wang saw the signs and wanted to take the initiative. They wanted to send Li Yifu, one of Concubine Wu's supporters, to a remote place to be a low-ranking official. However, before they could do anything, Li Yifu got wind of their plans and hastened to his best friend Wang Dejian, nephew of Xu Jingzong, for advice. Wang said, "His Majesty wants to make Concubine Wu the empress. That's for sure. His Majesty hesitates only for fear of the opposition of those senior courtiers. If you can openly state to the emperor that His Majesty should make Concubine Wu his empress, you will be in the favor of Concubine Wu and get a promotion in no time."

He nodded. Next day, He sent in a memorial to the emperor indicating that the present empress should be removed and Concubine Wu should be made empress. The emperor was pleased with him and granted him a bushel of pearls. Soon he received a promotion.

In the eighth moon, a courtier Pei Xingjian was demoted to be an official under the governor of Xichow (meaning West District) because he had made some remarks critical of Concubine Wu. Someone who had overheard it told Xu Jingzong, who reported it to Concubine Wu.

Empress Wang and the Crown Prince are Removed

On the first day of the ninth moon in 655, Xu Jingzong was restored to the position of the minister of the Etiquette Ministry. One day after the levee, the emperor summoned four courtiers to his personal office. They were Uncle Changsun, Li Ji, Zhu Suiliang and Yu Zhining (588–665), who was now a prime minister and the duke of YanGuo (Yan is the name of an ancient kingdom in China as well as a surname, and also can mean a swallow; Guo here means country). They all knew the reason for this reception. Everyone was thinking how he would reply to the emperor. Li Ji did not want to have any dispute with the other three. Therefore, he told them that he was suddenly not feeling well and went home.

The emperor received the three courtiers and said to Uncle Changsun, "As Empress Wang has no children and Concubine Wu has sons, it is reasonable for me to consider removing Empress Wang from her position and making Concubine Wu the succeeding empress. What do you think?"

Uncle Changsun astutely sidestepped, observing to the emperor that "The late emperor appointed Zhu Suiliang as Your Majesty's advisor. Your Majesty can ask his opinion."

Zhu Suiliang, without waiting for the emperor to ask him, said, "Empress Wang came from a noble family and the late emperor said that he had a good daughter-in-law. On his death bed, he held Your Majesty's hand and said to me, 'Now I trust my son and the daughter-in-law in your hands to help them in need.' I hope that Your Majesty still remembers it. Now, Empress Wang hasn't done anything wrong; how can she be removed? I can't agree with Your Majesty and betray the trust of the late emperor."

The emperor was unhappy, but once his late father had been invoked, he could not say anything more. He told them to think the matter over at home. The three courtiers left the palace.

Next day when the emperor summoned them into his presence again. Yu Zhining did not want to offend the emperor, but he did not want to agree with him either, and so he kept his mouth shut. Uncle Changsun was silent. Seeing this, Zhu Suiliang had to step forward, saying sternly, "If Your Majesty is determined to abolish the present empress and needs another one, there are so many other concubines from noble families. Why must Your Majesty want to make Concubine Wu the new empress? Everyone knows that she was a concubine of the late emperor. If she is made the empress, what will people think of Your Majesty? I know I'm guilty of opposing Your Majesty's will. I'm willing to die rather than betray the trust of the late emperor." Thus speaking, he took off his official cap, went down on his knees and knocked his forehead on the ground till it bled. (This was the way that a courtier in ancient China would attempt to force the emperor to accept his idea, but it was not always successful.) The emperor was incensed and ordered his bodyguards to drive Zhu out of the palace. Concubine Wu was sitting behind a screen listening to them. Now, from behind the screen, she shouted, "Why not kill that animal?" (That's a literal translation.) But the emperor gave no order to kill Zhu. Then another courtier, Han Yuan ran in, gasping. He asked, "Does Your Majesty order Zhu executed?" The emperor replied, "No. I have not given such an order." Han said, "Zhu is loyal to Your Majesty. He is right. Your Majesty can't depose Empress Wang and make Concubine

Wu the empress." Luckily for him, Concubine Wu had already left for her chamber. The emperor would not listen to him and sent him away.

Wu Becomes Empress

As there was such strong opposition from the older courtiers, the emperor was frustrated. Then he suddenly thought of Li Ji and secretly went to his residence. The emperor asked Li for his opinion. Li was dissatisfied with Uncle Changsun's clique and was really on Concubine Wu's side, but he was too wise a man to speak his idea openly. So he said, "This is Your Majesty's family matter, why ask the opinion of outsiders? Do the courtiers come to ask Your Majesty's opinion when they want to take someone to wife?"

What he meant was apparent. As it was the emperor's family matter, the emperor could make any decision about it he wanted, and no need to ask the courtiers for their opinions. Now the emperor took action. He demoted Zhu Suiliang and sent him out of the capital to be the governor of Tanchow (meaning Pond District), the present Changsha (meaning Long Sand) City in Hunan (Lake South) Province in the middle of China.

On the thirteenth day of the tenth moon, the emperor issued an imperial edict, stating:

> As Empress Wang and Concubine Xiao have attempted to poison me, they must be deprived of their titles and put in confinement. Their mother and brothers must be banished to the remote southern region.

The poisoning event went like this: As the emperor had been ignoring Empress Wang and Concubine Xiao and staying every night with Concubine Wu, Empress Wang and Concubine Xiao sent a jug of wine to the emperor one evening at dinner time. When the emperor was about to raise the cup to his lips, Concubine Wu stopped him and poured the cup of wine on the ground. The spot on the ground that the wine touched turned black, which meant that the wine contained poison. Thus the emperor had evidence that they intended to poison him.

Another version suggests that it was Concubine Wu who prepared the wine with the poison in it and had someone working for Empress Wang bring in the jug, making Empress Wang and Concubine Xiao look as if they wanted to poison the emperor. Either way, Empress Wang was deposed as empress.

Concubine Wu summoned Xu Jingzong to her presence and asked him to write a petition and gather signatures, as many as possible. In the petition they would beg the emperor to make Concubine Wu as the new empress. So Xu and other supporters went round to collect signatures on the petition. As the situation was so evident that the emperor abolished Empress Wang from the position and was determined to make Concubine Wu his new empress, many courtiers went along and signed their names on the petition.

On the nineteenth day of the tenth moon when the petition was handed in to the emperor, the emperor was glad that so many courtiers supported his idea. Then another imperial edict was issued, stating:

> Wu's family had great merits in the establishment of the Tang Dynasty. Concubine Wu herself had been chosen into the palace for her talents. After I was made the crown prince, I waited on the late emperor by his sick bed day and night. He appreciated my good conduct and gave me Concubine Wu as a reward. Therefore, I make her my empress now.

According to tradition in ancient China, a man could give any of his concubines (but not his wife) to anyone he wanted to as a gift. But a father giving his concubine to his son seldom happened — if ever.

After the imperial edict had been declared nationwide, on the first day of the eleventh moon, a solemn ceremony of crowning the new empress took place. Concubine Wu was sent to her mother's house beforehand. Then Li Ji was sent there as wedding envoy and Yu Zhining as deputy wedding envoy, followed by many carriers of wedding presents.

On entering the house, a eunuch carrying a tray with an imperial wedding certificate and the seal of the empress on it put the tray on the table. Some palace ladies went into Wu's room and attired her as an imperial bride. When they were finished, she came out accompanied by the ladies to receive the certificate and the seal, on her knees. In Chinese tradition these two things were more important than the crown. Then she took her seat and all the others kowtowed to her as congratulations.

Li Ji and Yu Zhining returned to the palace to report to the emperor that they had completed their errand. Then Empress Wu was carried in an imperial palanquin into the palace, escorted by an honor guard. Once in the palace again, she was led into the wedding chamber, waiting for the emperor to come in to spend the first honeymoon night with her. She became empress at last, at the age of thirty-one.

On the twenty-first day of the tenth moon, just three days after her wedding day, she wrote a memorial to the emperor to request he praise Han Yuan and Lai Ji, both of whom had opposed her becoming empress.

Although already empress, Empress Wu still felt some threat to her position as long as the ex-empress was still alive and those old courtiers, supporters of the original empress, still stayed in power. Now she had to do something to shore up her position. The chance came before long.

In the eleventh moon, the emperor gave some thought to the ex-empress Wang and ex-concubine Xiao, who were now in confinement. He went to see them. The ex-empress Wang begged his pardon and ex-concubine Xiao scolded Empress Wu for their confinement. Both implored the emperor to set them free. They would be willing to serve as palace maids to be near him. The emperor said that he would think it over and then left.

Empress Wu learned of this and asked the emperor to kill them. As the emperor so doted on her, he was at last persuaded to give an order that the ex-empress Wang and ex-concubine Xiao should hang themselves.

On the twenty-seventh day of the same moon, when both the women died, Empress Wu felt only half relieved. She heard that before ex-concubine Xiao hanged herself, she cried, "In the next life, I wish I may become a cat and Wu become a mouse. I will bite her head off."

The next issue was about the crown prince, the foster son of the ex-empress Wang, who had been made the successor to the throne at the request of those old courtiers. Empress Wu was afraid that if he should become emperor some day, he would have killed her out of vengeance for the ex-empress. Now as she was the empress and had her own sons, according to tradition, her eldest son should be the crown prince, which would help to strengthen her position. She waited for another chance to complete her wish.

Xu Jingzong, one of her chief supporters, also thought that now Concubine Wu had become Empress Wu, her son should be the crown prince. He knew that the emperor would like to please his new empress. Therefore, he wrote a memorial to the throne to request the replacement of the crown prince since the present crown prince had been born to a mother who was not even an imperial concubine.

The emperor was glad to receive such a memorial. He sent for Xu and asked, "What about making the eldest son of Empress Wu, Li Hong, the crown prince?" Xu readily agreed. This time Uncle Changsun and his clique did not say anything in opposition.

On the sixth day of the first moon in 656, the crown prince was deposed and sent to Liangchow (Liang here is a surname) as the magistrate there; hence, his former title Prince Chen was changed to Prince Liang. Li Hong, the eldest son of Empress Wu, four years old then, was made the crown prince. He had been born in 652 in the nunnery when Empress Wu was still a nun there. Soon after the birth of the son, Empress Wu had been brought back to the palace and next year the son was made Prince Dai.

If she had not met Emperor Gaozong when was still the crown prince, or if she had met Emperor Gaozong and he had not fallen in love with her, she would have remained a nun for the rest of her life. What can we conclude from this? Was it fate or something more? She did meet Emperor Gaozong and he did fall in love with her. However, if she had not been so clever and known how to use a variety of ploys to deal with Empress Wang, she might have remained a concubine or even been killed by Empress Wang. But she knew how to get support, from the emperor and courtiers to the eunuchs and maids, and knew how to seize opportunities and take decisive measures. That was why she succeeded and the ex-empress Wang failed.

CHAPTER 3. FROM EMPRESS TO EMPRESS DOWAGER

ADVANCING SUPPORTERS AND ANNIHILATING OPPONENTS

The supporters of Empress Wu were not quickly promoted because those older courtiers still held the center of power. Only Zhu Suiliang had been demoted and sent to a remote place. Since there were no vacancies among the important official positions, how could the supporters be promoted? So the next task was to get rid of those old courtiers. As long as they were still in power, they could yet be a threat to Empress Wu.

On the nineteenth day of the first moon in 656, Yu Zhining was appointed tutor to the crown prince, and Han Yuan, Lai Ji (both were friends of Uncle Changsun) and Xu Jingzong, were appointed as counselors of the crown prince.

On the seventeenth day of the second moon, Wu Shiyue, the late father of Empress Wu, was endowed with an honorary posthumous title of Duke of Zhouguo.

On the twelfth day of the ninth moon, Empress Wu presented to the emperor as an official document a book entitled "Commandments for the Imperial In-Laws," which she had written herself.

On the fifth day of the eleventh moon, Empress Wu begot her third son in the capital ChangAn City. He was named Li Xian (Xian here means Show, pronounced in the third tone, distinguishing it from other "Xians").

In the twelfth moon, a courtier, Han Yuan, handed in a memorial to the throne saying essentially that the imperial edict to demote Zhu Suiliang to be the governor of Tanchow was improper because Zhu had done nothing wrong and he should be pardoned. The underlying meaning was that Zhu should be summoned back to the capital and restored to his former position. After reading the memorial, the emperor said to Han, "I knew him. He offended me and deserved the punishment. You seem to think I was wrong. How can you think so?"

Han pleaded, "Zhu is a loyal courtier. I, Your Majesty's humble servant, am afraid that it was because some evil courtiers spoke ill of him." He implied that Zhu was demoted on hearsay, ill words spoken to the emperor by certain persons, namely Xu Jingzong and Li Yifu. The emperor ignored him. Then Han resorted to resigning to show his insistence in his opinion. But the emperor did not accept his resignation.

As all their efforts were in vain, those old courtiers thought that they would do something within their power to improve Zhu's situation. On the sixth day of the third moon in 657, without getting permission from the emperor beforehand, those senior courtiers gave the order to transfer Zhu from Tanchow to Guichow (meaning Cinnamon District), presently Guilin (Cinnamon Forest) City in Guangxi (meaning Wide West) Province in southwestern China, still as governor.

Xu Jingzong and his group watched every move of their opposite party. When they learned that Zhu Suiliang had been transferred, they thought it an opportunity to deal another blow to those old courtiers. They reported it to the emperor, saying that Guichow City was a strategic place in case of warfare; that it was a conspiracy that Han Yuan and Lai Ji transferred Zhu to that place; and that when needed, they could occupy this important place to raise a rebellion.

The emperor was easily persuaded and issued edicts on the eleventh day of the eighth moon to demote Han Yuan to magistrate of Zhenchow (Shake District) to the west of the present Sanya Town in HaiNan (meaning Sea South) Island, the second largest island in south China Sea, and Lai Ji to be the magistrate of Taichow (Platform District), the present Linhai (meaning Near Sea) Town of Zhejiang (Jiang means River and Zhe, here, is its name) Province in southeastern China, and to demote Zhu again to be the magistrate of Aichow (meaning Love District) in the territory of the present Vietnam and Liu Shi again to be the magistrate of Xiangchow (meaning Elephant District), to the northeast of the present Xiangchow Town in the Guangxi Province.

On the thirteenth day of the twelfth moon, the emperor decided that Luoyang City would be the eastern capital of the Tang Dynasty. Since the emperor had to live in the capital, he made Luoyang City the second capital so that he could often go to live there. It showed that he liked Luoyang City better than ChangAn City, the main capital, because the environment was pleasanter.

On the fifth day of the first moon in 658, Uncle Changsun working with some other courtiers presented to the emperor the book "New Etiquette" in one hundred and thirty volumes. The emperor wrote the preface himself and ordered it to be circulated as the standard of official behavior.

In the tenth moon, Li Yifu, the favorite courtier of the emperor and main supporter of Empress Wu, had a quarrel with another courtier, Du Zhenglun, who was an upright man and often clashed with the corrupt courtiers. Li Yifu often took bribes and sold official positions. They came to complain to the emperor about each other. The emperor reprimanded both of them, and then demoted Li Yifu to be the magistrate of Puchow (meaning Common District) and Du Zhenglun the magistrate of Hengchow (Across District), and he died in office there soon.

On the nineteenth day of the eleventh moon, Zhu Suiliang died of grief at the age of sixty-three. Now only Uncle Changsun stayed in the capital, although in recent times he had kept out of political activities. He was working with a group of scholars to compile history books under the order of the emperor. However, his rivals would not let him live peacefully. They were waiting for a chance. That was the way of political warfare In China.

On the twenty-eighth day of the second moon in 659, the emperor himself held the final government test. Nine hundred men participated in it. The government tests consisted of several levels. First was the town or city level. Second was the province level. Third was the central government level. The final test was held in the presence of the emperor.

In the fourth moon, almost half a year after Zhu's death, there came a report that two officials, Wei Jifang and Li Chao, had formed a clique. Since the emperor hated his courtiers to fall into any kind of clique for fear that they could end up getting together to do something harmful to his reign, Xu Jingzong seized this opportunity to report to the emperor that Uncle Changsun and Li Chao were plotting a mutiny.

The emperor had been resentful to his uncle since he did not support him in his desire to abolish the former empress and crown the new empress. Therefore, he was ready to believe whatever Xu reported to him, and he demoted his uncle Changsun to the position of the governor of Yangchow (Yang here means the Sun) on the twenty-second day of the fourth moon, but sent him to live in Qianchow (Qian here means Black), so that he was a governor only in name.

Before long, after Changsun left the capital, Xu reported to the emperor again that Changsun had been instigated to rebel by Zhu Suiliang, Liu Shi and Han Yuan, and that Yu Zhining also belonged to Changsun's clique. So the emperor issued orders to deprive Changsun of any titles, to delete the names of Liu Shi and Han Yuan from the official list (which meant that they could never be appointed to any official positions anymore), and to dispense Yu Zhining from his office. The name of the son of Changsun Wuji was deleted, too, from the official list, and the son was exiled to the remote region in southern China. The two sons of Zhu Suiliang were banished to Aichow (meaning Love District), but were killed on the way there.

In the seventh moon, the emperor ordered Li Ji, Xu Jingzong and three others to organize a group to make the final decisions on those who had been accused of treason. Xu sent someone to Qianchow to force Changsun to hang himself and then reported to the emperor that Changsun had committed suicide.

Presently the emperor gave orders to execute Liu Shi, and as Han Yuan already died, his corpse was dug up and his head was cut off as a form of execution, which was a tradition. All the kinsfolk of both families were exiled to remote southern China to be slaves. Thus ended the case.

Lai Ji, who had also opposed Empress Wu, had already died in a battle with the Tujue Clan. His father had been a general in the Sui Dynasty. In the event when Yuwen Huaji killed Emperor Yang, his family was also killed in the chaos. Only he escaped. He had studied hard and become learned. When he began to work for the Tang government, he was by degrees promoted to be a prime minister. If he had not died in a battle, he would have been executed as a traitor, too. To die in a battle against the invaders was honored as a way of dying for the country. He was a national hero. A national hero was certainly not a traitor.

Taking Part in Politics

Now those who had been supporters of Empress Wu all received promotions, especially Xu Jingzong and Li Yifu. Both had the trust of Emperor Gaozong. Even if Li Yifu had done many wrong things, against the law and against moral standards, the emperor let him go without punishment.

Once a beautiful woman, wife to a Mr. Yuchun, had offended the law with adultery and was put in the prison of the Supreme Court belonging to the central government in the capital. When Li learned that there was a beautiful female in prison, he wanted to take her to be his concubine. He asked Bi Zhengyi, who was the second in charge in the Supreme Court, to release the woman to him by twisting the law and making her appear guiltless. It was against the law. Wang Yifang (615–669), a courtier whose duty it was to watch the behavior of other courtiers, learned of it and reported to the emperor. Li was afraid that Bi Zhengyi would confess to the emperor and so compelled him to kill himself in the prison. Though the emperor was told all of this later, yet he let Li Yifu go without inflicting any penalty on him.

Courtier Wang Yifang wanted to impeach Li Yifu. He talked to his mother first. "I'm not a loyal courtier if I don't right the wrong. If I impeach the bad courtier, I will get myself in danger. Then I won't be a filial son, if I make my mother worry about me. So I am in a dilemma and can't make up my mind." His mother said, "If you can be loyal to the emperor, I won't complain even if I die for it." So next day Wang Yifang said to the emperor at the levee, "Li Yifu killed a judge right under the nose of Your Majesty. He said that the judge committed suicide. But the judge was forced to do so by Li Yifu, who wanted to annihilate the potential testifier. So Li Yifu must be tried." But the emperor did not say anything about Li Yifu. On the contrary, he accused Wang Yifang of insulting a courtier and demoted him to be an official in Laichow (Lai here means Radish). Li Yifu said to Wang Yifang, "You talked nonsense before His Majesty. Are you ashamed of yourself?" Wang Yifang replied, "I feel ashamed of myself for being not able to get rid of bad, corrupt courtiers."

Li Yifu often sold official positions and took bribes. His family members followed suit. When the emperor was told about all this, he sent for Li and said to him, "I heard that your family members did many wrong things. You must restrain them." Li flared up and asked, "Who told Your Majesty?" The emperor said, "If it is true, you don't need to ask me who told me so." Li did not show any remorse and left.

Li Yifu was as sly as a fox. He always smiled at people, but if necessary, he would do something harmful behind their backs. So people said that Li Yifu had "a knife hidden behind his smile." This has become an idiom in the Chinese language.

Xu Jingzong, when charged with compiling history books, put false facts in them. It had happened at the end of the Sui Dynasty when his father was killed by the general Yuwen Huaji, who also killed the emperor of the Sui Dynasty, Xu had not stepped forward to save his father but had begged Yuwen on his knees for his own dear life. The courtier Feng Deyi knew it and told this tale to everybody he knew. So Xu hated Feng and then wrote some spurious things to discredit Feng in the history books.

Feng Deyi (568–627) was a courtier in the Sui Dynasty. When he was young, his uncle said, "This boy is cleverer than other boys. He will surely be a prime minister some day." A prime minister Yang Su of the Sui Dynasty looked upon him with great expectations. Once Yang Su patted his own bed and said, "No doubt, Feng will sit on this bed." He meant that since he himself was a prime minister, Feng would be a prime minister and sit on this bed. Yang Su married his brother's daughter to Feng. When the general Yuwen Huaji killed Emperor Yang of the Sui Dynasty, Feng Deyi worked for Yuwen, and when Yuwen was killed by Dou Jiande, he went to ChangAn City to work for Li Yuan in the second moon of 619. He was promoted to be the minister of Official Ministry in 623. Two years later, he was granted the title of the Duke of Miguo and was finally made a prime minister.

In the contention between the sons of Li Yuan, the first emperor of the Tang Dynasty, he sometimes looked like he was on the side of the first son, but sometimes he seemed to side with the second son. But from the fact that the second son rewarded him with many things when he became emperor, one can deduce that he really stood on the side of the second son. But once when Li Yuan had discussed the problem of abolishing the first son from the position of the crown prince, he was opposed to it. Therefore, he was considered a two-faced person.

By the sixth moon of 660, Prince Liang, who was the eldest son of the emperor and had been the crown prince, was nervous and in considerable fear that he would be assassinated. He was often disguised as a woman so that if anyone came after him, he could not be recognized. When someone reported this to the emperor, the emperor deprived Prince Liang of his title and sent him to live in Qianchow in confinement.

On the second day of the tenth moon, the emperor began to suffer from severe dizziness and could not read the memorials the courtiers handed in. Therefore, he let Empress Wu read them and then express her opinions or decisions about the problems mentioned in the memorials. He often agreed with her.

In ancient China, it was a rule that women should not interfere in, nor even be concerned with, politics. For allowing Empress Wu to become involved in political affairs, some considered the emperor a complete fool. However, that was hardly the case.

Firstly, his father had been a famously wise emperor; it is unlikely that he would have chosen an idiot son as his successor to the throne. On the contrary, he was proven to be prudent and wise. As crown prince, he had helped his father to make certain decisions about national affairs. When he had become emperor, he never missed a day for levees with his courtiers. Only when the prime ministers reported to him that the whole country was enjoying peace and there was no revolt anywhere did he agree to their suggestion to hold the levee every other day.

Furthermore, he had even improved on past administrations by having the courtiers make new laws that were more detailed and fairer than the old ones. He also encouraged his courtiers to freely give their advice and opinions. For example, there was the hunting incident mentioned earlier, during which the emperor asked Gu Naluu what to do about the leaks in his rain gear. When the official responded by hinting that he should stay under his own tile roof instead of neglecting state affairs by hunting, he was not offended but rewarded him handsomely for the sage advice. And when he set about to gather laborers from Yongchow to strengthen the walls of ChangAn City, a courtier voiced the superstitious notion that repairing the walls of ChangAn City could be fatal, the emperor was wise enough to let the remark go. So he could not have been a complete fool.

Prince Teng, who was the youngest son of the first emperor of the Tang Dynasty and the uncle of the present emperor Gaozong, and Prince Jiang, who was the seventh son of the late emperor and the brother of the present emperor, accumulated their wealth by the exploitation of people. When the emperor gave gifts to other princes, he said to them, "As both of you seem to be able to bring in a fortune all by yourselves, I don't need to give you anything. I grant you only two cartfuls of flax that you can have made into cords to string together your coins." Thus he embarrassed the two princes, in a clever and good-humored way.

In 652 when Prince Wu (the third son of the late emperor and the step-brother of the present emperor), Princess Gaoyang (seventeenth daughter of the late emperor and sister of the present emperor), and her husband Fang YiAi plotted to usurp the throne, the emperor learned of their conspiracy and was decisive enough to order Fang YiAi executed and his brother and sister to hang themselves.

When the emperor was about to travel to Luoyang City in 657, to save money he gave an order that the road should be left as it was. Generally the local government would repair the road surface to make it safer and more comfortable when the emperor was planning to use it. But it started to rain when the emperor set out, and as he reached Baqiao (Ba is the name of a river and Qiao here means Bridge), his horse stumbled and the emperor almost fell. A courtier accused the officer in charge of horses of choosing a poor horse for the emperor and said that he should be executed. The emperor said, "You can't execute a man for the fault of a horse."

In previous dynasties a system had been set up to divide the arable land. When the Tang Dynasty was established, the first emperor had also adopted the system. The present emperor expanded the system to the farthest districts in the territory. The system stipulated that every male adult could get almost seven acres of fields to grow whatever crops were suitable for the region. Of that land, 20% would belong to the man forever. If he died, he could bequeath it to other family members. The remaining 80% belonged to the government. When the man died, the government would take it back and allot it to someone else. good-for-nothing, he might not have improved the system.

At the last years of the late emperor, the annexation of the fields became a serious problem. Then the present emperor issued a law to forbid anyone to sell or buy the assigned fields.

All these facts showed that Emperor Gaozong was no fool. Then someone started another rumor, that the emperor was henpecked, that is, afraid of his wife, Empress Wu, so that he could not restrain Empress Wu from interfering with the national affairs. But that was groundless, too.

As a matter of fact in the Tang Dynasty there were quite a few high-rank officials who were afraid of their wives. Yuan Song, the mayor of Guiyang (meaning Cinnamon Sun) Town, once held a feast. His wife was jealous and when she heard that her husband had sent for some singing girls to entertain the guests, she rushed out with a knife in hand, clothes untidy and hair disheveled. The guests dispersed and the singing girls ran for their dear lives. The mayor hid under the bed. Another story was about Yang Hongwu, the vice minister of Military Ministry, who was also weaker than his wife. Once he had given someone a position, and this came under question. Then the emperor asked him why he had selected that man, Yang replied that his wife had insisted upon it and "if I refuse, she'll make my life miserable." The emperor appreciated his frankness, if not his strength, and pardoned him. There was another story about "drinking vinegar." Fang Xuanling, the famous prime minister of Emperor Taizong, had a jealous wife. Once Emperor Taizong wanted to give him some girls as his concubines, but he did not dare to accept them. Emperor Taizong sent a eunuch with a container of poisoned wine to his residence, with an imperial order that if the wife would not let her husband have these girls as concubines, she should drink the poisoned wine. The wife bravely took up the vessel and drank up the contents in it. But she did not die because it was vinegar inside. Since then, "drink vinegar" means "jealous" in the Chinese language.

In any event, if Emperor Gaozong was unable to stand up to women, how did he dare to give the order to abolish the previous empress and Concubine Xiao? The truth was that, in the tenth moon of 660, the emperor was seriously dizzy and could not even open his eyes to see.

Under such circumstances, how could he manage the national affairs? Generally, when the emperor was ill, the crown prince would help to administer the affairs. But the present crown prince Li Hong was then only eight years old. He surely could not help. As for the courtiers, if the emperor entrusted everything to them, they might usurp the power. Who knows? Therefore, the most trustworthy person was his wife, Empress Wu. Besides, Empress Wu was a woman of talent and ambition. She had learned how to manage national affairs when she had waited on the late emperor and the present emperor.

At the age of thirty-six, Empress Wu commenced her political career. The emperor was already ill and later caught malaria; he could not hold levees so the courtiers had to hand in reports or memorials to the throne instead of discussing important things or asking for imperial decisions at court meetings. The emperor then let Empress Wu read all the reports or memorials and make decisions, in consultation with him.

On the twenty-fourth day of the sixth moon in 662, a courtier Shangguan (double surname) Yi was appointed the chief prime minister. His father had been a courtier in the Sui Dynasty. At the end of the Sui Dynasty, when the whole country was in chaos, the father of Shangguan Yi had been killed and Shangguan Yi himself went to a temple to be a monk. When the Tang Dynasty was established, he grew his hair long. Then he took part in and passed the government tests and became a courtier. As he was a learned scholar, the late emperor liked him. Whenever the late emperor wrote something, he would have Shangguan to read it to see if there would be anything to be corrected. The present emperor also had high opinion of him and so appointed him to be an advisor of the former crown prince Li Zhong, later Prince Liang. After Li Zhong was deposed, the emperor made him a prime minister. After he held the position for only one year, he became so powerful he seemed to administer the country all by himself. He was also famous for his poems, which had a special style.

In the third moon of 663, the emperor learned again that his favorite courtier Li Yifu was still selling official positions. He sent for Li and said to him, "I was told that you, your sons and your son-in-law have done quite a few illegal things. When other courtiers complained, I even cover for you. You should restrain yourself and your family." Li asked angrily, "Who told Your Majesty?" The emperor said, "If what I say is true, it doesn't matter where I heard it." Li didn't even apologize; he just left. The emperor was irritated. It happened a second time.

In the fourth moon, Li Yifu was put into prison for breaking so many laws. At the order of the emperor, the case was tried and all the accusations were supported by facts. Therefore, on the fifth day, he was exiled to Xichow (Xi here is the name of a place) and died there in the first moon of 666. The names of his sons and son-in-law were all deleted from the official list and they were all banished to Tingchow (Ting here means Courtyard). The courtiers and people were all delighted at the news.

In the fourth moon of 664, Li Xiaoxie, duke of XunGuo and the magistrate of Weichow (Wei here is a surname), was ordered to commit suicide by the emperor because he accepted bribes. A courtier said to the emperor, "His father died for the government and he has no brothers. If he dies, his lineage will be cut off. (In feudal China, a man's most important duty was to hand down the family name and last the lineage.)" The emperor said, "Everyone is equal before the law. Even if the crown prince does something against the law, he cannot be pardoned. I know he has a son. So his lineage won't be cut off." Li Xiaoxie had to commit suicide at home. His father Li Shuliang had died in a battle against the invasion of the Tujue Clan.

Empress Wu often had nightmares. In the twelfth moon, she found a sorcerer called Guo Xingzhen, who was said to be able to drive away nightmares by using his magical power. He exercised his magic in the chamber of Empress Wu. Such things were against the palace rules. The head eunuch of the emperor, who had served the deposed crown prince and disliked Empress Wu, learned of this and reported it to the emperor. The emperor sent for Shangguan to ask his opinion. Shangguan had also served the deposed crown prince and detested Empress Wu. So he said, "The empress is so dictatorial that the whole nation is against her. Better to abolish her from the position of empress."

In his illness, the emperor was somewhat less clear-headed. He agreed with Shangguan and let him draft an edict to that effect. A eunuch reported to Empress Wu and she hurried in to see him. The draft was still on the table. Empress Wu pleaded for herself. Although both she and the former Empress Wang had used sorcery, the nature of the crime was different in character. Ex-empress Wang had used sorcery to try to murder Empress Wu, but Empress Wu had used sorcery to cure the nightmares that troubled her at night. The emperor was so fond of her that he pardoned her. Then he added, "I didn't even think of it. Shangguan suggested it." Anyway, the sorcerer was arrested and executed by the order of Shangguan Yi. He did it without asking permission from the emperor.

Empress Wu gave Xu Jingzhong, her supporter, a hint and Xu Jingzong handed in a memorial, saying that Shangguan Yi was helping the former crown prince in a conspiracy to rebel.

On the thirteenth day of the twelfth moon, the head eunuch was put in prison, and so was Shangguan Yi with his son Shangguan Tingzhi. All three died in the prison. But Shangguan Yi's new grand-daughter fared better.

Shangguan WanEr (664–710) was just born in the year her grandfather and father died. She and her mother were taken into the palace as slaves. Under the instruction of her mother, she became a learned girl. She was clever and could write poetry and essays. In 677, at the age of thirteen, Empress Wu came to know the condition of WanEr and summoned her to her presence. Empress Wu bade her to write an essay right before her. Shangguan WanEr quickly wrote a good essay with beautiful wording. Empress Wu was delighted and ordered to free her from the status of a slave and placed her in charge of her documents and the like. WanEr worked for Empress Wu as a kind of a modern secretary till the death of Empress Wu. Once WanEr did something against the will of Empress Wu, which deserved death, but Empress Wu pardoned on the basis of for her literary talent and only gave her a slight punishment by pricking a plum flower on her forehead and coloring it with vermilion. (In feudal China, one punishment for a criminal was to prick on his forehead the word "crime" and blacken it with ink so that when he went about, everyone knew that he was a criminal.) After that, WanEr acted very carefully and never displeased Empress Wu. From 698, Empress Wu let WanEr help her deal with political affairs. So WanEr began to have some power. She was also a famous poetess and had thirty-two poems handed down.

The former crown prince began to prepare a revolt. He often sent spies to the capital to gather information. To avoid detection, he was often dressed in woman's clothes as a disguise. When his plot was discovered, he was ordered to die, too. Ever after, if the emperor felt well enough to hold levees, Empress Wu would sit behind a pearl-covered screen behind the throne and hold levees together with the emperor. They were thus called "Duo-Saints" in the history book and were so addressed by all the courtiers in their reports and memorials to them. It was in the twelfth moon of 664.

Empress Wu was very strict on her own relatives. Before Empress Wu had the chance to join in political activities, she had written a pamphlet about "Commandments to In-Laws". It was because she had read in the history books that the collapse of a dynasty was often caused by in-laws of the emperor.

When she acquired some power in making decisions, she restrained her relatives, that is, the in-laws of the present emperor. She had two stepbrothers, Yuanqing and Yuanshuang, and two male cousins, Weiliang and Huaiyun, who were all officials of the government. At the request of the empress, the emperor sent Huaiyun to be the magistrate of Shichow (meaning First District), currently JianGe (meaning Sword Pavilion) Town in Sichuan Province, Yuanqing to be the magistrate of Longchow (meaning Dragon District), to the north of the present Longchow Town in Guangxi Province, and Yuanshuang to be the magistrate of Haochow (Hao is the name of a river), the east of the present Fengyang (meaning Phoenix Sun) Town in Anhui (meaning Safety Badge) Province. Huaiyun was already the magistrate of Zichow (Zi is the name of a river). Since they were not courtiers in the capital, they could not influence those in power.

In the second moon of 665, when talking about Emperor Yang of the Sui Dynasty, the emperor said to the courtiers, "The Sui Dynasty collapsed because Emperor Yang wouldn't listen to good advice. I learned from the lesson and always take good advice. But recently, no one is giving me any advice.

Why is that?" Li Ji replied, "It is because Your Majesty is doing everything properly, and so no one feels in need to offer any advice."

The history book records the following about the stepbrothers and cousins of Empress Wu. In 666, Yuanqing died of a disease. Weiliang and Huaiyuan both came to the capital that year. Empress Wu treated them with a dinner party. Putting poison in the minced meat dish, she made her niece eat it and the niece died right away. It was said that the niece often went into the palace to see Empress Wu and once the emperor saw her and took an immediate fancy to her, and had taken advantage of her. Empress Wu was jealous and seized this opportunity to poison her. Then Weiliang and Huaiyuan were accused of the murder and on the fourteenth day of the eighth moon they were executed. Another cousin, Yuanshuang, was exiled to the remote southern province as an accomplice and died there. It was said that since her stepbrothers and cousins had maltreated her mother, her sister and herself before, she took her revenge on them by killing two birds, or rather four birds, with one stone.

In the ninth moon of 666, Liu Qixian was appointed an officer in charge of the local troops in Jinchow (Jin here is the name of a place). When once the emperor was hunting in the imperial park, a general said to him, "Your servant has heard that the hawks in Jinchow are the best. As Liu Qixian is now in Jinchow, Your Majesty could order him to catch some hawks." The emperor said, "Liu Qixian is not a hawk catcher. He's an officer. What do you think he is?"

In the first moon of 667, the emperor wanted to hold a ritual to begin the spring farming. Usually he used a tool in the shape of a spade to do it. A specially-made tool was offered to him with a decoratively carved long handle. The emperor said, "A tool is used for farming and should not be ornamented with carvings."

In the third moon, the emperor rebuked the courtiers for not recommending talented men. One courtier, Li Anqi said, "There are talented men throughout the nation. Every courtier wants to recommend someone, but when any courtier does give a recommendation, he is accused of having the intention to form a clique with those he had recommended. Then he is charged with a crime. Who would dare to recommend anyone now? It is up to Your Majesty, not the courtiers." The emperor saw the merit of the argument. Li Anqi (?–670) was a clever boy and could write essays at the age of seven. At the end of the Sui Dynasty, his father had been demoted to work in Guichow. When he passed by Tai Lake in Jiangsu (Jiang here means River and Su here is a surname) Province one time, he met with robbers. The robbers wanted to kill his father, but he begged them, on his knees, to spare his father's life. He said that he was willing to be killed instead of his father. So the robbers let them go.

In the second moon of 669, comments and grades were being given on every courtier and official according to the work he had done. The grades were from 1 to 9. By courtier, I refer to those who could attend levees and talk directly to the emperor. By official, I refer to those who could not attend levees and talk directly to the emperor. If an official wanted to say something to the emperor he had to write a memorial and hand it in to the registrar at the gate of the palace. When the emperor read the memorial, if he wanted to ask him some questions or need some explanations, the emperor would send for him. Only thus could an official talk directly to the emperor.

A courtier, Lu Chengqing, was made responsible for this work. An official in charge of transporting grain by ship had lost some sacks of the grain, it was said, due to the strong wind. Lu wrote the comment: "Lost grain in his charge." The grade was 4. The official did not plead for himself and was about to leave. Generally many officials would enumerate such and such reasons to plead for themselves. So this official made a good impression on Lu, who then added something: "There was nothing he could do, given the rough weather," and changed the grade to 5. Then when Lu saw that the official did not show on his face that he was happy or ashamed, Lu added another sentence: "He's a calm person and nothing can affect his mood." The final grade went up to 6.

On the third day of the twelfth moon, Li Ji died a natural death. When Li was still in sick bed, the emperor sent for all his sons and relatives who were away from the capital so that they could see or speak to him before his last breath. Whenever the emperor or the crown prince sent him medication, Li would take it. But when his sons offered him medication, Li would not take it, saying, "I was a farmer in Shandong Province. I met the good emperors who promoted me to the position of a prime minister. I am satisfied with my life. Now I am approaching eighty and it's my fate to die. Why should I seek a longer life through medication?"

On the nineteenth day of the third moon in 670, Xu Jingzong, who was the main supporter of Empress Wu, was retired.

Helan (double surname) Minzhi (?–671) a nephew of Empress Wu, the son of her sister, Lady HanGuo (a title granted to the wife of a high-rank courtier) was a handsome fellow. When her step-brothers died, Empress Wu wanted to find someone to be the successor to the Wu family. She thought that Helan was a suitable candidate and asked the emperor to change his surname to Wu and thus let him take over the title of Duke Zhouguo, which her father had been granted posthumously, together with the Wu estate.

Minzhi should have been grateful and well-behaved to deserve the sur-name Wu and the title of duke. But he was not a man of good character. He often broke the law, which made life difficult for Empress Wu. The worst thing he did had to do with the daughter of the courtier Yang Sijian. She was very pretty. The emperor and the empress both decided to make her the wife of the crown prince, but right before the wedding Minzhi raped the girl, who could no longer become the wife of the crown prince since a crown prince should marry a virgin. While Princess Taiping, now the sole daughter of Empress Wu, was little, she went to visit her grandmother, Lady RongGuo, the mother of Empress Wu. Minzhi, who was staying with the grandmother, had also harassed her and raped the maids accompanying her.

On the second day of the eighth moon, Lady RongGuo, mother of Em-press Wu, died of old age at ninety-two. Empress Wu herself was forty-six years old. She mourned her mother till her heart would bleed. She had a grand funeral held and a magnificent tomb built for her mother. She gave Minzhi scrolls of brocade and some hundred thousand coins from the palace store room to build a statue of Buddha as a contribution so that her mother would be blessed in the nether world. But Minzhi embezzled the money, and besides, he took off the mourning garments, put on fine clothes and sent for some singing girls for merry-making, which was greatly against the tradition and the funeral rules set up by the government.

In the sixth moon of 671, when Empress Wu learned of Minzhi's embez-zlement, she was very angry and reported it to the emperor, suggesting that Minzhi should be removed from office and banished to Leichow (meaning Thunder District), now Haikang (meaning Sea Health) Town in Guangdong (Wide East) Province. The emperor issued an order to that effect. On the way to there, Minzhi was strangled by his personal foe, using the rein of his horse.

In the sixth moon, the emperor let Wu Chengsi (?–698), another nephew of Empress Wu, inherit the title of Duke Zhouguo originally granted to his grandfather.

On the nineteenth day of the eighth moon in 672, Xu Jingzong, the former supporter of Empress Wu, who had retired two years ago, died.

On the twenty-sixth day of the second moon in 673, the crown prince came back from the east capital and the emperor wanted him to marry the daughter of General Pei Judao.

In the third moon, the emperor ordered a courtier, Liu RenGui, to revise the contemporary history compiled by Xu Jingzong to correct certain facts. Liu RenGui (601–685) was an upright courtier. When he was an official in Chencang (Chen here is a surname and Cang here means Barn) Town in charge of security, a high-ranked officer Lu Ning violated the law and was put into prison. When Liu was interrogating him in the yamen, Lu cursed Liu badly in public — his rank was higher than that of Liu. Liu had him beaten to death. When the emperor heard of the event, he was furious that an official with a lower rank had killed an officer of a higher rank. He wanted to execute Liu RenGui, but upon second thought, he recognized that there must have been some reason for Liu to do it. So he summoned Liu to his presence and questioned Liu himself. When the emperor was told the reason, he appreciated the courage of Liu in punishing the bad behavior of an officer whose rank was higher than his. The emperor thereby appointed him to be the vice mayor of Liyang (Li here means Oak and Yang here means the Sun) Town and before long promoted him to be the mayor of XinAn (meaning New Safety) Town. Then he became a courtier.

In 656, Liu RenGui offended the mischievous courtier Li Yifu, who was at that time a prime minister, when he sought to apply the law in judging a certain case. Li Yifu began to hate him and in 659, he found fault with Liu and demoted him to be the magistrate of Qingchow (meaning Black District).

In the seventh moon of 656, there was a deluge in Wuchow (Wu here is the name of a river). Five thousand people were drowned.

In the eighth moon, the emperor came down with malaria and let the crown prince read the memorials and reports handed in by the courtiers.

On the first day of the tenth moon, a prime minister, Yan Liben, died (601–673). He was born with a gold spoon in his mouth. He learned how to paint in his youth and was a famous painter of the early the Tang Dynasty. One of his famous paintings is of thirteen emperors in Chinese history, including Emperor Taizong.

On the fifteenth day of the eighth moon in 674, the emperor formally named himself Heavenly Emperor and so the empress was Heavenly Empress.

On the twenty-third day of the eighth moon, an imperial edict was issued about the ranks of the courtiers and officials. There were nine ranks. To indicate different ranks, the courtiers and officials had different uniforms, which mainly consisted of a gown and a girdle. Those above the third rank wore gowns of purple with a girdle made of jade set in gold. Those of the fourth rank wore gowns of dark red with a girdle of gold and those of the fifth rank had gowns of light red with a girdle of gold. Those of the sixth rank and of the seventh rank had gowns of dark green and light green respectively, both with a girdle of silver. Those of the eighth and ninth ranks were respectively given gowns of dark blue and light blue, both with girdle of a special kind of stone. Those not belonging to any rank had yellow gowns with brass or iron girdles.

On the seventh day of the ninth moon, the emperor gave an edict to return the official title to Changsun Wuji, his maternal uncle. The title had been removed when he was demoted. His great grandson, Changsun Yi, inherited the title of Duke Zhao.

On the eighth day of the ninth moon, a banquet was given in Hanyuan Hall and the courtiers attended in their new uniforms. The emperor divided the musicians into two groups stationed respectively in the east side and the west side of the hall. He then let Prince Yong head the east group and Prince Zhou head the west group for a competition to see which group was better. The courtier Hao Chujun said, "As the princes are still young, they must be taught how to love and be friendly to each other, not to compete with each other." The emperor thought that was right and stopped the competition.

Hao Chujun (607–681) passed the government tests and became a courtier. He was gradually promoted and in 674 was made a prime minister. Once when Emperor Gaozong was severely ill and wanted to leave the throne to Empress Wu, it was Hao that dissuaded the emperor from the decision. So Empress Wu disliked him, but could not find any fault with him. Hao Chujun lived to seventy-five without any disaster.

In the eleventh moon of 674, an official, Zhang Junche, and three men in Jichow (Dustpan District) falsely accused Prince Jiang and his son of treason. The emperor sent a courtier to investigate. But Prince Jiang committed suicide out of fear. When the emperor found out that the accusation was false, he mourned over Prince Jiang and had Zhang Junche and three men executed.

On the twenty-seventh day of the twelfth moon, Heavenly Empress Wu wrote a memorial to the Heavenly Emperor, stating that it should be government policy to encourage agricultural activities, decrease taxes, stop unnecessary military activities, improve the people's morale, forbid dissipation, encourage criticism and suggestions, discourage slandering, appoint officials based on ability, and have everyone from princes and dukes to the petty officials learn the book *Laotze* written by Li Er (said to have lived between 600 BC and 470 BC, during the West Zhou Dynasty, 1121 BC–771 BC). She emphasized this because the Tang Dynasty was established by the Li family and so all the emperors considered that Li Er had been their ancestor. The Heavenly Emperor approved her suggestions, which showed that Heavenly Empress Wu had become a mature politician now.

A man named Liu Xiao sent in a memorial to the emperor about the selection of the officials and courtiers. He said, "The government currently chooses officials and courtiers only on the basis of their calligraphy and essays, but doesn't question their morality and ability. What if they ask others to do the calligraphy and write essays for them? What is more, the testees only know how to write good essays, but they do not care about improving their moral strength and ability, and as a result, a man can pass the test in the morning and become a criminal in the evening. What's the use of those persons even if they can recite ten thousand words a day? If in the selection of the officials and courtiers Your Majesty could take into consideration their morals and ability first, and their essays and calligraphy second, the morality among testees will improve in no time."

In the third moon of 675, the vertigo of Heavenly Emperor got worse and he could not sit up to manage his daily routines. Heavenly Empress Wu performed his duties alone for him. Therefore, he wanted to abdicate and leave the throne to Heavenly Empress Wu. But some prime ministers opposed it.

In the fourth moon, Wei Hongji was appointed the head of the department for the agriculture and also was put in charge of the repair of the palace park near the east capital. A eunuch violated the regulations. Wei had him beaten and then reported it to the emperor. The emperor thought that Wei was a capable man and allowed him to beat any offending eunuchs without reporting to him later.

In the ninth moon of 676, the Supreme Court sent in a report that two generals had chopped down some cypresses in the graveyard of the late Emperor Taizong, by mistake. Mistake or not, this was regarded as disrespect to the late emperor. The Heavenly Emperor was infuriated and ordered the two generals beheaded. Di Renjie, the deputy general judge of the Supreme Court, argued, "The two generals don't deserve death, even though they are guilty." Heavenly Emperor said, "If I don't execute them, I won't be seen as a filial son." Di retorted, "Their crime doesn't deserve death, and if Your Majesty insists in executing them, how will you be seen? If I carry out the order, I will make Your Majesty be viewed as inhumane." So the two generals were exiled. A few days later, Di Renjie received a promotion.

Di Renjie (630–700) was born in a courtier's family. He passed government tests and received an official position. Then he was falsely accused of a crime. Yan Liben was, at that time, the minister of Construction Ministry and was sent to investigate the case. He cleared Di Renjie of the trumped-up charge and found Di a man of talent and probity. Under his recommendation, Di was appointed a law official under the governor of Bingchow (Bing here means Emerge). Between 676 and 679, Di Renjie was made the deputy general judge of the Supreme Court. The case above happened during this period. When Empress Wu became the sovereign, he was by degrees promoted to be a prime minister.

In the tenth moon, Prince Xun was driven out of the capital to be the magistrate of Shenchow (Shen here means Explain). Prince Xun was the son of Concubine Xiao, who had hated Heavenly Empress Wu and died with Empress Wang. Heavenly Empress Wu disliked her son and demoted him.

In the tenth moon of 677, the emperor wrote the epitaph for Li Ji, who had the title of the Duke of Yingguo.

In the twelfth moon, the emperor ordered each of the courtiers in the capital above the third rank to recommend someone with ability for the position of a governor or a general.

On the fourth day of the first moon in 678, Heavenly Empress Wu met all the courtiers and the chieftains of the ethnic minorities in the capital as a New Year's ritual.

In the first moon of 679, Di Renjie impeached a courtier who was in charge of constructing Shangyang Palace for the emperor. The magnificent palace was built at the side of Luo River with a corridor as long as half a kilometer. Di Renjie thought he was enticing the emperor into leading a life of dissipation. So the courtier was removed from the position.

A courtier named Wang Liben was a favorite of the emperor and he got away with several illegal things. Di Renjie exposed him to the emperor and begged to put him into prison. But the emperor wanted to pardon him. Di said, "Your Majesty can't bend the law to pardon a courtier. If Your Majesty should insist on forgiving him, Your Majesty had better banish me so that all the honest courtiers can learn a lesson from it." So the emperor had to agree with Di Renjie.

On the nineteenth day of the first moon in 680, Heavenly Empress Wu gave a feast in Luoyang City to all the princes, the courtiers above the third rank, and the governors and magistrates from provinces and chows (districts).

In the second moon of 681, Heavenly Empress Wu wrote a memorial to the Heavenly Emperor to beg him to pardon Prince Qi, the son of Concubine Yang, and Prince Panyang, the son of deceased Concubine Xiao. Then Prince Qi was appointed to be the magistrate of Mianchow (Mian here is the name of a river in Shaanxi Province) and Prince Panyang the magistrate of Yuechow (Yue here is a surname).

In the third moon, a courtier who was a shrewd businessman proposed to Heavenly Emperor Gaozong that if the horse manure in the imperial stables were sold, they could make twenty thousand *taels* of silver in a year. Heavenly Emperor asked another courtier, Liu RenGui, about it. Liu said, "The profit is good, but it will bring Your Majesty a bad reputation." So the emperor did not agree to the proposal.

On the twenty-fourth day of the bissextile seventh moon in this lunar leap year, the Heavenly Emperor's illness took a turn for the worse again and he ordered the crown prince to hold the levee for him. In this year, an epidemic broke out among domesticated animals. One hundred eighty-four thousand nine hundred horses and eleven thousand six hundred cattle died.

In 682, there was a disaster in the suburbs of the main capital ChangAn City caused by locusts which damaged the wheat crop.

In the fourth moon of 682, there was a famine in the area around ChangAn City. The emperor went to Luoyang City, the east capital, and left the crown prince behind to manage national affairs with the aid of Liu RenGui, Pei Yan and Xue Yuanchao, all being prime ministers. The emperor thought that there might be robbers on the way and so ordered a courtier, Wei Yuanzhong, to look after his safety. Since they left in a hurry, there were not enough bodyguards to be gathered. Wei was struck with a wonderful idea. He went to a prison and selected a gang leader there. He put an official uniform on him and let him follow the procession on horseback. The gang leader was delighted at being treated that way. When the robbers and thieves saw the gang leader, they did not dare to approach. Therefore, nothing was lost or stolen all the way to the east capital.

Pei Yan (?–684) came from an official's family. After he received an official position, he was gradually promoted to be a prime minister in 680. Heavenly Emperor Gaozong trusted him and on his death bed in 683 AD, gave Pei Yan his imperial will and asked him to help his son to be a good emperor. However, as he was opposed to Heavenly Empress Wu, he was killed in 684.

Xue Yuanchao (621–683) lost his father at three years old. His father Xue Shou (died a natural death at the age of thirty-three) had worked for the late emperor when the late emperor was still Prince Qin. He was given a title of Baron of Fenying (Fen here is the name of a river and Ying here means Cloudy) Town. Xue Yuanchao succeeded to the title of his father at the age of nine. When growing up, he became a learned scholar. The late emperor regarded him highly and married his niece Princess Heqing to him. Princess Heqing was the daughter of the younger brother of the late emperor, that is, the third son of Emperor Li Yuan. When the present emperor ascended the throne, Xue was promoted. In 654, he took a funeral leave when his mother died. He came back the next year and was appointed the magistrate of Raochow (Abundance District). Before long he was summoned back to the capital for a higher position. But when the wicked prime minister Li Yifu was exiled to Sichuan Province, he asked that Li be given a horse to ride. (By tradition, an exile must walk.) His request was looked upon as an offense. So Xue was demoted to be the magistrate of Jianchow (Simple District). In 674, he was pardoned and upon his return to the capital he was given an official position. In 676, he became a prime minister. Since Heavenly Emperor Gaozong liked traveling, especially between the main capital and the east capital, he let the crown prince take care of the administration and often ordered

Xue to help his son. In 683, Xue retired due to illness and died in the winter of that year at the age of sixty-two.

Wei Yuanzhong (?–707) began his career as a student in the government school and learned the art of war. Then he became a courtier. In 678, he wrote a memorial to the emperor to discuss why the Tang army was often defeated by the Tibetan army. In 684, he went with General Li Xiaoyi to fight rebels in Yangchow City (related separately in chapter IV). He was the subject of numerous false accusations by the courtiers and was banished several times. In 699, he was back and made a prime minister.

In the fifth moon, Heavenly Emperor Gaozong sent a eunuch to get special bamboos to plant in his imperial garden. Everywhere the eunuch passed through, he made a great deal of trouble for the people and the local government. When he arrived in Jingchow (Bramble District), the administrator there, by the name of Su Liangsi, imprisoned the eunuch and sent a report to Heavenly Emperor. "To search for peculiar things and bring trouble to the people is not what a saint of an emperor should do." Heavenly Emperor acknowledged his error and wrote to Su that he could throw all the bamboos away.

Su Liangsi (604–689) was an honest courtier and always abided by the law. When he was appointed a law official in the fief of Prince Zhou, he always advised Prince Zhou not to do illegal things. He even went so far as to put those working in the fief into prison for their unlawful actions. Emperor Gaozong appreciated his integrity and promoted him to be the administrator of Jingchow. During the Zhou Dynasty, established by Empress Wu, he was made a prime minister and granted the title of Duke of WenGuo. Then he was falsely accused by some less honest courtiers and was sentenced to death. But when he was still in prison, Empress Wu learned that he had been falsely charged and released him. Before long he died of disease at the age of eighty-five. Empress Wu ordered all the courtiers to go to his funeral. It was a great honor.

In the fifth moon of 682, Xie You, the governor of Qianchow (Black District) wanted to please Heavenly Empress Wu and forced Prince Lingling to commit suicide. The next night he was sleeping in his own bedroom, but in the morning his servants found him in bed without his head. Some years later when Heavenly Empress Wu established her new dynasty and killed the son of Prince Lingling, the head of Xie You was found in the son's residence. The head had been painted and made into a urinal for night use with the name Xie You written on it.

On the fifth day of the tenth moon, there was an earthquake in the main capital ChangAn City. It was followed by some kind of epidemic.

An imperial edict was issued to prohibit the private mintage of coins, upon penalty of death.

In the second moon of 683, Prime Minister Li Yitan made plans to relocate the tomb of his parents. He forced his maternal uncle to remove his old family graves. When Heavenly Emperor Gaozong learned of it, he was angry and said, "If he can bully his own uncle, he is not suitable to be a prime minister." When Li Yitan heard about that, he was afraid and sent in a resignation on the pretext of having foot illness. Heavenly Emperor approved his resignation.

Li Yitan passed the government tests in his youth and later was sent to work under General Li Ji, who was very strict on everyone. Most persons under Li Ji were afraid of him, but Li Yitan would contradict him when he thought he was right. So Li Ji thought highly of him. Then he was promoted to be the mayor of Baishui (meaning White Water) Town. Before long he was summoned to the capital and gradually promoted to the position of a prime minister. He was one of the prime ministers who opposed the Heavenly Emperor's decision to abdicate and leave the throne to Heavenly Empress Wu. Li Yitan led a simple life and had no magnificent residence. His younger brother, also a courtier, bought some lumber for his elder brother so that he could use it to build a new house. But Li Yitan said, "I'm embarrassed to be a prime minister since I'm not a man of talent. If I build a splendid house, it will hasten my misfortune. How can you show your love to me in such a way?" His brother said, "Anybody who reaches the position of a prime minister builds a new house. Now you are a prime minister, how can you still live in such a shabby home?" Li Yitan replied, "Good things don't come in pairs. If I yearn for both, disaster may befall me. It's not that I don't want it, but I do not want any disaster that might come with it." So he let the lumber decay where it was. In 685, he was appointed the magistrate of Huaichow (Huai here means Chest), but ever since he had opposed Heavenly Empress Wu, he had always feared what ill fate could be in store for him. So he declined the appointment. He died in 688.

On the third day of the eleventh moon, the illness of Heavenly Emperor turned far worse. He could not see anything. A famous imperial doctor at that time by the name of Qin Minghe suggested that he would stick acupuncture needles into His Majesty's head. Heavenly Empress Wu would not agree, fearing that it might cause some fatal harm, but the Heavenly Emperor himself gave his consent. So the doctor exercised his skills. After the operation, Heavenly Emperor's vision seemed to improve a little. He was delighted, hoping that he would get better this way. Heavenly Empress Wu granted the doctor a hundred scrolls of colored satin. But toward the end of that month, the situation of Heavenly Emperor worsened significantly.

On the fourth day of the twelfth moon in 683, Heavenly Emperor died at the age of fifty-six. He stated in his will, "On the seventh day of my funeral the crown prince should be crowned as the emperor and if he cannot decide on any important national or military affairs, he should go to Heavenly Empress who will make final decisions." That year Heavenly Empress Wu was fifty-nine.

In ancient China, when an emperor died, his funeral and burial was of the first importance to the whole nation. An order was always issued that any entertainment, like singing, dancing and feasts, were forbidden for a certain period of time.

Now a tomb had to be built for the burial. The tomb of this emperor's grandfather, the first emperor of the Tang Dynasty, and that of his father, the famous emperor Tang Taizong, were both located on the north side of ChangAn City, the main capital. The tomb of Emperor Gaozong should have been built there, near his grandfather and father's. That was the tradition. Besides, the emperor said that if Heaven could allow his life to last for one or two more months, he could return to the main capital and die there. So his last wish could be explained as a wish to be buried with his grandfather and father. But a courtier, Chen ZiAng, suggested that the tomb of this emperor should be built here, in the suburbs of Luoyang City, to save the trouble of conveying the heavy coffin for a long way to the main capital. Besides, there was famine in the area of ChangAn City. When the imperial coffin was conveyed there, thousands of soldiers and workers would have to go together; and there was not enough food for them. Since Heavenly Emperor had been ill, he had stayed in Luoyang City, because conditions here were better than in ChangAn City; and there he died.

Chen ZiAng (661–702) was a renowned poet and came from a rich family. In 682, he passed the government tests and became a courtier. Although Heavenly Empress Wu appreciated his literary talent, he had to resign and return to his hometown, because he had offended Wu Sansi, a powerful nephew of Heavenly Empress Wu. But he did not live peacefully at home. The mayor of that town coveted his riches and made a false accusation against him. He died in woe and ire.

Heavenly Empress Wu decided that the tomb must be built outside the main capital so that her husband could lie near his grandfather and father. Construction work began soon after his death. The deceased emperor now lay in his expensive coffin, waiting to be carried into his magnificent tomb, called Mausoleum Qian.

There were two kinds of tomb for a ruler or his important family member. One was to pile up earth on top of the coffin to make a tomb. The other was to dig a deep cave into a mountain to make the tomb inside the cave and then seal it securely so that no one could dig in to steal precious things buried inside.

The Liang (a surname) Hill to the north of ChangAn City was selected to be Emperor Gaozong's tomb site and the digging work began right off.

On the eleventh day of the twelfth moon, the crown prince Li Xian3, who had been born on the fifth day of the eleventh moon in 656 in ChangAn City, was crowned emperor at the age of twenty-eight. He was called Emperor Zhongzong. Heavenly Empress Wu had become the empress dowager and she still managed the national affairs.

THE PLEASURES OF TRAVELING

As has been noted, Emperor Gaozong always liked to travel. When he was ill, he traveled lying in a warm imperial coach. His late father, Emperor Taizong, did not travel much unless it was necessary.

Back on the twelfth day of the third moon in 654, the emperor traveled to Myriad Year Palace. In ancient China every residence for the emperor was called a palace, including his temporary dwellings for the summer or for the lodging at night when he was traveling. He only took Concubine Wu along with him, leaving Empress Wang and Concubine Xiao behind. That year Concubine Wu was with child again.

There was a hot spring called Phoenix Spring at the foot of Mount Qi to the north of Myriad Year Palace near Mei (Mei here is the name of a place) Town in Qichow (Qi here is the name of a mountain). Since the establishment of the Tang Dynasty, common people were excluded from the spring. Only the imperial family members could come. The hot spring flowed into a bathing pond, about thirty meters long, fifteen meters wide, and two meters deep at the deepest, according to the records of that time. On the nineteenth day of the third moon, they went to Phoenix Spring and returned to Myriad Year Palace on the twenty-third day.

On the fifteenth day of the fifth moon, the emperor wrote "Epigraph of Myriad Year Palace" and had it engraved on a stone tablet.

On the twenty-third day of the first moon in 660, after they spent Chinese New Year's Festival there, the emperor and Empress Wu left Luoyang City for Wenshui Town in Bingchow, the home town of Empress Wu.

On the tenth day of the second moon, after a separation of more than twenty years, Empress Wu returned to her home town on a visit, accompanied by the emperor and her favorite courtiers and escorted by imperial guards.

On the fifteenth day of the same moon, in her home town, banquets were given for three days to entertain her relatives, neighbors, and local officials. Everyone received something as a gift.

It was a tradition in ancient China that anyone rising to power or wealth from his original low status would return to his home town to show off. About this tradition an old saying goes like this: if anyone rises to power or wealth but does not return to his home town, the expensive new clothes he wears make no more impression than if he were walking in the dark of night.

On the eighth day of the fourth moon, the emperor and Empress Wu left Bingchow and returned to Luoyang City. Empress Wu felt happy and satisfied with her life. No one would threaten her position now. She was a woman of ambition and this is when she started her political career by taking part in political activities and helping the emperor make decisions on national affairs.

On the sixteenth day of the first moon in 662, the government school was set up in the east capital Luoyang City, since they were there at the time.

On the fifth day of the third moon, the emperor and Empress Wu left Luoyang City for ChangAn City. On the first day of the fourth moon, the emperor and Empress Wu returned to ChangAn City, the main capital. The emperor was ill.

On the eleventh day of the tenth moon in 662, the emperor and Empress Wu went to Mount Li (Li here means a Black Horse) for a dip in the hot spring there. The crown prince was put in charge of handling routine matters with the help of the senior courtiers. On the twenty-first day of the same moon, they returned to the main capital.

On the tenth day of the second moon in 664, the emperor and Empress Wu left the capital and arrived in Myriad Year Palace. On the first day of the eighth moon, they returned to the capital and lived in Penglai (Penglai is the name of a mountain on the east sea, where it was believed that gods and goddesses lived) Palace, which had just been built. It was because since the death of her daughter, Empress Wu had always had nightmares when living in the old palace chambers. That was why the emperor agreed with Empress Wu to make Luoyang city the east capital and live there. Now they moved into the new palace in the hope that no more nightmares would haunt Empress Wu. But no such luck for her.

In the tenth moon of 665, the emperor decided to worship Heaven and Earth on the top of Mount Tai, which located in Shandong (Shan here means Mountain and Dong here means East) Province in the eastern part of China close to the East Sea. His father, the late Emperor Taizong, had not done it in his life though the courtiers had proposed it for three or four times. Once Wu Shiyue, the father of Empress Wu, had also suggested it, but the late emperor had refused then, too, because he had thought that his merits were not so glorious as to deserve the honor.

On the fifteenth day of the tenth moon, Empress Wu asked to take part in the activity with the wives of the high-rank courtiers, to which the emperor consented.

On the twenty-eighth day of the same moon, Emperor Gaozong and Empress Wu started on the journey. The procession went on for some hundred miles, including many courtiers and their wives, the imperial bodyguards and guards of honor.

In the eleventh moon, they arrived in Puyang (Pu here is a surname and Yang here means the Sun) City. A courtier named Dou Dexuan rode beside the emperor, who asked him why Puyang City was also called the Emperor Mound. Dou could not answer and confessed it frankly. Another courtier Xu Jingzong rode up and said to the emperor, "Because Emperor Zhuanxu once lived here." The emperor praised him for the knowledge. Then Xu said to others, "A courtier should be learned. When I saw that Dou could not reply, I felt ashamed of him." When Dou was told so, he said, "Everyone may know or do certain things, but not everything. I didn't answer what I didn't know. That's all I can do." Li Ji said, "It's good that Xu is so knowledgeable, but what Dou said is correct."

On the ninth day of the twelfth moon, they arrived in Qichow (meaning Even District) and took a rest for ten days. On the nineteenth day, they reached Mount Tai.

On the first day of the first moon in 666, Emperor Gaozong and Empress Wu held the ritual of worshipping Heaven and Earth at the foot of Mount Tai. Mount Tai is a sightseeing place close to the sea. Tourists often go to the top of it to watch the sunrise from the horizon on the sea. There are five famous mountains in China, situated respectively in the eastern, western, southern and northern parts of China with one in the middle. Emperors in feudal China liked to hold a ritual to worship Heaven and Earth on top of one of the mountains, especially on Mount Tai. It was deemed a sign of glory of their reign and of peace in the country, though that was not always the case. The first emperor of the Qin Dynasty (221 BC–207 BC) had done so on Mount Tai even though he had done nothing glorious and the country had not been peaceful. Now Emperor Gaozong and Empress Wu came for the same purpose. On the second day, they went to the top of Mount Tai and performed the ritual once more. An earthen platform had been built there and the ritual would be performed on it. The emperor was the first to do it, followed by Empress Wu. In feudal China, women could not even be present at such a ceremony, let alone to take part in it. But Empress Wu did it.

On the nineteenth day of the same moon, they left Mount Tai. Then on their way back, they went to Qufu (meaning Curved Mound) Town in Shandong Province, where the Temple of Confucius (551 BC–479 BC) was situated. They offered sacrifices to him in the temple.

On the eleventh day of the third moon, they arrived in the east capital and had a rest there for six days. On the eighth day of the fourth moon, they returned to the main capital ChangAn City and held a feast for all the courtiers.

Later Emperor Gaozong and Empress Wu wanted to go to Mount Song for the same ritual. Mount Song is not far from Luoyang City. However, they failed to do so because of the poor health of the emperor and the heavy national duties to attend to.

On the seventh day of the first moon in 671, Emperor Gaozong and Empress Wu left the main capital. The emperor let the crown prince handle the national affairs. On the twenty-sixth day of the same moon, they arrived in the east capital Luoyang City. In the ninth moon of 672, the emperor summoned the crown prince to the east capital. On the second day of the tenth moon, when the crown prince arrived, the emperor told him to go on taking charge of the national affairs there so that he could see how the crown prince was handling the administration.

On the seventh day of the second moon in 676, Heavenly Empress Wu suggested to the Heavenly Emperor to worship Heaven and Earth on Mount Song, the central mountain in China.

On the fifteenth day of the same moon, the Heavenly Emperor made up his mind to go in the winter and ordered the preparations to be made for the journey.

In the bissextile third moon of 676, as the Tibetan army invaded Tang territory, Emperor Gaozong cancelled the journey to Mount Song and sent Prince Xiang with troops to resist the aggression.

On the eighth day of the second moon in 680, the Heavenly Emperor, Heavenly Empress Wu and the crown prince went to the hot spring in Ruchow (Ru here means You).

On the twelfth day of the same moon, they visited Mount Shaoshi, which was later famous for the Shaolin (Shao here means Young and Lin here means Forest) Temple, in which Shaolin kungfu was taught. On the twentieth day, they returned to the east capital after visits to other places.

In the seventh moon of 683, the Heavenly Emperor gave an order that he would go to Mount Song to worship Heaven and Earth in the eleventh moon. But soon his illness took a turn for the worse and he cancelled the plan till the first moon next year. But he never made the trip, as he died that year.

Generally speaking, traveling would cost a great deal of money. But no courtiers came forth to dissuade the emperor from traveling. If a country was poor, the courtiers should be concerned about the cost of travel. If the country was rich, no one would care about the cost. Apparently the Tang Dynasty at that time was very wealthy.

RELATIONSHIP WITH HER CHILDREN

Empress Wu had five children. How was her relationship with her children, good or bad? The relationship between parents and children cannot always be good, especially in an imperial family. There is too much involved, power and benefits. Sometimes even a conflict of ideas would cause a disruption in their relationship.

In 656, the crown prince Li Hong was taken seriously ill. All the imperial doctors were at their wits' end to cure him. He suffered from the fatal disease tuberculosis. But he would not die soon.

On the twelfth day of the second moon in 657, the third son of Empress Wu, Li Xian3, was made Prince Zhou.

On the first day of the sixth moon in 662, Empress Wu gave birth to another son, named Li Xulun. On the first day of the seventh moon, the new son was one month old and the celebration lasted for three days. An edict was issued for an amnesty. On the eighteenth day of the eleventh moon, Xulun received the title of Prince Yin.

Since the first crown prince Li Zhong had been deposed, Li Hong, the eldest son of Empress Wu, was the present crown prince. Although he was suffering from tuberculosis, he could still walk and manage things. Therefore, on the first day of the tenth moon in 663, the emperor wanted him to hold levees every five days and make decisions on trifling matters.

In 665, Princess Taiping (665-713), the daughter of Empress Wu, was born. Hence, Empress Wu had four sons and a daughter, excluding the daughter who had died before.

On the third day of the ninth moon in 667, the emperor was ill and let the crown prince hold levees for him.

In the twelfth moon of 672, since the crown prince seldom had visitors at meal time, the official in charge of his meals reduced the number of dishes provided to the crown prince. (There was a certain number of dishes for every meal provided for the emperor, the empress, the crown prince and the concubines respectively.) The emperor praised the official and promoted him.

One day in 673, the crown prince was strolling in the palace garden and came across a deserted place, but he noticed that there were still some palace sentinels guarding the place. He approached to ask the sentinel there and was told that two women were confined inside. The women looked to be over thirty years old; they were Princess Yiyang and Princess Xuancheng, the daughters of the deceased Concubine Xiao. They had been confined there for nineteen years. The crown prince released them and reported it to the emperor. Then Empress Wu married them to two of the palace guards. Generally princesses would be married to men of higher social status or men born into noble families. When Empress Wu became sovereign empress, the two guards, husbands of the two princesses, were killed, being found guilty of something or other. The two princesses went to a nunnery to be nuns. The relationship between Empress Wu and her eldest son began to unravel since the son had released the two princesses without getting permission from his mother first. Hence, the death of the son afterwards raised rumors.

On the first day of the tenth moon in 673, the wedding ceremony of the crown prince and the daughter of General Pei took place. The feast lasted for three days.

On the twenty-fifth day of the fourth moon in 675, the crown prince, Li Hong, died at the age of twenty-four. A rumor went round that Li Hong was poisoned by Heavenly Empress Wu, his mother, as he did not listen to her and did things his own way, and Heavenly Empress Wu could not tolerate a disobedient son. But it was long understood that Li Hong was already suffering from tuberculosis, which could not be cured at that time. Why should his mother take the trouble to poison him?

On the fifth day of the fifth moon, the emperor gave his deceased son a posthumous honorary title of Emperor Xiaojing (Xiao here means Filial and Jing here means Respect), which meant that if he had lived he would have been Emperor Xiaojing in due course. Generally in feudal China, an emperor only gave such a posthumous honorary title to his father or grandfather who had never been an emperor in life. This was the first time that such a title was given to a son. Emperors in the later dynasties followed suit.

On the fifth day of the sixth moon, Li Xianl, the younger brother of the late crown prince and the second son of Heavenly Empress Wu, was made crown prince. Li Xianl was already an adult and a man of ability. He had always resented his mother's interference in politics. Therefore, he gathered some scholars to annotate the book "History of the Later Han Dynasty." He indirectly criticized the in-laws of that time who usurped the power of the emperor, which was an innuendo to his mother.

When Heavenly Empress Wu learned of this, she was annoyed and had a book titled "Biography of Filial Sons" written. She gave a copy of it to her second son, in hopes that he could be filial to his parents. But Li Xianl did not like his mother to tell him what to do and so a breach arose between mother and the son almost at the beginning of his political career.

On the nineteenth day of the eighth moon, the late crown prince was buried in a tomb called Mausoleum Gong. The emperor wrote the epitaph himself and had it inscribed on the tombstone, which was set up on one side of the mausoleum entrance.

On the twenty-third day of the first moon in 676, Xulun, the youngest son of Heavenly Empress Wu, was re-titled Prince Xiang.

On the third day of the twelfth moon in 676, the annotation of the book "History of the Later Han Dynasty" was finished and the crown prince delivered it to the emperor, who praised him.

In the eighth moon of 680, there was a rumor in the palace that Li Xian was not born to Heavenly Empress Wu, but to her elder sister Lady HanGuo, who was married to the courtier Helan (double surname) Yueshi, who died young. Her son was Helan Minzhi. When her sister had become the empress she often came to visit her sister and stayed in the palace. It was said that the emperor occasionally had intimate relations with her and that that was why it was said that she was poisoned by her sister. If that were the truth, Li Xian was not qualified to be the crown prince. So he secretly harbored fear. Then a courtier, Ming Congyan, said to Heavenly Empress Wu that the present crown prince was not fated to be an emperor. Li Xian1 learned it and sent some assassin to murder Ming Congyan. That was not a clever move.

Ming Congyan was born into a scholar's family. In his youth, he went to live with his father, who was then the mayor of Anxi (An here means Safety and Xi here means Happiness) Town. A petty clerk in the yamen was versed in astrology and could exercise witchcraft for healing people. Ming Congyan learned all such things from him. In 666, he was recommended to the government and was appointed the vice mayor of HuangAn (Huang here means Yellow and An here means Safety) Town. When the daughter of the magistrate of this district was suffering from a serious disease, he went there to cure her. Before long, the emperor heard of his reputation and summoned him to the capital. After a conversation, the emperor liked him very much and gave him a courtier's position. Empress Wu often sent for him to come to the palace. Every time he wanted to express his opinion to the emperor or the empress, he would say that he had received it from a deity. When he saw that the crown prince would not make a good emperor, he couched it in terms of destiny. But this time he paid for what he said with his life. The murderer was still at large, though Heavenly Empress Wu suspected that the crown prince was behind it.

The crown prince sensed the approach of danger and was scheming something drastic. The crown prince liked music and sex. He was especially fond of a young eunuch called Zhao Daosheng. It was this eunuch the crown prince sent to kill Ming Zongyan with a poisoned arrow. Someone reported the assassin to Heavenly Empress Wu, who let the courtiers Pei Yan and Qian Weidao question him. The eunuch confessed to the murder and said that he did it at the order of the crown prince. So the palace guards were sent to search the residence of the crown prince and a great amount of armor and weapons were found in his stables, which was deemed a sign of treason because the whole palace had the imperial bodyguards to take care of defense and the crown prince had no need to store such things.

On the twenty-second day of the eighth moon, Li Xian1 was deposed as crown prince and was confined in the main capital. His younger brother Li Xian3 succeeded as crown prince. But he was too young to handle things alone. So Heavenly Empress Wu still helped the Heavenly Emperor in the administration of national affairs and she even held levees in behalf of the Heavenly Emperor.

On the tenth day of the first moon in 681, a banquet was given for the celebration of the new crown prince. On the twenty-second day of the third moon, Princess Taiping, daughter of Heavenly Empress Wu, was married to Xue Shao, who was the son of Princess Chengyang, the daughter of late Emperor Taizong, and also the stepsister of the present emperor. It meant that Xue Shao was the cousin of Princess Taiping. (People believed in marrying cousins to each other so as to make the close relationship closer.) Once before, a messenger had come from Tibet to beg the hand of Princess Taiping for their new king. The Heavenly Emperor and Heavenly Empress Wu were so fond of Princess Taiping that they would not marry her far away to Tibet. So the Heavenly Emperor had a Taoist temple built for her and Princess Taiping pretended to be a female Taoist. According to the tradition in the old time, a Taoist, whether a male or a female, could not get married — just like a monk. (Unlike monks, Taoists, whether male or female, did not need to be tonsured. They just tied their hair up in a specific type of knot on the top of the head. So it was easy to return to be an ordinary person, who could get married, by just changing the hairdo back into the style ordinary people wore.) Thus, Heavenly Emperor would not offend the Tibetan king by refusing to marry Princess Taiping to him.

Xue Shao came from a big noble family. There was a history of intermarriage between Li family and Xue family; for instance, Princess Chengyang married the father of Xue Shao. Their marriage lasted for seven years and they had two sons and two daughters. Xue Shao died in prison when he was accused of joining a mutiny against Heavenly Empress Wu, for whom the most unbearable and unforgivable crime was treason. He might have been falsely accused since he mingled with those Li princes who rebelled. Another factor in the death of Xue Shao was that Xue Shao was chosen by the emperor. Empress Wu did not like Xue Shao. She thought that the wife of the brother of Xue Shao came from an ordinary family, not suitable to be sisters-in-law with her daughter. If Xue Shao had been liked and selected by her, Heavenly Empress Wu might have pardoned him.

In the eleventh moon, Li Xianl, the ex-crown prince, was relocated to Bachow (Ba here is the name of an ancient nation in the eastern part of the present Sichuan Province), still in confinement

On the nineteenth day of the second moon in 682, the grandson Li Chong-zhao, born to the crown prince, was one month old. An edict of amnesty was issued. On the twenty-fifth day of the third moon, the little grandson was made the grand-crown-prince, which meant that he would succeed to the throne when his father, the present crown prince and presumed eventual emperor, died.

On the nineteenth day of the seventh moon in 683, the fourth son of Heavenly Empress Wu had his name changed from Li Xulun to Li Dan and his title changed from Prince Xiang to Prince Yu. The crown prince was summoned to the east capital.

On the fifth day of the third moon in 684, Li Xianl, the second son of Empress Dowager Wu committed suicide in Bachow, where he had been sent to live in confinement since being deposes as crown prince. General Qiu Shenji had been sent to watch over Li Xianl for fear that he might be scheming a mutiny, taking his chance when his father died. One hypothesis was that Li Xianl could not bear the thought that he would live in confinement for the rest of his life and so killed himself. Another supposition was that General Qiu forced him to commit suicide. When the sad news came, Empress Dowager Wu wept and held a memorial service for him and granted him the title of Prince Yong posthumously. General Qiu Shenji was demoted to be the magistrate of Diechow. But before long, he was summoned back to the capital. Does that mean that the second supposition was correct, or why else was General Qiu demoted and then summoned back so soon?

On the fifth day of the eighth moon in 685, the grandson of Empress Dowager Wu, Li Longji, was born, who would be a future emperor of the Tang Dynasty. (This emperor would kill Princess Taiping in the fight for power when he was already the emperor. Princess Taiping was an ambitious person like her mother. She could only run after power after her mother died, not when her mother was alive. But she failed in vying for power with her nephew, the lawful emperor.)

In 690, Princess Taiping, the only daughter of Empress Dowager Wu, was a widow now. Empress Dowager Wu wanted to marry her to Wu Youji, one of her nephews. This nephew had already married. According to Chinese tradition, any woman who married a man with a wife could only be a concubine, but a princess could not be a concubine, particularly her daughter. Therefore, Empress Dowager Wu had the wife secretly killed and then married her daughter to him. She loved her daughter very much because the daughter was very much like her in both disposition and behavior. Empress Dowager Wu often discussed political affairs with her.

The marriage of Princess Taiping with Wu Youji lasted for twenty-two years and they had two sons and a daughter. Wu Youji died one year before Princess Taiping did.

On the twenty-fourth day of the first moon in 693, two courtiers Pei Feigong and Fan Yunxian came to the palace to see the crown prince. Somehow, Holy Empress Wu learned of it and was afraid that they would plot against her. Then she had the two courtiers executed and prohibited her son to see any courtiers afterwards.

Holy Empress Wu liked a palace maid named TuanEr and believed whatever she said. TuanEr wanted to be a concubine to the crown prince. But the crown prince did not even like her. Besides, the wife of the crown prince, née Liu, and his Concubine De, née Dou, drove her away. Therefore, she carved a small wooden figure and buried it somewhere in the residence of the crown prince. Then she reported to Holy Empress Wu that the wife of the crown prince and his Concubine De had cursed Her Majesty by a kind of black art. At her guidance the figure was dug up. So when the wife and the concubine came to pay their respects to Holy Empress Wu, they were secretly murdered and buried somewhere in the palace. Later when the crown prince learned of it, he did not dare to say anything but pretended the ignorance. After a while, TuanEr wanted to make false report of the crown prince himself. But her plot was revealed to Holy Empress Wu, who killed TuanEr. That was in 693.

Someone instigated a servant working for the family of Concubine De's father by telling him how to make false accusations. The servant told a false story of something horrible that happened in their garden to the mistress of the family, i.e., the mother of Concubine De, who had already died. The purpose was to make the mother terrified, and it worked. Then the servant suggested that she should ask someone to practice black art to get rid of the horrible thing. The use of the black art was against the law at that time. The mother followed his advice and the servant informed the government about it. So the mother was arrested and tried by a courtier, Xue Jichang, who made a false report to Holy Empress Wu, saying that the mother had cursed Her Majesty by using the black art. Holy Empress Wu decided that the mother should be put to death. One of her sons came to see the just and upright courtier Xu Yougong, who told the executioner to delay the execution. He went to see Holy Empress Wu and revealed the false indictment, concluding that the mother was not guilty. Later the courtier Xue said to Holy Empress Wu that Xu Yougong had pleaded for the criminal and he deserved a death sentence. Someone told Xu Yougong and thought he must be in panic. But he was seen fast asleep. Next day, Holy Empress Wu sent for him and asked,

"How can the difference be so great between the verdict of a death sentence and not guilty?" Xu answered, "If the 'not guilty' verdict is a mistake, it's the fault of your humble servant; but if a life can be saved, it's the mercy of Your Holy Majesty." Holy Empress Wu fell in silence. Therefore, the sentence was changed from death to exile to a remote region together with her three sons. The husband, the father of Concubine De, was demoted from the magistrate of Runchow (meaning Moist District) to be a petty official in Luochow (Luo here is a surname). Xu Yougong was removed from the official position.

Xue Jichang (?–706) sent in a memorial to Empress Wu when she just had become the sovereign empress. Empress Wu liked the ideas expressed in his memorial and made him an imperial censor, the position for a courtier whose duties were to reveal to Empress Wu the illegal things any of the courtiers did. Then he did something Empress Wu did not like and so was demoted, but before long, he was restored to the former position.

Once courtier Hou Weixu was sent to fight Qidan Clan in the north and was defeated. Hou wanted to conceal that failure and sent in a false report to Empress Wu, saying that Qidan warriors had tigers and snakes as a vanguard so that the Tang army could not resist. Empress Wu did not believe it and sent Xue Jichang to investigate. Xue rushed directly into the military camp and arrested Hou. When Xue learned the truth and obtained evidence, he had Hou executed right away. Once Xue Jichang went to Bing (meaning Report) Town to gather proof against a law officer there. When his corruption was verified, Xue had him flogged to death. These actions won Xue a good reputation. When he returned to the capital, he was promoted, but soon he made some mistake and was demoted to be the magistrate of Dingchow (meaning Fix District). In 700, he was transferred to Yongchow (meaning Harmony District) as an administrator. There he punished many local rogues. In 705, he joined the coup d'état to force Empress Wu to abdicate and give the throne back to her son. Next year he poisoned himself when other five courtiers, who started the coup d'état, were killed by Wu Sansi, a nephew of Empress Wu.

Xu Yougong (641–702) was a just and upstanding judge who had saved lives of hundreds of families from the unprincipled courtiers. Three years after he was removed from his official position, he was appointed an imperial censor. He had three times been on the verge of death, under various accusations by the dishonest courtiers. But Empress Wu knew him well and would not agree to have him executed.

It was almost inconceivable that a woman would become a sovereign in feudal China since women had almost no status in the society. But Empress Wu had the wisdom to direct the development of things toward her goal. She also had the patience to wait for the right time.

After the death of Heavenly Emperor Gaozong in 683, his third son succeeded to the throne and became Emperor Zhongzong. On the first day of the first moon in 684, Emperor Zhongzong's wife, née Wei, was made the empress; hence, she was called Empress Wei. The father-in-law, Wei Xuanzhen, was promoted from an official in Puchow (Common District) to be the magistrate of Yuchow (Happy District).

At the beginning of the second moon the emperor wanted to make his father-in-law, Wei Xuanzhen, a prime minister, and the son of his wet nurse an official in the central government, but prime ministers Pei Yan and Liu Weizhi raised objections. The emperor was angry and spat out without thinking, "What if I want to give Wei Xuanzhen the whole empire? Why can't I make him a prime minister?" Pei Yan was afraid that the new emperor would actually do it and said so to Empress Dowager Wu, who thought that this son of hers was not suitable to emperor if he could even imagine giving away the empire so easily. If he was joking, he was a reckless person because that was not a matter to be joking about.

Emperor Zhongzong was really a good-for-nothing. He was not fond of studies, but led a loose life. When he was still the crown prince, the courtiers who worked for him all kept him at a respectful distance. He had divorced his first wife, née Zhou, in 675 and married this wife, who was ambitious and capable. He always listened to her. He had no supporters among the courtiers. He wanted to appoint his father-in-law as a prime minister that he could at least have one to side with him. But the head prime minister Pei Yan preferred his younger brother Li Dan to be the emperor and of course objected to his unreasonable decision.

Liu Weizhi was well-known for his literary and poetic talent in his youth. When he became a courtier, he was gradually promoted to be a prime minister. But he had the temerity to express his opinion that Empress Wu should return the power to the emperor, and he was ordered to end his own life at home on the third day of the fifth moon in 687.

On the sixth day of the second moon, Empress Dowager Wu held the levee in the Qianyuan (Qian here representing Heaven, and Yuan here means Beginning) Hall in Luoyang Palace, and the emperor was present. Prime ministers Pei Yan and Liu Weizhi and generals Cheng Wuting and Zhang Qianmao came in with the imperial bodyguards. They read to the emperor a decree issued by Empress Dowager Wu to depose him from the throne. The emperor asked, "What did I do to deserve this?" Empress Dowager Wu answered, "You wanted to give the whole empire to Wei Xuanzhen. Do you think that's right?" The emperor was taken by the bodyguards to a place of confinement and was given a title of Prince Luling.

Cheng Wuting (?–685) was a famous general in the Tang Dynasty. His father was also a general. Cheng Wuting went with his father to fight in battles in his youth. His bravery was well known in the Tang army. When he was made a general, he was sent to fight invaders here and there. The Tujue Clan dreaded Cheng so much that wherever Cheng was in defense of a city, the Tujue Clan never invaded that place. But they admired him so much that they built a temple to worship him after he was killed at the command of Empress Wu because he was deemed an accomplice of Pei Yan. (Details later in this chapter.)

On the seventh day, his brother Li Dan, Prince Yu, was made the emperor, called Emperor Ruizong. Li Dan was the youngest son of Empress Dowager Wu, born on the first day of the sixth moon in 662 and died in 716. At the age of twenty-two, he was directly made emperor, in the emergency, skipping the stage of crown prince. But he let his mother take care of all state matters anyway. He knew very well that he had no experience to handle such complicated affairs, and was unprepared for being made emperor. He would have to learn from his mother. Meanwhile, his wife, née Liu, was made empress, called Empress Liu. Although this son was not experienced and learned, he was at least wise. He knew very well that his mother would never give up power. So he just let his mother handle everything and never thought of taking things out of her hands.

On the eighth day, Chongzhao, the grandson of Empress Dowager Wu, was abolished from his position of grand-crown-prince, and Wei Xuanzhen was banished to Qinchow (meaning Admiration District). On the tenth day of the fourth moon in 684, Li Shangjin was re-titled again as Prince Ze and made the magistrate of Suchow (Su here is a surname). Li Sujie was also re-titled again as Prince Xu and made the magistrate of Jiangchow (Jiang here denotes the color of crimson).

Li Shangjin (?–690) was the third son of Emperor Gaozong. His mother was not even a concubine. After Emperor Gaozong attained the throne, he was given a title of Prince Qi. In 652, he was appointed the governor of Yichow (Benefits District). In 666, he was transferred to be the magistrate of Shouchow (Longevity District). As Empress Wu did not like his mother, he was later deprived of his official position and fief and sent to live in Lichow (Li here is the name of a river). In 682, he was made the magistrate of Mianchow (Mian here is the name of a river).

Li Sujie (648–690) was the fourth son of Emperor Gaozong. His mother was Concubine Xiao, killed by Empress Wu. He was clever and his father liked him very much. After his mother died, he was demoted to be the magistrate of Shenchow (Shen here means Narration). In 678, he was transferred to be the magistrate of Yuechow (Yue here is a surname). In 690, Wu Chengsi, nephew of Empress Wu, wanted the devious courtier Zhou Xing to make a false accusation that Li Shangjin and Li Sujie were stirring up trouble. They were summoned back to the east capital, Luoyang City, to be tried. When Li Sujie was killed, Li Shangjin was so fearful that he hanged himself. Seven sons of Li Shangjin were exiled to Xianchow (Xian here means Show), and six of them died there. Only one survived. Nine adult sons of Li Sujie were killed and four younger sons were banished to Leichow (meaning Thunder District).

On the twenty-sixth day of the fourth moon in 684, Prince Luling, the ex-emperor Zhongzong, was dispatched to live in Junchow (Average District), the present Jun Town in Hubei (Lake North) Province, still in confinement.

On the fifteenth day of the fifth moon, the new emperor Ruizong left Luoyang City with his late father's coffin for ChangAn City to bury his father there. Empress Dowager Wu wanted to go herself, but she was afraid that something might happen if she was away. The imperial coffin was carried on a sturdy wagon drawn by horses and escorted by a thousand soldiers. Everyone wore clothes of white linen with a hood of the same material on the head — traditional mourning clothes. The procession proceeded slowly and arrived at the destination in the sixth moon.

The tomb was not finished yet, though there were one hundred thousand laborers working at it. The imperial coffin was put in the old palace and the officials and courtiers in ChangAn City all came to pay their last homage to the deceased emperor.

On the ninth day of the seventh moon, Lu Yuanrui, the governor of Guangchow (Guang here means Wide) City was killed by a foreigner. Lu was a weak man and lost the control of the officials under him. The officials took full advantage whenever they could. Whenever ships came from other countries, they would make the merchants on board pay more money as tariff than necessary. Once when a foreign merchant complained to the governor, the governor did not reprimand his officials but sought to detain the merchant. All the foreigners were indignant. One of them went straight into the yamen and killed the governor with a sword. He also killed more than ten men there and then went aboard the ship, which sailed away right off. No one in the yamen dared to step forth to stop him.

A courtier named Feng Yuanchang was demoted to be the magistrate of Guangchow. Feng had advised the late Heavenly Emperor to suppress the power of Heavenly Empress Wu. The late Heavenly Emperor could not take that advice, even though he had thought it right. When Heavenly Empress Wu became Empress Dowager Wu, the mayor of Songyang (Song is the name of a mountain and Yang means the Sun) City, sent in a good luck stone (generally there was some picture or lines looking like some words with a good meaning on this kind of stone). Empress Dowager Wu showed it to the courtiers. Feng said that it was a fake, just a common pebble such as might be found in many places. Empress Dowager Wu did not like what he said and demoted him. As the governor of Guangchow, he put down the rebellion of Li Sixian. Usually he should be given a reward for that, but Empress Dowager Wu did not grant him any. At last he was summoned back to the capital and was killed in the jail at a false accusation of the cruel courtier Zhou Xing.

Early in the eighth moon, the tomb was completed. On the eleventh day, the funeral was held early in the morning. The emperor began to mourn the death of his father and funeral music played. Then the coffin was placed on the wagon. Generally for an emperor, there were three coffins: the basic one containing the body put in another coffin a little bigger in size and both put in another still bigger one. Six thick ropes, each ten meters long, were tied on either side of the wagon, which were not drawn by horses this time, but pulled by a thousand bodyguards in white linen. On each side walked sixty-four funeral musicians and backed up by one hundred and fifty criers to help the imperial family members, courtiers and officials with wailing at the mourning ceremony. When the coffin reached the entrance of the tomb, it stopped for a while. The princesses and all other females stood on the west side of the coffin while the emperor and the courtiers and other males on the east side. All started to cry loudly. Then wine was offered to the ghost of the late emperor and a libation followed. A courtier made the funeral speech. When all these were done, the coffin was rolled into the cave and raised and put down on a platform. It was covered with a quilt. The wagon was taken out and burned at the side of the tomb. Great quantities of porcelain and earthen wares, and gold and silver ornaments decorated the inside of the tomb. Tapestry hung on the cave wall. Pearls and precious stones, paintings and books that the late emperor had enjoyed when alive were all buried with him. Then the entrance of the tomb was closed with two stone gates and the space outside the gates was filled with stone slates. The gaps between the slates were sealed with melted iron. The late Heavenly Emperor was interred in the grand tomb built for him.

On the sixth day of the ninth moon, an edict was issued for an amnesty. The color of the flags was changed to golden. Empress Dowager Wu renamed the east capital, that is, Luoyang City, as the Divine Capital, and called her palace Taichu Palace. From then on, she lived there and never went back to the former capital, ChangAn City.

On the seventh day of the second moon in 685, an order was given that the big drum in front of the levee hall should not be guarded so that anyone who had any complaints to make could beat it and the concerned officials must take care of the person. This put an end to the guards' practice of preventing people from beating the drum, which led to trouble.

On the eleventh day of the third moon, Prince Luling, the deposed emperor, was relocated to Fangchow (House District).

In the fourth moon, a courtier who had been demoted complained to the prime ministers. Prime Minister Qian Weidao said that it had been decided by Empress Dowager Wu, by which he meant that he could not do anything to help him. Another prime minister, Liu Weizhi, observed that demotions were generally proposed by a courtier first, by which he meant that it had been the idea of a courtier and Empress Dowager Wu had just given her assent. When Empress Dowager Wu heard about the discussion, she demoted Qian to be the magistrate of Qingchow (meaning Black District) and granted Liu an honorary title. She said, "The sovereign and the courtiers are like a body. A courtier should not ascribe the bad to the sovereign and the good to himself."

In the same moon, an order was given that permitted men of talent to recommend themselves to the government so that the government might employ them, using their talent to serve the people and the nation. Before the Tang Dynasty, the government officials and officers were chosen from the families of nobility, and generally through official recommendations. At the beginning of the Tang Dynasty, Emperor Taizong had sought to widen the base of candidates and had started to hold government tests so that men of talent all over the nation could come to be selected. But many courtiers had opposed it.

Now, as Empress Dowager Wu was the first woman to rule the country in the history of China, her elevation to sovereign was against tradition and this irked many men, especially those from the noble families. Therefore, Empress Dowager Wu issued the order broadening the pool of candidates so that she could select courtiers from among the common people, who would be her supporters.

Every government has officials to serve it, but if the officials are corrupt, it is worse than no officials at all. Empress Dowager Wu wanted all her courtiers to be capable and moral. So she wrote an article titled "Rules for Courtiers" and listed ten rules for them to observe:

> 1) Courtiers must do everything in accordance with the sovereign, as limbs act in accordance with the body, and perform their duties faithfully. 2) Courtiers must base their behavior on mercy; not talk much about their merits; attribute goodness to the sovereign and errors to one's self. 3) Courtiers must not be greedy; behave well; and not allow fame or rewards to taint their morals. 4) Courtiers must be just to everyone in everything; forget personal interests while handling official affairs; avoid twisting the law while involving one's own relatives, and recommend men of ability to the government even if they are one's enemies. 5) Courtiers must point out any mistakes and faults of the sovereign, even at the risk of losing their life. 6) Courtiers must be loyal and honest to the sovereign and others; for when everyone trusts each other, no suspicion will exist. 7) Courtiers must preserve state secrets; never divulge what was said at court; be mindful what they say and what they do. 8) Eschew corruption; not seek what is not their due; and use the laws to serve, not to harm the people. 9) Courtiers must act like good generals, brave and decisive, and allow nothing to disturb their wisdom and cloud their insight; be trustworthy and not cheat; be upright and not crooked; the day they are ordered to go to war, forget their home; the day they leave for the battlefield, forget their family; when in the campground before the battle, forget their sovereign; when fighting, forget themselves. 10) A courtier's first thought should be to benefit the people, encouraging agricultural activities and sparing peasants from excessive tax and public service; avoid interfering with people's work so that every family will have enough and to spare.

In the first moon of 686, Empress Dowager Wu offered to turn the power over to the emperor, but the emperor was smart enough to refuse the offer and insisted that Empress Dowager Wu should continue to handle the administration. And so she did.

On the second day of the tenth moon, according to the history book, a hill emerged out of the ground to the southeast of Xinfeng (meaning New Abundance) Town, the present Lintong (Lin here means Near and Tong here is the name of a town) Town in Shaanxi (Shaan here is the name of a place and Xi here means West) Province). The courtiers thought that it was a good sign to the nation and handed in memorials to sing the praise of the sovereignty. Empress Dowager Wu renamed Xinfeng Town as Celebrating-Hill Town.

A man called Yu Wenjun sent in a memorial, saying that if Heaven was not in harmony, unusual weather would occur; if human body was not in harmony, disease would occur; if the earth was not in harmony, unusual things would occur; and that the emerging of the hill was an unusual thing. He added that as a female Her Majesty was occupying a position that should belong to a male, and that was why an unusual thing happened like the emerging of a hill. While Her Majesty thought it a good sign, he thought it a bad omen. He continued that if Her Majesty did not retire from power, disasters would unfold. Empress Dowager Wu was incensed and banished him to a remote region. He was killed, later, with other exiles.

Di Renji was at that time the magistrate of Ningchow (Calm District). He did a good job there. Empress Dowager Wu summoned him to the capital and appointed him a vice minister of the Construction Ministry.

In the fourth moon of 687, a courtier Pei Feigong inspected the imperial gardens in the capital and suggested to sell the vegetables and fruits growing there to get some profits. A courtier Su Liangsi said, "Never heard in the history that a sovereign sold vegetables and fruits." So Empress Dowager Wu did not agree to the suggestion.

On the seventh day of the fifth moon, a courtier Liu Weizhi said to another courtier Jia Dayin, "Since the empress dowager replaced her good-for-nothing son with the capable one, why does Her Majesty still hold levees? Why not return power to the emperor so that everyone will be at rest."

Jia Dayin reported it to Empress Dowager Wu, who was irate. Then someone sent in a false report that Liu Weizhi had taken the bribe from Sun Wanrong, the governor of Chengchow (Honesty District) and also had committed adultery with a concubine of courtier Xu Jingzong. Empress Dowager Wu ordered Wang Liben, the magistrate of Suchow (Respect District), to try the case.

When Wang read the edict from Empress Dowager Wu to Liu Weizhi, Liu boldly asked, "How can it be called an imperial edict if not issued by the emperor?" In ancient China the refusal or disdain of an imperial edict was a serious crime. So Liu was ordered to end his own life, at home.

Even as a teenager, Liu Weizhi had been famous as a scholar and later had been summoned to the palace as a counselor. When Empress Dowager Wu rose in power he had been promoted and finally reached the position of a prime minister. He had drafted almost all the imperial edicts for Empress Dowager Wu. He must have been entirely fed up with life to say such a fatal thing.

Originally Empress Dowager Wu had wanted to restrain the in-laws of the imperial family because those in-laws never did anything beneficial to the nation. The in-laws included her relatives. But as the situation changed, she needed supporters, as many as possible. Her relatives ought to have been her most faithful supporters. So she wanted to promote her relatives to higher positions. As a preliminary step, she had a temple built for the Wu family to worship their ancestors. In feudal China, only the Li family, founders of the Tang Dynasty, had had the right to build such a temple. Empress Dowager Wu had no right to construct a temple of the same sort as that of the Li family. Against tradition! Quite a few relatives of the Li family were more and more dissatisfied with her.

On the eleventh day of the first moon in 688, Empress Dowager Wu ordered Qianyuan Hall pulled down and Ming Hall (a place for all important ceremonies to be held) to be constructed on the site. Ming Hall had a specific style and structure, and was said to have first been built by Zhou Gong (?–1105), a prime minister at the beginning of the West Zhou Dynasty (1121 BC–771 BC). It had frequently been imitated by subsequent dynasties. Since all the important events would take place there, it would appear to have been very important to a sovereign.

Although the name of Ming Hall had been recorded in the history books, no one in subsequent dynasties really knew how a Ming Hall should be built — no one had any notion about its specific style and structure. In the dynasties previous to the Tang Dynasty, a Ming Hall had been constructed according to the imagination of the architect, approved by the emperor.

The second emperor of the Tang Dynasty, Taizong, had wished to build a Ming Hall and ordered the courtiers to discuss it, but no one could tell him what a Ming Hall looked like. There were too many different opinions. Emperor Taizong could not decide which version he would adopt and his dream never came true. The third emperor, Gaozong, the husband of Empress Dowager Wu, had also desired to build a Ming Hall. However, for the same reason, his desire had not been accomplished in his lifetime. Too many cooks spoiled the broth.

Aware of the reason for previous failures, Empress Dowager Wu did not discuss it with courtiers and just asked the opinions of a few of her loyal followers, called the North Gate Scholars, because they always gathered in a building at the north gate of the palace. Although the courtiers were not consulted over the construction of the Ming Hall, they were permitted to express their opinions about the plan of Empress Dowager Wu when it was announced. Some courtiers suggested that it should be built on a site three miles from the palace, but Empress Dowager Wu thought it too far and inconvenient for her to travel there and back so often. So she ordered the

Qianyuan Hall to be pulled down and Ming Hall to be built on the site. She ordered her favorite, the monk Xue Huaiyi, to take charge of the construction, though he knew nothing about architecture.

STANDING AT THE TOP

In the fourth moon of 588, Wu Chengsi, a nephew of Empress Dowager Wu, had a stone inscribed with the words "Holy Mother descends from Heaven; Her imperial career everlasting," and had it buried in the bank of the Luo River. Then he sent someone to dig it up and report to Empress Dowager Wu as a sign from Heaven that she should be the sovereign empress, not just the empress dowager. Empress Dowager Wu got the news and liked it very much. She also thought that she was destined to be the sovereign empress.

On the eleventh day of the fifth moon, Empress Dowager Wu decided to worship the Luo River in acceptance of the heaven-granted precious stone. She ordered the princes, imperial in-laws, governors and magistrates to gather in the capital ten days before the worshipping ceremony.

On the eighteenth day of the same moon, she took another noble title: Holy Mother Heavenly Empress.

Since the successive rebellions had been respectively conquered, it was now the high time for Empress Dowager Wu to be crowned as the first female sovereign in Chinese history. But in 688, before the coronation, she had to go first to worship the Luo River, where the stone from Heaven had been found. At the ceremony she could see whether the courtiers and people would support her becoming the sovereign empress.

On the twenty-fifth day of the twelfth moon, there was a fine snowfall. An earthen platform had been built on the north bank of the Luo River. Empress Dowager Wu went to worship the Luo River there. The ceremony was accompanied with special music composed for the occasion. Empress Dowager Wu wrote the words herself.

The procession stretched out for several *li* (one *li* is equal to half a kilometer), consisting of horse soldiers and foot soldiers all carrying either banners or weapons, of big drums and other musical instruments on horse-drawn wagons, and of all kinds of royal coaches, in one of which rode Empress Dowager Wu.

All the courtiers were present, and people came from far and near to watch the ceremony. The place was crowded, but no one made any sound. Empress Dowager Wu stepped down from her coach. When she started toward the platform, the music and singing began. The courtiers and soldiers held their positions in the ritual. No one stirred. Empress Dowager Wu walked to the platform and ascended it. She looked around at the snow-covered mountains at a distance and at the human throngs nearby. She was facing the Luo River, which flowed slowly from west to east. She worshipped the river with the accompaniment of the music and singing. Then the Heaven-granted precious stone was given to her by the master of ceremonies. The ritual thus ended, and Empress Dowager Wu returned to her palace.

Later the local people set up a stone tablet there with an inscription about the event. This indicated that the people supported her rule. But Empress Dowager Wu was a careful person, and was not in a hurry to be crowned as the sovereign empress of a new dynasty.

On the twenty-seventh day of the twelfth moon, just two days after the ceremony, the magnificent Ming Hall was finished, which was ninety-one meters fourteen centimeters high with square bottom and the circumference of ninety-three meters. It had three stories. The first floor had four doors and eight windows, representing four seasons. The second floor represented the twelve sections of the day's time (in ancient China the 24-hour cycle was divided into twelve sections, each section equal to two hours as we presently count time) with the circumference decorated on the outside walls with nine dragons. The top floor had a dome with a gilded flying phoenix on it.

The Ming Hall was intended as a place for Empress Dowager Wu to hold court and also for other important ceremonies to be held there. Empress Dowager Wu named it as Omnifarious Divine Hall and allowed the public to visit it for a certain period of time before she began to use it.

On the first day of the first moon in 689, which was the Chinese New Year's Day, Empress Dowager Wu held a feast in the Divine Hall. All the courtiers attended. Then the hall was officially used for political events.

Now the only thing wanting was a convincing reason why Empress Dowager Wu should be the sovereign empress of a new dynasty. Although a few small nations in the vicinity of China had had female sovereigns in previous or contemporary times, it had never happened in such a large country as China.

In Han Dynasty (206 BC–220), Buddhism was introduced into China from India and spread very fast throughout the country. Quite a few emperors had a pious belief in Buddhism, which made it more influential in the life and concept of Chinese people. The mother of Empress Dowager Wu had been a pious believer and used her influence to have a crumbled temple repaired and also a pagoda built at the site of Shaolin Temple when her daughter had risen in power. Empress Dowager Wu believed in Buddhism, too. She knew that the Buddhist sutras contained information that would be helpful about a woman being a sovereign.

The monk Xue Huaiyi, who had been in charge of the construction of Ming Hall, handed in a memorial (written by someone else) stating that according to a certain Buddhist sutra he had been reading, Her Majesty was the incarnation of Buddha Maitreya and should be the ruler of a new dynasty to replace the present Tang Dynasty.

Then many copies were made of that sutra and sent out to the remotest corner of the country to let people know that Buddha had foretold in this sutra that Holy Mother was sent down to rule the country.

On the first day of the eleventh moon, Empress Dowager Wu changed the calendar. She named the eleventh moon as the initial moon in the new calendar, the twelfth moon as the winter moon and the first moon still called the first moon. But actually, the initial moon would be the first moon of the year in the new calendar and the so-called first moon was the third moon.

Then she issued new policies for governors and magistrates to follow. The local government should take care of the bereaved family of deceased soldiers. If the son or sons were still too young to work, the local government must provide them with basic rations. The local rich families should help them with seeds for sowing in spring. The local government should uphold the customs and traditions that wealthy families should be frugal in their expenses for daily clothes and funerals and burials. The local government should also encourage people to marry when reaching an appropriate age.

On the eighth day of the initial moon in 690, Empress Dowager Wu created a new Chinese word for her given name. The new word was added to the dictionary. It consisted of three existing Chinese characters. One Chinese character meant "the sun," which was put side by side with the character meaning "the moon," and then both were put over the character meaning "the sky." So the new word meant "(she was like) the sun and the moon in the sky."

In the second moon, Empress Dowager Wu gave new tests in her palace for the selection of officials and courtiers. These tests were called palace tests. The tests lasted for several days. Before the Tang Dynasty, the selection of government officials had been made by recommendation by active officials, so many men of talent were left in the cold outside the political door. The selection of the officials and courtiers by tests had started in the Sui Dynasty, the dynasty previous to the Tang Dynasty. But as the Sui Dynasty was short-lived, the procedures for the tests were still evolving. The tests really commenced in the Tang Dynasty at the reign of the second emperor, Emperor Taozong, who had taken Empress Dowager Wu into the palace as one of his concubines.

On the twentieth day of the third moon, Empress Dowager Wu made her nephew Wu Chengsi a prime minister. He had been the minister of Official Ministry before.

On the third day of the ninth moon, a courtier Fu Youyi, together with nine hundred people, petitioned that Empress Dowager Wu should establish the Zhou Dynasty for the Wu family. Empress Dowager Wu humbly demurred, but promoted Fu Youyi to a higher position. Then people living in the capital and its vicinity, numbered more than twelve thousand, including a few courtiers and the famous poet Chen ZiAng, came to submit a petition to that effect. But Empress Dowager Wu still refused it.

On the fifth day, some courtiers reported that a phoenix had been seen perching on a Chinese parasol tree for a long while and then flying toward the southeast, and that hundreds of thousands of scarlet sparrows had gathered in the place where court was held. (Both were good omens, and that is how the history book recorded it.)

On the seventh day, all the courtiers, imperial relatives, chieftains of tribal groups, monks and Taoists, and people from far and near, over sixty thousand in number, handed in petitions. Even the emperor begged to change his surname from Li to Wu, his mother's family name. They said in their petitions that since Heaven sent Her Majesty down to this world to be the sovereign and since all the people wished Her Majesty to be the sovereign, Her Majesty would disappoint both Heaven and people if Her Majesty rejected the suggestion again.

How could Empress Dowager Wu disappoint both Heaven and the people? Therefore, she granted their petitions. On the ninth day, she deposed the emperor as successor to the throne (equivalent to the title of the crown prince) and changed his surname from Li to Wu.

She also changed the Tang Dynasty to the Zhou Dynasty, because the late emperor Gaozong, her husband, had conferred on her late father the title of the duke of Zhou-guo.

Now we can see clearly the steps she took on her way to the sovereignty. First she had annihilated all those courtiers who objected to her reign. Then she made superstitious people believe that she was sent down by Heaven to rule the country. Then she showed her modesty by refusing several times the petitions imploring her to become the sovereign, until the time was right. It was not that she herself wanted to be the sovereign, but that courtiers and people begged her to be the sovereign.

View from the Summit

On the twelfth day of the ninth moon in 690, she was crowned as Holy Empress Wu, the first and the last and the sole female sovereign in Chinese history. On the thirteenth day, she conferred the title of prince on all her nephews: Wu Chengsi as Prince Wei, Wu Sansi as Prince Liang and Wu Youning as Prince Jianchang, and also the title of princess to her female relatives. She was sixty-six that year. She also let certain courtiers, Fu Youyi, Cen Changqian, Zhang Qianmao, Qiu Shenji, Lai Zixun, etc., have Wu as their surnames, which was deemed an honor. All those were at that time her faithful supporters and favorites.

Fu Youyi was promoted from an imperial censor to be a prime minister. But several months later, on the twenty-fifth day of the ninth moon in 691, Fu Youyi was put into jail and killed himself there. It was because he had a dream that he was sitting on the throne. He told it to a relative, who reported to the authorities. What are friends and family for? Superstitious people interpreted it to mean that Fu would replace Holy Empress Wu someday.

Cen Changqian (?–691) was brought up by his uncle since his parents died early. In 682, he was promoted from the vice minister of Military Ministry to be a prime minister. In 688, he was made a commander-in-chief to conquer a rebellion and in 690, he was granted a title of Duke of Dengguo. He was then the second in power among the courtiers, just under Wu Chengsi, a nephew of Holy Empress Wu. In the tenth moon of 691, some courtier wrote a petition to Holy Empress Wu that Wu Chengsi should be made the crown prince. But he considered that there was already a crown prince and so he refused to sign onto the petition. Thus he offended Wu Chengsi. Furthermore, he opposed the decision of Holy Empress Wu to build a temple. He was demoted and sent to fight the Tibetan army as a commander-in-chief. But before long, he was summoned back to the capital and put into jail as an accomplice to treason. He was killed together with his five sons.

Lai Zixun was appointed an imperial censor when he wrote a memorial to Empress Dowager Wu in the fourth moon of 689. Once, when a courtier did not wear official boots at the levee, Lai criticized him, saying, "I heard that 'a courtier should put on a girdle to attend the levee'." Everyone thought it funny. Then he was made a judge and sent quite a few courtiers to the guillotine on false accusations. So he was deemed one of the cruelest courtiers. But in 692, he was banished to Aichow (Love District).

There was a story about Wu Yanzong, Prince Henei. In the Tang Dynasty, princes could collect goods or money as tax directly from peasants and merchants in their fiefdoms. When the Zhou Dynasty was established, Holy Empress Wu decided that the goods or money should be collected by local governments and then sent to the princes. Thus the princes could not exploit people for more than their due. Of course, some princes were dissatisfied. Wu Yanzong was one of them. Once when Holy Empress Wu gave a banquet to her family and relatives, Wu Yanzong, in the middle of the feast, suddenly stood up and said to Holy Empress Wu, "When a courtier has an emergency, he must tell the sovereign. When a son has an emergency, he must tell his father." It seemed that he had some emergency. Holy Empress Wu was so surprised to hear it that she asked him what the matter was. He responded that he used to collect taxes for himself before, but since Her

Majesty had changed the procedures he received less than his due from the local government. He meant that local government was not dependable and it would be better to go back to letting princes collect "taxes" for themselves. Holy Empress Wu was angry and looked up at the rafters under the roof for a long time, and then she said to Wu Yanzong, "I'm enjoying the revel with all my relatives. You are a prince, and should not bother me with such a trifling thing. You almost terrified me to death. You are not suitable to be a prince." She had her bodyguards drive him out of the feasting hall. Wu Yanzong immediately fell on his knees and begged for pardon. Other princes begged, too, saying, "He's an idiot. He's just joking." Holy Empress Wu pardoned him. But it showed that Holy Empress Wu never bent the rules once she had set them up, not even for her own relatives.

Then she decided that the capital of Zhou Dynasty would be Luoyang City, the present Divine Capital of the Tang Dynasty. Although the formal capital, ChangAn City, of the Tang Dynasty, was situated among mountains, easily defensible, yet Luoyang City had more advantages. The Yellow River flowed by to the north of the city with a mountain range further north. A fertile area lay to its south and if the traffic from the city went to the east, it could reach the Huai River region and so she could control the east part of the country. The location was almost at the heart of her territory.

On the thirtieth day of the second moon in 691, Wu Youning, a nephew of Holy Empress Wu, was made the general to head the brigade of her bodyguards. This was a very important position and Holy Empress Wu needed a trustworthy person to fill it.

In the ninth moon, Di Renji was summoned back to the capital from his demotion and was made the vice minister of the Etiquette Ministry. One day, Holy Empress Wu asked Di, "Do you want to know who spoke ill of you?" Di replied, "If Your Majesty thinks I have made an error, I will correct it. If Your Majesty thinks I have not made an error, I am pleased. I don't need to know who said what." The answer pleased Holy Empress Wu.

Holy Empress Wu had two ways to choose her courtiers. One was by taking tests. She was the first one to order that the name of the test-taker should be covered with a small piece of paper so that no examiner could know who was who, to prevent cheating. The other was by recommendation. She would give an official position to anyone recommended to her, but on a trial period. If she found anyone not suitable to the position she had assigned, she would demote him to a lower position more suited to his capabilities or even send him back where he had come from. She seems to have employed everyone recommended to her, no matter whether he was a good man or a bad man, or was talented or not. In 692, therefore, a sarcastic poem was circulated among the courtiers. A man called Shen Quanjiao said something more, even pointing his criticism directly to Holy Empress Wu. A courtier Ji Xianzhi arrested him and reported to Holy Empress Wu. He requested that the man should be beaten and put into prison. But Holy Empress Wu said, "If all you courtiers are doing everything right, why do you care what he said?" The courtier felt ashamed and the man was pardoned and released. It showed that Holy Empress Wu would pardon a man for anything other than treachery.

A courtier Guo Ba was promoted from the vice mayor in Ningling (Peaceful Mound) Town to the position of an imperial censor by flattering Holy Empress Wu. Once when a prime minister Wei Yuanzhong had been ill, Guo had paid a visit to him and tasted his excrement, saying, "If the excrement is sweet, I will worry about the illness of Your Excellency, but now as it tastes bitter, Your Excellency is okay." Wei despised him for it and told the story to everyone.

In the fifth moon, an edict was issued to forbid the slaughter of animals and the catching of fish and prawns except for important occasions. However, Zhang De, a courtier, held a feast to entertain his friends. It was the third day after his son was born to him. He furtively cooked a sheep. Du Su, another courtier, was invited to the feast. He ate to his heart's content, and then hid a piece of meat in his pocket and went back home. Next day he wrote a memorial to the throne to expose the event with the piece of meat as proof. The day after that, at the levee, Holy Empress Wu said to Zhang De, "I'm glad you have been given a son." Zhang thanked Her Majesty, who added, "Where did you get the meat?" Zhang fell on his knees and kowtowed to beg the pardon. Holy Empress Wu continued, "When you invite guests, you must choose carefully whom to invite." Then she showed Zhang the memorial Du had sent in. Du was ashamed of himself. Other courtiers spat on him as a sign of disdain.

Holy Empress Wu liked good or lucky signs. Someone came up with a stone that had red lines on it. A prime minister, Li Zhaode, asked the man what was so special about this stone. Pointing to the red lines, the man said that it had a red heart, which meant loyalty. Li Zhaode said angrily, "If this stone is loyal, are all other stones rebellious?" The courtiers all laughed. Another man came in with a turtle having red words on the belly: "Long Live the Empress." Li took the turtle from the man and scraped the words with a small knife. The words came off because they had been written on with red paint.

Li Zhaode was born from a courtier's family and was a man of talent and determination. In 693, he was appointed one of the three vice ministers of the Etiquette Ministry. The other two were Lou Shide and Hou Zhiyi. As Holy Empress Wu trusted Li Zhaode, she made him a prime minister later.

But gradually Li used the power given to him too independently. So many courtiers began to dislike him, and some wrote memorials to Holy Empress Wu to complain about him. Li Zhaode then lost favor of Holy Empress Wu. On the twenty-first day of the ninth moon in 694, Li was demoted to be a petty official in Qinchow (Admiration District). A few days later, he was exiled. But before long, he was summoned back to the capital to be an imperial censor. The cruel courtier Lai Juncheng hated him and falsely accused him of treason. Li was executed — together with Lai. (The story is detailed further on.) On the day of the execution, people said that there was sad news and there was happy news, the former of which referred to Li and the latter of which referred to Lai.

On the twenty-fourth day of the eighth moon, Holy Empress Wu grew new teeth where the old ones had dropped out. It showed that Holy Empress Wu was a special person and was still in good shape. She had always taken good care of herself.

On the first day of the initial moon in 693, Holy Empress Wu gave a feast to entertain all the courtiers in the Omnifarious Divine Hall and nine hundred dancers danced to the "Music of the Divine Hall" composed by herself.

A prime minister, Lou Shide, said to his younger brother, "I'm afraid that you will offend people." The brother said, "From now on, even if someone spits on my face, I will just wipe it off." He meant that he would not quarrel with people anymore. Lou said, "That's why I'm afraid. If anyone spits on your face, it means he's angry with you. If you wipe your face, it won't assuage his anger. You should let it dry by itself." (This example of forbearance was often cited in the subsequent dynasties just like the example of turning the other cheek, in the Bible.)

Lou Shide (630–699) was quick-witted as a youth. He passed the government tests at twenty and immediately received the position of law official in Jiangdu (meaning River Capital) City. His ability in maintaining law and order astonished Lu Chengye, the administrator of the city. He said to Lou, "You will be a prime minister some day. Will you please look after my offspring when I'm gone. I can't even see you as my subordinate." In 674, he was promoted to be an imperial censor in the capital. In 677, when Emperor Gaozong felt the threat of invasion from Tibet, he wanted persons of military capability. Lou recommended himself and later became a famous general in defending Tang territory from Tibet. In 692, he was summoned back to the capital as the vice minister of the Etiquette Ministry, but in charge of all the responsibilities the minister should perform. (The history book did not say what happened to the actual minister.) In 693, he was made a prime minister. Several times Lou was sent to the frontier on some emergency and then summoned back to the capital; he died in on the saddle at the age of seventy in Huichow (Meeting District), where he was sent to defend the place.

There are more anecdotes about him in the history book. Once, when Lou was traveling to the frontier, he sent his men to go ahead and he himself sat on a large wooden block outside the city gate, waiting for his coach to be brought along, because he had some trouble walking on his foot. The mayor, who did not know Lou by face, came to sit beside him and introduced himself to Lou. Then his subordinates came, who had seen Lou before, and told him who Lou was. The mayor stood up at once, apologizing to Lou that he had not paid due respect to him. Lou said, "It's not your fault, since you never saw me before." (In China, even nowadays, if a subordinate does not show due respect to his superior, the superior will deem it a grave offence.) He was frugal and never took an illegal coin. When he was a prime minister, he still led a veer modest life.

Once when Lou was still an imperial censor, he went to a town for inspection. At that time, slaughter of animals and fish was forbidden. The mayor told his cook to get some lamb meat for Lou. When the cook served the meat, Lou criticized him. The cook said that he did not kill the lamb but the lamb was bitten to death by a wolf. Since the lamb was already dead, he just cooked it. So Lou said smilingly, "This wolf knows how to treat a guest." Then the cook served a fish. When Lou was about to accuse him, the cook said that the fish was also bitten to death by the wolf. Lou said, "You idiot. You should have said that the fish was bitten to death by an otter. Then I wouldn't know you're lying." The story of a wolf biting a fish to death was recorded in the history book.

On the ninth day of the ninth moon, Holy Empress Wu gave herself another title, Golden-Wheel Holy Empress Wu. Golden Wheel came from the Buddhist sutras, referring to the King of the Golden Wheel. It meant that she would be as great and holy as the King of the Golden Wheel.

In the fifth moon of 694, Prince Wei, Wu Chengsi, the nephew of Holy Empress Wu, together with more than twenty-six thousand people, suggested presenting to Holy Empress Wu another title: Superior (meaning she was superior to all the past emperors) Golden-Wheel Holy Empress Wu. On the eleventh day Holy Empress Wu accepted the new title.

On the first day of the initial moon in 695, Holy Empress Wu had another title, Merciful Superior Golden-Wheel Holy Empress Wu. But even she seems to have thought that was a bit much, for on the sixteenth day of the same moon, Holy Empress Wu deleted the words "Merciful Superior" from her full title.

A man named Wei Shifang, coming from Mount Song, boasted that he had been born in 237, which meant that he was already 457 years old. (That year was during the times of Three Kingdoms from 220 to 280 in Chinese history.) People at that time believed such things and deemed him a saint. So did Holy Empress Wu, who summoned him to her presence in the seventh moon and endowed him with an official title. Besides, she changed his surname to Wu, her own surname, as a special honor. But the man really was very old and in the eighth moon he begged to return to where he had come from — Mount Song. Holy Empress Wu consented to his wish.

When he had first emerged from his hermitage and come to the capital he lodged in the Unicorn-Toe Temple. He bragged that he could make pills endowing longevity. So before he returned to Mount Song, Holy Empress Wu wanted him to make some longevity pills for her. Instead of letting him go back to Mount Song, Wei was then sent to Lingnan (Ling here means Hill and Nan means South) to gather the necessary herbs for the pills. Lodged together with him in the Unicorn-Toe Temple there was an old nun who boasted that she could foretell things that would happen. After Ming Hall had been burned (details to come), the old nun went to see Holy Empress Wu to comfort her. Holy Empress Wu asked her in anger, "If you can foretell things, why didn't you tell me that Ming Hall would be burned down?" The nun was silent, for she had nothing to say. Holy Empress Wu sent her away from the capital and her disciples escaped from the temple. Then someone reported to Holy Empress Wu all the bad things the old nun and her disciples had done. During the daytime, the old nun ate only rice before the public, but at night she feasted with her disciples and led a lewd life. Holy Empress Wu then commanded the old nun and all her disciples come back to the temple. They thought they were safe, and they all came back. But they were arrested and sent to work as maidservants to the nobility. When Wei Shifang heard the news, he was afraid that his lie would be exposed and so committed suicide.

As wars were continually waged, with invasions from the peoples in the north and in the west, a prime minister called Doulu (double surname) Qinwang put up a proposal that all the courtiers and officials, from the lowest to the highest ranks, should donate two months' salary for the support of the wars. Wang Qiuli, an official of the lower rank, said to Qinwang, "The salary of Your Excellency is much higher than mine. It makes almost no difference to Your Excellency when Your Excellency donates some of it. But as for me, I am poor, just working from hand to mouth. Why didn't Your Excellency consult us, the low-ranking officials, before Your Excellency made the proposal?" Qinwang refused to be persuaded. Therefore, Wang Qiuli sent in a memorial to the throne, saying, "Your Majesty has all the wealth of the nation and great resources for wars; why to take away our small salaries?" As a result, Qinwang's proposal was ignored.

Wu Shansi, another nephew of Holy Empress Wu, together with the chieftains of all the tribal peoples, requested that some Heavenly Columns should be made to inscribe on them the record of the great deeds of Holy Empress Wu. The Heavenly Columns should be erected outside the southern gate of the capital. For that purpose, the chieftains donated a great deal of money. Holy Empress Wu consigned the task to the courtier Yao Shou (632–705), who collected two hundred fifty thousand kilograms of brass and one million six hundred fifty thousand kilograms of iron for the work. He ordered the technician Mao Poluo to make the molds for eight brass columns in octagonal shape. The design was that each of them would be thirty-five meters high and the diameter would be four meters. The pedestal on which a column would stand would be made of iron in the shape of a mountain. All around a column there were reliefs of dragons, lions and unicorns in brass, and on top of it was brass shaped in clouds and above the clouds were four dragons holding a "fiery pearl" (a globe with fire-shaped carvings on it). The circumference of the whole sculpture on the top was ten meters and the "pearl" was three meters thirty-three centimeters high. The Heavenly Columns shone when the sunlight was struck them.

On the first day of the fourth moon, the Heavenly Columns were finished, and on them were engraved the names of the courtiers and the chieftains of the tribal groups besides the eulogies to the great deeds of Holy Empress Wu. Many courtiers wrote poems and articles of praise for the occasion. On the ninth day of the ninth moon, she was called "Heaven-Granted Golden-Wheel Great Holy Empress Wu."

On the sixteenth day of the third moon in 696, a new Ming Hall was finished after the old one had been burned. It was named Heavenly Hall, and was smaller in size than the old one: one hundred meters on each side and ninety-eight meters high. A gilded phoenix was set on top, but later it was damaged by strong winds.

Since now her new dynasty was established, Holy Empress Wu wanted to realize the desire of her late husband, Emperor Gaozong, to go to Mount Song for the ritual of worshipping Heaven and Earth. Mount Song was a famous mountain in the middle of Zhou territory, not far from the present capital. Therefore, on the first day of the winter moon, Holy Empress Wu went to Mount Song with her courtiers and a large troop of her bodyguards. It was very cold and windy that winter. The ritual had to be performed on the highest peak of the mountain range. It was 1440 meters high. On the eleventh day, at the age of seventy-two, she stood on the mountain top and worshiped Heaven and Earth on an earthen platform built there beforehand, bathing in all the glory a monarch could attain.

Wu Youxu, another nephew of Holy Empress Wu, was a man of a different kind. Although he held the title of Prince Anping, he hated all the etiquette of the officialdom and loved a simple life. After coming back from Mount Song for the ritual, having accompanied his imperial aunt there, he resigned from his position as a general and retired to live at the southern side of Mount Song. Holy Empress Wu suspected that he would plan something harmful to the nation and sent someone to watch over him. But he actually took to living in a hut in the summer and in a cave in the winter, as a recluse. He put aside all the precious things granted to him by Holy Empress Wu or given to him by other nobilities.

Wu Youxu (655–723) loved a quiet life in his youth. He hated the killings that went on in political circles. n the process of Holy Empress Wu's struggle to get to the throne, she had killed all her opponents, including members of Li family. Wu Youxu could foresee that someday, when Holy Empress Wu was gone, the members of Wu family would be killed, too. That strengthened his determination to get away from politics. When he retired to the hut and cave at the age of forty-one, he never went back to the capital for ten years, while Holy Empress Wu was alive. After her death, he returned to the capital twice at the summons of his cousin, Emperor Zhongzong: once for the coronation of the emperor and once for the wedding of the emperor's daughter. Although the emperor granted him many gifts , he returned to his hut and cave without taking anything. So when many members of Wu family, such as Wu Sansi, Wu Yanxiu (son of Wu Chengsi) and others, were killed one by one, he survived and died a natural death at the age of sixty-nine.

In the initial moon of 698, Holy Empress Wu grew new eyebrows. In the same moon, she issued a decree to forbid the mutual slander between the Taoists and the Buddhist monks. The Taoists and the monks were always attacking each other as they were different in their religious beliefs. The edict stated that if a Taoist or a Buddhist monk did anything disrespectful to the other party, he would be caned and expelled from the temple.

On the eleventh day of the eighth moon, Wu Changsi died of a disease. It was said that the disease was developed from depression, because he could not attain his aim of being crown prince.

In the winter moon of 699, a courtier Zong Chuke and his brother were found guilty of taking huge bribes and having built an over-luxurious residence. So Zong Chuke was demoted to Bochow (Bo here means To Sow) and his brother was banished to Fengchow (Peak District). When Princess Taiping went to see their residence, she sighed with envy, saying, "When I saw their residence, I felt that I was leading a poor life."

Zong Chuke (?–710) was also a distant nephew of Holy Empress Wu. He was gradually promoted to be the vice minister of the Household Ministry.

In 697, he was made a prime minister. One year or so after his demotion, he was summoned back to be a prime minister again. But later when he had a disagreement with Wu Yanzong, plus he took bribes again, he was demoted again. In 704, he returned and was restored to the position of a prime minister once more. After the death of Holy Empress Wu, he was executed.

In the second moon of 699, Holy Empress Wu was taken ill. A courtier, Yan Chaoyin, went to Mount Shaoshi (Shao here means Young and Shi here means Chamber) and prayed to Buddha that he would die in lieu of Holy Empress Wu. When Holy Empress Wu recovered and heard what he had done, she granted him several favors.

A courtier Wang Jishan, though not learned, was a man of character and unselfish. In the eighth moon when he attended the palace feast and saw the Zhang brothers flouting the rules of palace etiquette, he advised Holy Empress Wu not to let the brothers conduct themselves in such a way. Holy Empress Wu was not happy and said to him, "You are too old. You must not come to the feast anymore. Just do your duties as a prime minister." Then Wang Jishan pretended to be sick and asked for a month's leave. During the month, Holy Empress Wu never sent anyone to inquire about his illness, which was a bad sign: according to tradition, a sovereign should send someone to inquire about the illness of a prime minister. Wang decided he had better resign, but Holy Empress Wu did not consent.

Wang Jishan inherited his father's title as the Duke of Xingguo at the age of fourteen, because his father died in the war with Korea. While he was growing up, he was ordered to work for the crown prince. Once the crown prince had told the fellows working for him to wrestle together, for fun. When it was Wang Jishan's turn, he refused, saying, "I only do my duties here and this is not my duty." The crown prince had to let him go. When the emperor heard of it, he thought that was a good answer and granted him a hundred scrolls of muslin. Then he was made a general. When Holy Empress Wu was on the throne, he was appointed the minister of the Etiquette Ministry and later the governor of Qinchow (Qin here is a surname). When he was sick and old, he asked to retire. His request was granted. Then the Qidan Clan revolted in Shandong (Mountain East) Province. Holy Empress Wu made him the magistrate of Huachow (Slide District) to deal with the Qidan Clan. She said to him, "Though you are ill, you can go slowly. When you reach there, you can lie in bed and handle the matter." Then she asked him how to rule the country well. He made some suggestions. Holy Empress Wu found these suggestions even more important than dealing with the Qidan uprising, so she sent someone else and made him a prime minister. He died in 699 at the age of eighty-two.

In the initial moon of 700, prime minister Ji Xu was demoted and sent out of the capital. Once when Ji and Wu Yanzong, a nephew of Holy Empress Wu, were debating in her presence, Ji, tall and stout, looked down at Yanzong, who was small in stature, and shouted at him disdainfully. Seeing this, Holy Empress Wu was unhappy and said to Ji, "In my presence, you are already scornful to Wu family members. How can I depend on you to treat them well when I am gone?" These Wu princes hated him for his support of the crown prince and they exposed his brother pretending to be a courtier. So he was demoted. On the day he was supposed to leave, he went to bid farewell to Holy Empress Wu and said, "Now I will leave Your Majesty and won't see Your Majesty again for the rest of my life. May I say my last words?" At her assent, he asked, "Is there any problem if water and clay mix together?" Holy Empress Wu said "No." "Is there any problem if half of the temple belongs to Buddhists and half to Taoists?" "Yes." "The nation will have peace if the imperial family members and the imperial in-laws can mix without any conflict. But now Your Majesty has the crown prince as a successor, and yet the in-laws remain in power. In this way Your Majesty sets them up for conflict in the future. No peace for either side." Holy Empress Wu said, "I know. But things are already as they are. What can I do?"

Ji Xu was really not a man of great integrity. Once his father, the magistrate of Yichow (Yi hear means Easy), received a death sentence for taking bribes. Ji Xu blocked the way of Prince Wei, Wu Chengsi, nephew of Holy Empress Wu, at Tianjin Bridge. He prostrated himself before Prince Wei, who asked him what the matter was. Ji said, "I have two sisters who would like to wait on Your Highness." Prince Wei accepted the offer and took the two sisters home. For three days the sisters did not say a word. When Prince Wei wondered why, the sisters said that they were so sad that their father would soon be executed. Then Prince Wei begged Holy Empress Wu to pardon their father from death sentence.

In the wintertime Holy Empress Wu was always concerned how the common people were faring. Once she asked Lu Yuanfang, a prime minister, about the living conditions of the people, but Lu answered that it was not necessary for Her Majesty to be concerned with such trifling things. Holy Empress Wu was irritated and removed Lu from his position as a prime minister.

In the eighth moon, a courtier Su Anheng implored Holy Empress Wu to return the power to the emperor and restore to the Tang Dynasty. The history book does not say what happened to him. Generally such a courtier would at least be demoted.

Holy Empress Wu planned to build a colossal statue of Buddha and ordered all the nuns and monks each to donate one coin a day for the work. Di

Renjie sent in a memorial to state his reason for opposing the plan. He wrote, "The pomp of the statues nowadays already surpasses that of the palace. Buddha should make the ghosts work for him, but now he makes people do it. Building materials can't fall down from Heaven. They must come out from the earth. If they are not obtained through the toil of people, how can they come into use?" He went on, "The donation of the nuns and monks cannot cover all the expenses. And the statue of Buddha can't sit in the open. He should have a roof over him and walls round him. The doctrine of Buddhism is always to have mercy on people. It is against the doctrine to make people toil for the statue." Holy Empress Wu said to him, "Since you advise me to have mercy, how can I do otherwise?" So the plan was cancelled.

Di Renjie was accustomed to arguing with Holy Empress Wu on certain important issues. As he was always right, Holy Empress Wu yielded to his opinion. Once Holy Empress Wu asked Di, "I'd like to have a talented courtier to help me. Who you think is fit?" Instead of answering, Di put a question, "What's the purpose Your Majesty want to use the person for?" She said, "I want him to be a prime minister." Di replied, "Then, Zhang Jianzhi is the right man for Your Majesty, though he's a bit old." So Holy Empress Wu promoted Zhang Jianzhi to be in charge of the local army in Luochow (Luo here is the name of a river). Several days later, she asked Di again to recommend someone to her. Di said, "I already recommended Jianzhi to Your Majesty. Your Majesty has not used him yet." Holy Empress Wu said, "I already promoted him." Di said, "I recommended him as a prime minister, not to be in charge of the army." So Holy Empress Wu promoted Zhang to be a vice minister and finally made him a prime minister.

Zhang Jianzhi (625–706) was a scholar and passed the government tests. Then he was appointed the vice mayor of Qingyuan (meaning Clear Source) Town. In 689, he was promoted to be an imperial censor. Then he became the magistrate of Hechow (He here means To Close), and later of Shuchow (Shu here is the name of a place). At the time when Di Renji recommended him, he was the administrator of Jingchow. At the recommendation of Di Renji, he was appointed the vice minister of the Judicial Ministry and then a prime minister. In 705, he was the leader of a coup d'état seeking to force Holy Empress Wu to abdicate.

On the twenty-sixth day of the ninth moon, her helpful courtier Di Renji died. Holy Empress Wu wept and said, "From now on, there is no one in my court I can rely upon." Since then, if there was some problem that no one could suggest a means to resolve, Holy Empress Wu would sigh, "Why did Heaven deprive me of my helpful courtier so early?"

During 700 and 701, encouraged by Holy Empress Wu, many Buddhist temples were built all over the country, some even surpassing the palace in splendor, as well as Buddhist statues and pagodas. She often held gatherings for the worship of Buddha in the capital. On such occasions, throngs of men and women participated and Holy Empress Wu would have ten cartfuls of coins strewn everywhere on the ground and let people vie for the collection of the money.

In the third moon of 701, a courtier Zhang Xi was sentenced to decapitation for two reasons. First, he gave out palace secrets. Second, he embezzled some ten thousand units of money. But later he was pardoned from the death sentence and banished to Xunchow (Xun here means Observe Rules). Before he was dispatched to his destination, he had to go back to the jail and wait there. Another courtier named Su Weidao (648–705) also broke the law and went to jail too. Zhang Xi rode there on a horse and lived and ate expensively, as if he was still at home, while Su Weidao walked there, slept on the prison floor and ate only vegetables. When Holy Empress Wu learned of this, she pardoned Su Weidoa and restored him to his former position.

In the same moon, it snowed heavily. A prime minister Su Weidao considered it a good omen and thought he would go with other courtiers to see Holy Empress Wu to congratulate her for it. But an imperial censor, Wang Qiuli, said, "If snow in the third moon is called good snow, then, thunder in the third moon is good thunder." In the presence of Holy Empress Wu, when other courtiers congratulated her, Wang refused to do so, saying, "Now it's spring, the trees, flowers and grass are returning to life. The heavy snow will do them harm. How can it be called good snow? Those who say so are flatterers." Holy Empress Wu thought he was right.

In the initial moon of 702, Holy Empress Wu began a test of martial arts to select fighters for the army.

In the twelfth moon, Holy Empress Wu sent a courtier Zhang Xunxian on an inspection tour to Tingchow (Courtyard District). When the inspector had some problem he asked a local official, "Is there any talented person that I can consult?" The official mentioned a man called Zhang Jiazhen. When the man came, the inspector received him and consulted him about the problem. The man analyzed the situation logically and clearly for him. The inspector was satisfied. Afterwards, the inspector asked the man to write a memorial to the throne for him. The ideas he wrote in the memorial were so clever that the inspector would never even have thought of them. When the inspector returned to the capital he was summoned to the presence of Holy Empress Wu, who praised him for his wonderful ideas. Zhang Xunxian told Holy Empress Wu about the talented man he had found. So Holy Empress Wu sent for the man to be brought to the capital. Zhang Xunxian suggested giving the man his official position, but Holy Empress Wu said that she had several positions to give, and so she made the man an imperial censor and also promoted Zhang Xunxian as a reward for the recommendation.

The history book records the first interview of Zhang Jiazhen with Holy Empress Wu like this: Holy Empress Wu received Zhang Jiazhen, sitting behind a screen because he was still a stranger to her. But Zhang Jiazhen said boldly, "It's a rare occasion for your servant, a petty official, to come to the palace. Though the distance is short, your servant feels like he is looking at the sun through dense clouds." Hearing that, Holy Empress Wu ordered the screen rolled up and had a hearty conversation with him.

On the twenty-first day of the fourth moon in 704, Holy Empress Wu was going to tax the monks and nuns all over the nation and use the money to build a colossal Buddha's statue. However, dissuaded by a courtier named Li Jiao, she gave up the idea. Li Jiao handed in a memorial, saying, "The budget for the building of the Buddha's statue is seventeen thousand cords of money. (In ancient China, besides silver and gold used as currency, there were bronze or brass coins with a hole in the middle. The coins could be put on the cord through the mid-hole. There were a thousand coins on one cord. But there are still poor people out there. If we give a cord of money to one family, we can save seventeen thousand families from starving. Buddha always teaches us to have mercy on poor people. Why don't we give the money to them? This serves Buddha better than the statue." Holy Empress Wu thought it right and gave up her plan.

Li Jiao (645–714) was a poet and passed the government tests at twenty years old. He was appointed the law official in Anding (Quiet and Peaceful) Town. Gradually he was promoted to an imperial censor, then the minister of Official Ministry and at last a prime minister.

In the eighth moon, Holy Empress Wu was sick in bed. She was eighty that year.

In the twelfth moon, Holy Empress Wu fell ill again. Prime ministers could not see her for months. Only the Zhang brothers waited on her. When Holy Empress Wu felt better, a courtier sent in a memorial saying, "The crown prince and Prince Xiang are both sons of Your Majesty. They should wait on Your Majesty. Your servant thinks that those who have no blood relationship with Your Majesty should not be allowed to come in." He was referring to the Zhang brothers, whose relations with the Empress have raised questions we won't go into here.

In the initial moon of 705, the illness of Holy Empress Wu was much worse. The Zhang brothers were still in power. A prime minister Zhang Jianzhi and other courtiers planned to kill the brothers. They went to see Huan Yanfan (653–706), the leading general of the palace bodyguards, and secured his support. Then they went to see the crown prince, who agreed to their plan.

On the twenty-second day, Zhang Jianzhi and other courtiers followed the crown prince with the five hundred palace bodyguards to see Holy Empress Wu in her chamber. They met the Zhang brothers on their way there and killed the brothers just outside the chamber. They went into the chamber. Holy Empress Wu saw them with the bodyguards and asked, "Is there a rebellion?" They said, "The Zhang brothers were rebelling and were executed by order of the crown prince." Then Holy Empress Wu saw the crown prince and said, "It's you! Now that the rebels have been killed, you can go back." General Huan Yanfan came forth and said, "Now, the crown prince is old enough. All the people are thinking of the Li family. We beg Your Majesty to return the power to the crown prince." Thus they forced Holy Empress Wu to abdicate and give the throne back to the crown prince. Then the other Zhang brothers were also executed and their followers were banished.

On the twenty-fifth day, the crown prince was made emperor and the Zhou Dynasty was changed back to the Tang Dynasty. This crown prince was Prince Luo, the ex-emperor Zhongzong, who had been sent to live in Fangchow. At the persuasion of the courtiers, Holy Empress Wu had sent for him and made him the crown prince again.

On the twenty-seventh day, the emperor with all the courtiers went to see his mother and presented her with the honorary title Holy Empress Zetian (meaning Like Heaven) Wu the Great.

On the fourth day of the fifth moon, all the Wu princes were demoted to the rank of duke.

On the twenty-sixth day of the eleventh moon, Holy Empress Wu died at the age of eighty-one.

On the eighth day of the fifth moon in 706, Holy Empress Wu was buried. According to her last will, a blank tombstone was set in front of her tomb, by which she meant to let people in the future to judge her merits or demerits by inscribing whatever they thought on it.

CHAPTER 5. REBELLIONS

In every dynasty there were rebellions, generally one of two types. People at large might, for various reasons such as starvation or oppression, rise up in desperation against the government or those who were oppressing them. Otherwise, some ambitious persons who wished to seize power would stir things up, aiming to overthrow the sovereign and hoping to take his place.

THE LARGEST REBELLION

Some courtiers and officials thought that once the emperor was an adult, Empress Dowager Wu should return the power to him and that her further administration was unlawful. Even the prime minister Pei Yan thought so. Her conferring the posthumous titles of princes on the ancestors of the Wu family engendered further rancor. Her nephew Wu Chengsi had suggested it and Empress Dowager Wu happily went along, thinking it was no big deal to honor the dead. However, some courtiers and officials did think it was a big deal, in the overall scheme of rivalry between great families.

On the twenty-ninth day of the ninth moon in 684, an official Xu Jingye (?–684) in Yangchow City took up arms in revolt against Empress Dowager Wu, asking her to return the power to the emperor. He was the grandson of Li Ji (Li Ji's surname was originally Xu. The emperor had granted him permission to use the surname Li, an honor in feudal China.) Xu Jingye gave himself the title of Grand Governor of Yangchow as well as the title of Grand General of Restoration Yamen, by which he meant that his goal was to restore the power to the emperor from the hand of Empress Dowager Wu. Xu was a clever and brave man, and also ambitious and greedy. He had been the magistrate of Meichow (meaning Eyebrow District) and had been demoted because of embezzlement. His brother Xu Jingyou had been involved and was demoted too.

They came to Luoyang City and met other officials who had been demoted. One of them was Luo Binwang (640–684), was a famous scholar and poet. When he was only seven years old, he wrote a famous poem about the goose, with the renowned couplet: "The white feathers float on the green ripples; the red web-feet paddle in the emerald water." He was an official in the central government in 678, but was put into jail on a false indictment of taking bribes. He was pardoned in the sixth moon of the next year and was appointed as the deputy mayor of Linghai (meaning Near Sea) Town in Zhejiang (the name of a river there) Province, but as a smart man he thought that he deserved a higher position. So he refused the assignment and went south to Yangchow City. When they rallied disgruntled figures in rebellion against Empress Dowager Wu, Luo wrote the famous denunciation around which they gathered. When Empress Dowager Wu read a copy of it sent to her, she thought it was well written. She even said that it was the fault of the prime ministers that such a talented man had not been given a position corresponding to his talent.

Before they rose up in arms, they wanted to get some support in the capital. As they had been officials, they knew some courtiers there, of course. They tried to contact General Cheng Tingwu, who was a friend of the prime minister Pei Yan. Both were important courtiers. If they could support their "cause," victory would be on their side. Since Luo Bingwang knew General Cheng, Xu sent Luo to see Cheng when he arrived in the capital. Through General Cheng he visited Pei Yan. He tried to persuade them to support their cause and force Empress Dowager Wu to return power to the emperor. Pei and Cheng had always had such an intention, but they were old enough not to act rashly. What if the rebellion failed? Besides, they knew that Xu Jingye was a man of ambition. What if he succeeded in ousting the Empress only to take the power into his own hands?

They said to Luo, "It is a good thing to force Empress Dowager Wu to return power to the emperor. But she may do it after the late emperor is buried. It's better to wait for a while. If she doesn't return the power after that, you can do as you are planning."

Luo was dissatisfied with the response. But when he reported to Xu Jingye, Xu thought that it was at least a good sign. In the seventh moon, he sent a messenger to contact Xue Zhongzhang, their accomplice, who was the nephew of the prime minister Pei Yan. Then Xue Zhongzhang asked Empress Dowager Wu to send him to work in Jiangdu (meaning River Metropolis), which she did. He was sent there for inspection as an imperial censor, but in reality he wanted to go there to help Xu Jingye.

In the eighth moon, when the late emperor was laid in his tomb, Empress Dowager Wu continued her reign without any sign that she ever intended to let the emperor manage the national affairs. On the contrary, she set about to give honorary titles to the ancestors of the Wu family. Pei Yan opposed it in vain. Therefore, he and General Cheng made a plan to gain their goal by force. If they succeeded, Xu Jingye would not need to rebel in Yangchow City. They did not send anyone to contact him. They preferred to act without him. The history book puts it like this: Pei Yan planned to spring his trap when Empress Dowager Wu made her tour to Dragon Gate on a certain day. He would send soldiers to capture her and force her to turn the power back over to the emperor. But on that day, it rained hard and the trip was cancelled. The plan was aborted.

Pei Yan felt that he could not make his plan successful on his own and so he sent a messenger with a letter to Xu Jingye in Yangchow City. The letter contained only two words "Green goose," which must have been a secret code agreed upon between Luo Bingwang and him. Somehow, the letter fell into the hands of Empress Dowager Wu, who then held a suspicion against Pei Yan.

As Xu Jingye did not get any message from Pei Yan, he thought that Pei was still hesitating. He also thought that it was the right time to rebel since many courtiers and officials were disgusted with Empress Dowager Wu's granting of honorary titles to the ancestors of the Wu family.

Xue Zhongzhang had a temporary yamen in Yangchow City at that time Chen Jingzhi was the administrator there. (The governor there was only in name. The Administrator was in charge of everything.) Xu Jingye sent one of his followers to the temporary yamen of Xue Zhongzhang and reported that Chen Jingzhi would soon rebel. Xue knew what the report meant and put Chen in prison.

A few days later, Xu Jingye came to announce that he was the new administrator. So all the officials met him in his yamen, including Xue Zhongzhang. Thus they had the command of the local government army. Then Xu pretended that he had brought the imperial order to execute Chen Jingzhi. Chen was soon killed.

Furthermore, Xu told them false news that the chieftain in Gaochow (meaning High District) was revolting and he had another imperial order to go fight him. He wanted to gather troops. But one of the officials opposed it; they did away with him and then no one dared to say anything in disagreement.

Therefore, he summoned troops and distributed arms. When everyone was gathered, Xu declared that the revolt of the chieftain was not a big problem; that the really big problem for the country was Empress Dowager Wu, who had abolished the ex-emperor, the present Prince Luling. Xu went on to say that Wu refused to return power to the present emperor and that they wanted to support the ex-emperor to get back the throne that was due to him. Finally, Xu said that if anyone refused to support their cause, he would be executed under martial law.

Then they distributed the denunciation written by Luo Bingwang. Quite a few people who did not like Empress Dowager Wu received the message and came to support Xu. Within ten days, Xu had an army of a hundred thousand strong.

When the news of the rebellion came to the capital, the courtiers were in panic. However, Empress Dowager Wu was very calm because she knew about it beforehand and was ready for it. Xu Siwen, the uncle of Xu Jingye, admired Empress Dowager Wu and was loyal to her. He had sent a secret report to her. He was then the magistrate of Runchow (Run here means Moist).

A few days later, more news came. A law official, Li Chongfu in Chu-chow (Chu here is a surname) had surrendered to the rebels and three towns under his charge were occupied by Xu's troops. When the rebels went to attack Xuyi (name of a town) Town in the present Jiangsu (Jiang here means River and Su here is a surname) Province, they met strong resistance. Two brothers, Liu Xingju and Liu Xingshi, were responsible for the defense of this town and they fought fiercely. Empress Dowager Wu praised and promoted them.

Empress Dowager Wu had not forgotten the puzzling words "Green Goose" in the letter sent by prime minister Pei Yan to the rebels. Now she wanted to test his loyalty and solve the puzzle. She ordered Pei Yan to make a plan to conquer the rebels so she could see how Pei Yan would act.

Pei Yan thought that this was the opportunity to force Empress Dowager Wu to return power to the emperor. So was in no rush to present a plan; he just waited to see how the rebels would proceed. The delay made Empress Dowager Wu more suspicious of him.

To prove her suspicions, Empress Dowager Wu sent for Pei Yan one day and asked him point blank how to wipe out the rebels. But Pei said, "As the emperor is now an adult and doesn't manage the national affairs himself, it gives the rebels an excuse. If Your Majesty can let the emperor take care of the administration, they have no more excuse to rebel."

A courtier Cui Cha said, "Pei Yan worked for the late emperor for more than twenty years and has reached the position of the chief prime minister. He should know that it was the will of the late emperor to entrust the state affairs in the hands of Your Majesty. If he doesn't side with the rebels, why is he asking Your Majesty to return power to the emperor like the rebels do?" Empress Dowager Wu liked Cui's line of reasoning and so ordered Pei Yan to be thrown into jail. In a levee, a courtier Li Jingzhan vowed that Pei Yan would certainly betray the Empress. But courtiers Liu Jingxian and Hu Yuanfan were equally sure in their opinion that Pei Yan would not betray her. Empress Dowager Wu said, "I have proof that Pei will betray me. You don't know." Then she sent Liu Jingxian and Hu Yuanfan to prison and promoted Li Jingzhan to be a prime minister.

On the sixth day of the tenth moon, she made General Li Xiaoyi the commander-in-chief and General Li Zhishi and General Ma Jingchen the deputy commanders-in-chief and Wei Yuanzhong the military counselor. They marched with an army three hundred thousand strong to put out the rebellion.

Among the rebels, there were different opinions as to where to assault next. Their military counselor Wei Siwen suggested that they should gather all the forces and march directly to the capital Luoyang City. But Xue Zhongzhang had a different opinion. He said, "Jinling (meaning Gold Hill) City (now Nanking City) has been the capital of many dynasties. It has the Yangtze River as a natural trench. We'd better take it first as our military base and then march toward Luoyang City."

Wei retorted, "People hate Empress Dowager Wu. If we march north they will come to meet us even with hoes as weapons. This is a favorable situation. If we don't go north now, people will be disappointed and then we will lose their support."

Xu Jingye agreed with Xue and so they marched toward Runchow (Moist District) in what is now Zhenjiang (meaning Town River) City, very close to Nanking City. The magistrate in Runchow was Xu Siwen, the uncle of Xu Jingye. Xu Siwen had always opposed the idea of rebellion and had sent a secret report to Empress Dowager Wu. Now he made preparations to strengthen the defense of the city against the assault.

When Xu Jingye reached the city, he met with strong resistance. But as the defensive force was much less than the rebel troops the city was soon taken and Xu Siwen was captured and imprisoned. Yin Yuanzhen, the mayor of QuE (Qu here means Curved and E here means Flatter) Town, tried to come to the rescue, but was defeated and captured by the rebels. He would not surrender and was killed.

The government army under Li Xiaoye now arrived at Linghuai (Ling here means Near and Huai is the name of a river there) Town. The rebellious troops under Xu Jingye lined up in war formation to meet a detachment of the government army and defeated it.

Commander-in-chief Li Xiaoyi was the son of Li Shentong, Prince Hua-iAn, a relative of the imperial Li family. He was a good general, but a little over scrupulous. Since his detachment was defeated, he had withheld his army from any further action.

When Empress Dowager Wu heard the news of the situation, she was infuriated and had Pei Yan executed on the eighteenth day of the tenth moon, as she thought that Pei was an accomplice of the rebels. As for the other two courtiers who were imprisoned together with Pei Yan, one of them, Liu Jingxian was demoted to be the magistrate of Puchow (Common District), and the other courtier, Hu Yuanfan, was banished to Qiongchow (Qiong here is a sort of jade), and he died there. Then Pei Youxian, a nephew of Pei Yan, came to see Empress Dowager Wu, who reprimanded him, "Your uncle betrayed me. What do you have to say?" Pei Youxian answered, "I haven't come to complain. I am planning for Your Majesty's future. I have pity on Your Majesty for what Your Majesty did. If Your Majesty can give power back to the emperor, the members of Wu family will be safe; otherwise, they cannot be saved." Empress Dowager Wu was enraged. "How dare you say such a thing!" She ordered the guards to take him out. He was caned, and exiled to Rangchow (Rang here is the name of a river).

A courtier Jiang Sizong was sent to ChangAn City, the former capital, where a prime minister Liu RenGui was in charge. Empress Dowager Wu wanted to know Liu's attitude. When Liu asked Jiang about the situation in Luoyang City, Jiang said, "I felt that Pei Yan had not behaved normally for a long time." Liu said, "So you did feel it?" The reply was "Yes." Liu said, "I have a memorial. Can you take it back to Her Majesty?" Jiang said, "I can." Next day, when Jiang was leaving, Liu gave him a sealed envelope. As Jiang got back in the capital, he handed in Liu RenGui's memorial to Empress Dowager Wu. What was written in the memorial was, "Jiang Sizong knew that Pei Yan would betray Your Majesty, but he did not report it." When Empress Dowager Wu read that, she ordered Jiang Sizong to be hanged. Jiang could never dream that he had brought back his own death verdict. Liu played this nasty trick on him because he hated him as a two-faced person.

Then big rewards and grant of official positions were offered to any who could kill Xu Jingye and his followers and bring their heads to the government as evidence. A messenger was sent to Commander-in-chief Li Xiaoyi to exchange information.

On the fourth day of the eleventh moon, General Heichi Changzhi was sent as reinforcement to fight Xu Jingye. Meanwhile the military counselor Wei Yuanzhong said to Commander-in-chief Li Xiaoyi, "The government entrusts Your Excellency with such a large army because Your Excellency are an imperial relative. If Your Excellency fails to fight the rebels, the nation will be disappointed. What if Her Majesty sends someone else to replace Your Excellency?"

Commander-in-chief Li thought what he said was right and ordered his army to attack the rebellious troops and they conquered two detachments, and then surrounded the Duliang (Du means Metropolis and Liang is a surname) Mountain occupied by the rebels.

Now the situation was favorable to the government army. They had a meeting to decide on tactics. Most of the generals under Li thought that the Duliang Mountain was easy to defend and hard to attack since the slopes were so steep. They suggested that the commander-in-chief should leave a detachment here to continue the assault and the main part of the army should go to attack Xu Jingye's troops, which was the main force of the rebels.

But Xue Kegou, the official in charge of provisions, said, "There are not many rebels on the mountain. If we leave a detachment here, it will weaken our main striking force on Xu's troops. If we can conquer the rebels on the mountain first, we can concentrate our force to attack other rebels." Commander-in-Chief Li agreed and followed that strategy. After a severe attack, the rebels on the mountain were put to rout. Now where would the government army go next?

Xu Jingyou, the brother of Xu Jingye, occupied Huaiyin (Huai here is the name of a river and Yin here means Dark) City while Xu Jingye was in Jiangdu (River Metropolis) City. The question now was which city they should attack first. Most of the generals said that they should attack Jingye and then Jingyou would be easy to take, but if they attacked Jingyou first, Jingye would come to his brother's rescue and they would be attacked on both the front and the back. Military counselor Wei Yuanzhong disagreed, reasoning that as Xu Jingye had a stronger force, he would not be so easy to conquer. It would take more time. But Xu Jingyou was seen as the weak link and should be easier to conquer; it would take far less time to defeat him. Then they could swoop down on Xu Jingye with all might and main.

It sounded like a good plan and Commander-in-Chief Li accepted it. They marched toward Huaiying City. Xu Jingyou was not a fighter but a gambler. When he learned that the government army was after him, he was in great panic. He fled to his brother and the city was easily taken by the government army.

The news of his brother's defeat came to Xu Jingye, who was so angry that he wanted to fight a final decisive battle against the government army. Commander-in-Chief Li sent a detachment forward as the vanguard, which came face to face with the rebels across a river. Under cover of night, five thousand government men-at-arms under Officer Su Xiaoxiang and Officer Cheng Sanlang stole across the river and made a surprise attack, but they were outnumbered and defeated. Officer Su was slain in the fighting and Officer Cheng was captured.

A rebel officer wanted to boost the morale of his men and pointed to Officer Cheng, saying, "This is their commander-in-Chief Li." But Officer Cheng cried, "I'm not Li. I'm Cheng. The government army will soon come and you will all be wiped out." He was not given a chance to speak again.

A few days later the main force of the government army arrived under Commander-in-Chief Li. Battle after battle followed between the government army and the rebellious troops. Neither could conquer the other. Military counselor Wei offered a stratagem to attack with fire. The wind was favorable to them. So Li ordered his army to get across the river and set fire everywhere in the enemy's camp. The rebels were in panic and were put to rout. Xu Jingye, his brother and Luo Binwang escaped into Jiangdu City.

Li's army pursued them there. Xu Jingye and his brother got on board a ship. They wanted to flee to Korea. But when they arrived at Hailing, the wind was strong against them and their ship could not sail. The pursuers would reach them soon. At the critical juncture, a general Wang Naxiang, who was originally a follower of Xu Jingye, killed Xu and his brother and submitted himself to Commander-in-Chief Li — with their heads in hand. This happened on the eighteenth day of the eleventh moon in 684. Then Commander-in-Chief Li Xiaoyi sent his men after the other followers of Xu Jingye. The mutiny in Yangchow City was finally conquered. General Cheng Wuting was executed as an accomplice of the rebels since he was a good friend of Pei Yan. Luo Bingwang escaped — no one knew where. Or, it was said, he became a monk. This was the largest rebellion during the reign of Empress Dowager Wu.

Since General Li Xiaoye, who had conquered the Xu Jingye rebellion in Yangchow City, earned a great reputation, Wu Chengsi, the nephew of Empress Dowager Wu, envied him and so he often spoke ill of him to Empress Dowager Wu. In the second moon of 686, this bad-mouthing got Li Xiaoye demoted to be the magistrate of Shichow (Give District).

In the eleventh moon, General Li Xiaoye was exiled to Danchow (Dan here is the name of a place) in the present Guangdong (meaning Wide East) Province from his office in Shichow, because Wu Chengsi, Empress Dowager Wu's nephew, told his aunt that the name of the general implied that he would be a ruler some day. (The second Chinese character YE in his given name has part of the word meaning rabbit in it. A Chinese tale has it that there is a rabbit in the moon. People at that time thought that anything in heaven, including in the moon, is supreme. A man with something supreme in the meaning of his name would cause suspicion from a ruler.) Li died soon thereafter.

In the fifth moon of 689, Xu Jingzhen, a brother of Xu Jingye, escaped from his banishment in Xiuchow (Embroidery District). He intended to flee to the Tujue Clan in the north. When he went through Luoyang City, two officials, Gong Siye and Chang Siming, gave him money to use on the way. As he reached Dingchow (meaning Fix District) he was caught by the local government. He confessed everything. Gong Siye committed suicide and Chang Siming was arrested. Both Xu Jingzhen and Chang Siming supplied false information about the treachery of many courtiers they knew in hopes of saving their own lives. Their false accusations caused several courtiers to be executed. They themselves were executed, too. Zhang Chujin, the minister of Judicial Ministry, and other three courtiers were exiled to a southern province. They had originally been sentenced to death, but on the execution spot an imperial edict came from Empress Dowager Wu to commute their death sentence to exile. The history book records that the clouds cleared up and the sun came out when the pardon edict was read to them.

The failure of Xu Jingye's rebellion was due to his adoption of a poor strategy. If he had marched directly north to the capital, a number of local noblemen, who were opposed to the reign of Empress Dowager Wu as a woman, might have come to join him. His army would thus have been enlarged and he might have defeated the government army and taken the capital. But instead, he marched south to the present Nanking City in order to set up his military base. He ran into the stronger government army before he reached Nanking. So he failed.

THE REBELLIONS OF THE PRINCES LI

Prince Yue was the eighth son of Emperor Taizong, the stepbrother of the husband of Empress Dowager Wu, that is, her brother-in-law. He was talented but crafty, without any respect to ethics. Therefore, people in his district had a poor opinion of him.

Prince Yue was always opposed to Empress Dowager Wu staying in power. Supported by Prince Han and his son Duke Huangguo, Prince Lu and his son Prince Fanyang, Prince Huo and his son Prince Jiangdu, he was plotting a mutiny in 688.

Prince Han, named Li Yuanjia (618–688), was the eleventh son of the first emperor of the Tang Dynasty and thus the uncle of Empress Dowager Wu on her husband's side. He was titled Prince Han in 638. He had a hobby of collecting books which amounted to ten thousand volumes. He was versed in cursive calligraphy and could paint dragons, horses, tigers and leopards.

Prince Huo, by name Li YuanGui, was the fourteenth son of the first emperor of the Tang Dynasty, also the uncle of Empress Dowager Wu on her husband's side. He was the son-in-law of Wei Zheng, the favorite prime minister of Emperor Taizong. In 636, he received the title of Prince Huo and was appointed the magistrate of Xuchow (Xu here is a surname). But he just enjoyed reading and let his subordinates take care of everyday routines. In

649, he was transferred to be the magistrate of Dingchow. There he fought the Tujue Clan.

These princes had a thousand servants and several thousand horses. The servants were all trained to be fighters. They had not started their rebellion after the death of Emperor Gaozong, the husband of Empress Dowager Wu, because Empress Dowager Wu had maneuvered her troops in preparation for such events.

Later when Xu Jingye had risen in revolt in Yangchow City, they knew that Xu was a man of ambition and they could not unite with him against their common foe, Empress Dowager Wu. If they had overthrown the reign of Empress Dowager Wu in a joint effort with him, Xu would then have fought them to attain his own goal of achieving the imperial power. Xu had failed, and luckily they had not joined him.

Now every action of Empress Dowager Wu showed that she would create her own dynasty and be the sovereign empress. Once the new dynasty was established, it would be more difficult for them to drive her out of power. So they accelerated their preparations for the rebellion.

In the seventh moon, Duke Huangguo wrote to those princes, saying, "My wife's health has deteriorated. If let matters go on till winter, it will be hopeless. The earlier it is cured, the better." Code language. It meant that Empress Dowager Wu would soon establish her own dynasty. The situation would get worse if they waited longer. Therefore, they had better start their action as quickly as possible.

Prince Han wrote to the others, "Empress Dowager Wu has ordered us to gather in the capital. When we are all there, she will find some excuse to kill us all so that there are no more members of the Li family left alive to oppose her usurpation."

Duke Huangguo forged a letter from the present emperor, saying, "I am being confined. You princes should come and rescue me." He sent the forged letter to Prince Langxie. Duke Huangguo forged another letter, "Empress Dowager Wu will usurp the throne of the Tang Dynasty and establish her own dynasty of Wu family."

Prince Fanyang suggested that they should stage a coordinated uprising on the same day so that Empress Dowager Wu could not deal with each of them simultaneously. Thus the victory would be theirs.

Princess Changle, the seventh daughter of the first emperor of the Tang Dynasty, an aunt of Empress Dowager Wu on her husband's side, sent word to Prince Yue, saying, "You princes, if you are men, why have you not acted yet, after so much talk?"

So Prince Yue fixed a date and sent the information to all others. But owing to the distance, some of them did not get the information in time.

On the seventeenth day of the eighth moon, Prince Langxie began to implement the plan ahead of the fixed time. Even his father, Prince Yue, was not ready yet.

When Empress Dowager Wu received the news of the rebellion, she sent General Qu Shenji as Commander-in-Chief to fight Prince Langxie, who was leading his five thousand men across the Yellow River. Before meeting with General Qu's army, Prince Langxie took Jichow (Ji here means Help) and was marching toward the capital. He had to pass Wushui (Wu here means Karate and Shui means Water) Town on his way to the capital. However, Guo Wuti, the mayor of the town would not let him pass, so Prince Langxie had to attack the town first. Guo sent a messenger to the magistrate of Weichow (Wei here is a surname) for help. The magistrate sent Ma Xuansu, the mayor of Xin (name of a place in the present Shandong Province) Town (located to the west of Wushui Town), to the rescue with seventeen hundred soldiers for reinforcement.

Prince Langxie ordered his men to stuff some carts loaded with dry straw in the southern gateway of Wushui Town and ignite the straw. He wanted to burn a way into the town, but the wind was against him, and his plan failed. Now he was in trouble. His general Dong Xuanji said to his men, "Prince Langxie is acting against the government. That's rebellion." Prince Langxie found out and killed Dong. As a result, most of his men scattered, leaving only his servants still following him, a few dozen in all. Prince Langxie had to escape to his Bochow (Bo here means Learned), but he was slain by his gatekeeper on the twenty-third day of the same moon when he arrived at the gate. His action lasted only for a few days. General Qu's army had not even arrived yet.

On the twenty-fifth day, Prince Yue was up in arms in Yuchow (meaning Happy District) and soon took over Shangcai (Shang here means Upper and Cai here is a surname) Town. He declared his mutiny two days after his son died, before he received that bad news. The other princes did not follow suit. They were hesitating, watching how the father progressed. The father had sent a messenger to the Duke of Dongwan (Dong means East and Wan here means Smile), who did not know how to respond. At the advice of his subordinates, he detained the messenger and reported the incident to the central government.

Only when the father took over Shangcai Town did he get the bad news that his son had been killed. Now he was between the devil and the deep sea. He was in a panic and wanted to surrender himself to the government. Then he changed his mind, when someone brought two thousand men for his support. He began to recruit and scared up some seven thousand men in all. To raise the morale of his men, he lied to them with the false news that his son had taken over several districts and gathered two hundred thousand people, and that his son would come to meet him soon, with his troops of course.

On the first day of the ninth moon, Empress Dowager Wu sent General Qu Chongyu as Commander-in-Chief, the minister of the Etiquette Ministry Cen Changqian as Back-up Commander-in-Chief and a vice minister Zhang Guangfu as coordinator, with one hundred thousand soldiers. At the same time she announced she was divesting the father Prince Yue and his son Prince Langxie of their titles as princes.

On the eleventh day of the ninth moon, General Qu Chongyu arrived with his troops to the east of Yuchow, and set up his bivouac forty *li* (about twenty kilometers) from the city.

Prince Yue did not really have any confidence in the victory of his mutiny. He had hired Buddhist monks and Taoists to pray for his success. Most of his subordinates and soldiers were forced to join him, and so they would not fight to death for him. The only person faithful to him was his son-in-law Pei Shoude, skilful in martial arts.

When the government army camped outside the city, Prince Yue ordered his youngest son Li Gui and his son-in-law Pei Shoude to go out to attack. As soon as the two sides met on the battlefield, Prince Yue's men were defeated and scattered. The son was killed. The son-in-law was wounded and escaped back into the city. Prince Yue was in panic again and did not know what to do next.

The government army surrounded the city. Prince Yue looked out from the battlement at the formation of the government army and felt that his final day was upon him. He sighed and one of his followers came up to say to him, "Since the failure is certain, Your Highness must not let them execute you in disgrace. Do what Your Highness thinks fit." Prince Yue committed suicide by drinking poison. His son-in-law hanged himself. Others lay down their arms and surrendered. The whole event lasted for less than twenty days. His head and the head of his son were cut off and were hung high above the main gate of the capital city for a certain period of time, which was the tradition in those days to warn others who might rise up against the government.

The end of their rebellions came so fast that the other princes had not even had time to respond and support them. But Empress Dowager Wu knew of the extent of the conspiracy and had those princes and Princess Changle arrested and sent to the capital on the thirteenth day. All of them were forced to end their own lives. Princess Changle was the nineteenth daughter of the first emperor of the Tang Dynasty and the aunt of Empress Dowager Wu on her husband's side.

According to the law at that time, all those who had a connection with Prince Yue should die, too. That would amount to six or seven hundred families. Die Renji, the magistrate of Yuchow (meaning Happy District) at the time sent in a personal memorial to Empress Dowager Wu to beg her mercy for them, saying, "Those people were involved by error. Now, if I openly plead for them, it will look like I am pleading for the rebels. Yet if I learn the truth and don't let Your Majesty know, it will make Your Majesty look like a merciless person." So Empress Dowager Wu commuted the death verdict and banished them to Fengchow (Abundance District).

On the sixth day of the eleventh moon, Empress Dowager Wu had Xue Shao flung into jail and he starved to death there. Xue Shao was her son-in-law, the husband of her daughter Princess Taiping; he had also been involved in the treason.

In the fourth moon of 689, Prince RuNan and Duke Poyang wanted to support the ex-emperor in Luling in a revolt, but the plot was brought to light and Prince RuNan and Duke Poyang were executed. A vice minister of Official Ministry by the name of Deng Xuanting was also executed because his daughter was the wife of Duke Poyang and he himself was familiar with Prince RuNan. When Duke Poyang was contemplating his treachery, he asked Deng for advice but Deng kept silent. Prince RuNan had also talked to him about treason. He did not report it to Empress Dowager Wu. Deng Xuanting had been a friend of Shangguan Yi, and for that he had been demoted to be the mayor of Dunqiu (Dun here means Stop and Qiu here means Mound) Town. He had done a great job there and was praised by the emperor. When Empress Dowager Wu was in power, he had been promoted to be the vice minister of Official Ministry. Nevertheless, he had not distinguished himself in that position, and besides, he suffered from diabetes. So he had been demoted to be the magistrate of Lichow (Li here is the name of a river). There he had also done a great job and been promoted and then restored to the former position. Strangely, he had performed less admirably as the vice minister of the Official Ministry till his death.

On the thirteenth day of the seventh moon in 690, a secret message came to report that Prince Ze and Prince Xu were about to rebel, and as a result Prince Ze killed himself and Prince Xu was hanged.

On the eighth day of the eighth moon, twelve imperial relatives of Li family were killed. By then most of the Li family members had been killed. Only Princess Qianjin survived because she often flattered Empress Dowager Wu, and even begged to be her "dry" daughter though she was really older than Empress Dowager Wu, and to change her surname to Wu. So Empress Dowager Wu liked her very much and gave her the title of Grand Princess YanAn. (In the Chinese tradition, a dry daughter or son is not a foster one, one who is wet-nursed. She or he has her or his own family to live with. A woman or man calls someone dry father or dry mother because the so-called father or mother is rich or powerful so that the dry daughter or dry son can use their influence for her or his own benefits.)

The failure of the Li princes showed that people in general never supported them. They had only a handful of followers. Besides, they were not up to scheming on this grand scale and acting strictly in accordance with their original plan. If all of them could have marched together toward the capital on the same day, the result might be different. As for the general populace, they did not really care who was the ruler, Li or Wu, male or female, as long as they could have a comfortable life.

OTHER REBELLIONS

In 653, a woman named Chen Shuozhen, born in Muchow (Friendly District) staged an uprising together with her brother-in-law Zhang Shuyin. She called herself Empress Wenjia (now, that was really the first time a woman gave herself the title of sovereign in China), but as the event and the woman involved were extremely short-lived, it barely registered in Chinese history). The brother-in-law attacked Tonglu (Tong here means a Paulownia Tree and Lu here means House) Town and took it over. She herself attacked led two thousand men and occupied Muchow. Then she sent one of her followers to attack Wuchow (Wu here is the name of a river) with four thousand men. Cui Yixuan (585–656), the magistrate of Wuchow, went to meet the rebels with his men. In the battle, one man moved to shield the magistrate lest he should be killed or wounded but he said, "If I'm afraid of arrows, how can I encourage the soldiers to fight?" He rode into the battle in front of his soldiers. His men fought so bravely that the rebels were routed. They slew thousands of and allowed others to surrender. In the eleventh moon, Cui Yixuan marched towards Muchow and finally captured the woman and her brother-in-law, who were executed later.

In 683, a man called Bai Tieyu living, in Suichow (meaning Safety District) buried a brass Buddha statuette in the ground. After some time, grass grew over it. Then pointing to the spot, he told his neighbors, "I've seen a halo over here like the one we see around the head of Buddha, several times at night." The credulous neighbors dug into the earth and found the brass statuette of Buddha. Bai said, "The Buddha will bring us good luck." Many people believed him and so he had numerous followers. In the fourth moon that year, he held up a banner of rebellion and called himself Bright Holy Emperor. He attacked some towns and killed the officials there. General Cheng Wuting was sent to fight him. General Cheng took over Chengping (Cheng here means City and Ping means Peace) Town Bai Tieyu was occupying and captured him. The mutiny was quelled.

In the mid-ninth moon of 687, a man by the name of Yang Chucheng, in Guochow (Guo was the name of an ancient kingdom in China) lied, saying that he was a general, and started recruiting soldiers. He also lied that he had received an imperial edict from Prince Luling (the ex-emperor who had been abolished for his rash words about giving the throne to his father-in-law) in Fangchow (House District), where he had been transferred to live on the eleventh day of the third moon in 685. His conspiracy was revealed and he was executed.

In the fifth moon of 696, Li Jinzhong, the governor of Songmu (Song means Pine Tree and Mu here means Desert), and his brother-in-law Sun Wanrong, the magistrate of Guichengchow (Gui in this case means Return and Cheng here means Honesty), attacked Yingchow (Ying here means Camp) and killed the governor, Zhao Wenhui. Governor Zhao Wenhui was supposed to provide them with various necessities but had treated them badly. Anyway, when the news came, Holy Empress Wu sent Cao Renshi, Chang Xuanyu, Li Duozuo, Ma Renjie, and others, twenty-eight generals in all, to set them straight.

In the seventh moon, Li Jinzhong called himself Superior Khan. A man of the Chidan Clan, a tribal people living to the north of Zhou territory, he sent Sun as a vanguard to invade the territory of the Zhou Dynasty. They took over some towns and their army grew to some ten thousand in number. Then they began to assault Tanchow (Sandalwood District), but were defeated by General Zhang Jiujie there.

In the eighth moon, the government army led by Cao Renshi was defeated by the rebels. Here is what happened: rebels captured hundreds of government soldiers when they took over Yingchow. Now they released these captives and said to them, "We have no extra food to feed you and we would regret killing you. So we have to let you go. Besides, when the government army arrives, we will have to surrender anyway." The released captives met the government army marching to fight the rebels in Youchow (Reclusive District). When the generals heard what they had to say, they were happy in the thought that they could easily quash the rebellion without fighting. As they reached Yellow Deer Valley, they came across a few groups of old men who gestured to them to come with them. Therefore, the generals left all the foot-soldiers behind and went ahead with only the cavalry. Further ahead, they were caught in an ambuscade; the government army was defeated and two generals, Chang Xunyu and Ma Renjie, fell captives.

The rebels made the two generals write to those left behind, saying that the government army was victorious and the remaining army should hasten there. But along the route they were waylaid by the same ruse and most of the government army were slaughtered.

Needing more soldiers, in the ninth moon Holy Empress Wu thought she would free all the prisoners and the slaves of the courtiers to form an army to fight the rebels. She appointed the general Wu Youyi, her nephew, as the commander-in-chief and Chen ZiAng as a counselor to Wu Youyi. Chen was also a famous poet. He handed in a memorial, stating, "Prisoners and slaves are not suitable to form the national army. Besides, since false accusations are no longer being made, there are fewer and fewer prisoners, and the slaves are not trained fighters. Even if they are gathered up, they are no match for the rebels. There are so many loyal people in the nation to recruit; why use prisoners and slaves?"

On eighth day of the ninth moon, the rebels attacked Liangchow (Cool District) and took the governor Xu Qinming captive. His brother Xu Qinji resisted the rebels in Chongchow (High District), and was defeated and taken prisoner, too. He was told to talk of sedition to Pei XuanGui, the general who was guarding the city where the rebels were pressing the siege. When Xu Qinji reached the closed gate of the city and came within hearing distance, he shouted to Pei, "The rebels will perish soon. You must guard the city." He was slain on the spot.

On the twenty-first day of the ninth moon in 696, the chieftain Mochuo of the Tujue Clan offered to fight the rebels with his own Clansmen. Holy Empress Wu dubbed him with the title of Good Khan.

In the tenth moon, Good Khan Mochuo led a surprise attack and captured the family of Li Jinzhong, who escaped, but died before long. Mochuo took Li's captive Xu Qinming as his captive. Then Li's brother-in-law Sun Wanrong gathered his warriors and made himself their leader of them. Sun took over Jichow (Ji here means Hope) by force and killed the magistrate, Lu Baiji. Then Sun marched toward Yingchow (Ying means Sea). Holy Empress Wu made the courtier Di Renji the magistrate of Weichow (Wei here is a surname) to fight Sun Wanrong. The ex-magistrate Dugu (double surname) Si was afraid of a surprise attack from Sun and so moved all the people in the outskirts into the city. When Di Renji came, he let the people return to their homes. He told the ex-magistrate that the rebels were still some distance away and that when they came nearer, he would deal with them.

In the initial moon of 697, Mochuo, the Khan of the Tujue Clan, besieged Lingchow (Ling here means Sprite). He turned to fight the government now. He took his captive Xu Qinming along with him and wanted him to persuade the defenders to surrender. When they reached the bottom of the town walls, Xu shouted to the defenders on the battlement, "I need arms, rice and ink." On the surface, he was asking the defenders to give Mochuo those things, but the implication was that the defenders should choose someone as general and have him lead an army — with a full stomach — and attack Mochuo in the inky dark. But no one in the town understood the hint.

But on the twenty-fifth day of the tenth moon in 697, Good Khan Mochuo invaded Shengchow (Sheng means Victory), but was defeated by the government army guarding the place.

In the third moon, generals Wang Xiaoji and Su Honghui went with seventeen thousand soldiers to fight Sun Wanrong in the East Xiashi (Xia here is the name of a place and Shi here means Stone) Valley. They fought hard and the rebels retreated. Wang Xiaoji gave chase and reached the top of a cliff. The rebels came back and approached them. In the second battle, most of the government soldiers were killed and Wang Xiaoji fell from the cliff and died. Another general, Su Honghui, escaped beforehand. When the news came, Holy Empress Wu granted Wang Xiaoji an honorary title and sent a herald to execute the escaped general. Luckily for him, before the herald arrived, the general won a victory and his execution order was annulled.

In the same moon, courtiers Yan Zhiwei and Tian Guidao were sent as envoys to the Tujue Clan to appoint Mochuo actually as khan, not just in title. On the way, they met with one of Mochuo's messenger. Yan Zhiwei gave the messenger a crimson robe and a silver girdle, which was the uniform of a courtier of a certain rank. Furthermore, he sent back word to Holy Empress Wu suggesting that the messenger should be treated well. But Tian Guidao also sent word to Holy Empress Wu, saying, "Mochuo has betrayed the trust of Your Majesty and regrets it now. He must wait for the pardon of Your Majesty. Now Zhiwei did not have the right to give his messenger the robe and girdle unless he received permission from Your Majesty first, which puts Your Majesty in an awkward position. Your Majesty should order Zhiwei to take back the uniform till Your Majesty grants it. Besides, a messenger from a tribal unit does not deserve such an honor." Holy Empress Wu agreed with him.

When Yan Zhiwei and Tian Guidao arrived and were received by Khan Mochuo, Zhiwei went down on his knees and kissed the Khan's boot while Guidao stood there just holding up his hands as a salute. Mochuo detained him and wanted to kill him. But Guidao reproved him for avarice. One of Mochuo's men warned that it was not wise to make an enemy of such a big powerful country as China, so Mochuo just detained him.

Mochuo's messenger brought a request from Mochuo that China should provide them with seeds of grain, rolls of cloth, agricultural equipment and iron. Some courtiers wanted to grant the request while others opposed it. These things would make Mochuo stronger; but since now the government had enough enemies to fight, it was better to grant Mochuo's request so that the government would not fight on another front. Holy Empress Wu agreed with the latter opinion and granted Mochou's request. Mochuo released Yan and Tian. When they returned, they debated before Holy Empress Wu. Tian felt that Mochuo would betray them again while Yan insisted that Mochuo would never betray again.

In the fourth moon of 697, General Wu Yanzong, a nephew of Holy Empress Wu, was sent to fight the rebels as commander-in-chief with two hundred thousand soldiers.

In the sixth moon, General Wu Yanzong arrived in Zhaochow (Zhao here is a surname). When he heard the news that the rebels were on their way, he wanted to escape south. Someone said to him, "We must guard the place. When the rebels cannot occupy it, they will leave to attack somewhere else. That's their way. Then we can chase and fall on them. The victory is surely ours." General Wu would not listen and took off for Xiangchow (Xiang here means Visage). The rebels took the city and killed many people.

After defeating the government army, Sun Wanrong built a town named New Town. He let his brother-in-law guard it and he himself went to attack Youchow. He was afraid that Mochuo would assault him from behind, and so he sent five messengers to Mochuo to ask him to come and attack Youchow together. Three messengers arrived first with the words from Sun. Mochuo was glad and gave a red robe to each of them. When the other two messengers arrived, Mochuo was piqued that they were so late and wanted to kill them. The two late ones asked to be granted the privilege to say something before they were killed. With the permission of Mochuo, they told him the truth about Sun. So Mochuo killed the three messengers and gave the two late messengers a red robe each. Then he made them his guides. He killed Xu Qinming, the governor of Liangchow, whom he had captured, as a sacrifice to Heaven and marched to attack New Town. He surrounded the town for three days and captured it. He released the brother-in-law of Sun Wanrong and let him return to Sun so that he could report to him the fall of the town — revenge for his cheating.

At that time Sun was fighting the government army. When the bad news came, his men all feared the worst. The people of the Yi Clan, originally supporting Sun, now betrayed him. They attacked Sun from behind while the government army under another general Yang Xuanji attacked Sun from the front. Sun's troops were put to rout. He himself fled east with several thousand men, but he was ambushed by the government army. He escaped with one of his slaves into a forest. There was nowhere to go. His slave killed him and went to surrender himself with Sun's head to the government army. It was the thirtieth day of the sixth moon in 697.

In the seventh moon, General Wu Yanzong came back. He demanded that all the people who had sided with the rebels should be executed. A courtier Wang Qiuli contradicted him, saying that those people had had to go with the rebels under the threat of death. They were innocent and should be pardoned. Besides, he revealed that Wu Yanzong had fled before the rebels. That left Wu Yanzong with very little to say. Holy Empress Wu gave her assent that those people should be pardoned.

In the seventh moon of 700, Holy Empress Wu gave a feast to celebrate the victory over the remaining rebels of the Qidan Clan. The victory had been won by General Li Kaigu, a former general of the rebels who had often defeated the government army. After Sun Wanrong died, he surrendered himself to the government army. Someone had suggested executing him, but Di Renjie thought it would be far better to coopt him. Such a brave and capable man, pardoned and welcomed as one of them, would be a valuable asset for the government army. Holy Empress Wu accepted his idea, and furthermore, made him a general of the government army at the proposal of Di Renjie. Thus Li Kaigu fought for the government and defeated the remaining rebels.

All these rebellions failed because the populace as a whole did not support them. People preferred a peaceful life and did not like disturbances. Most rebels could only come up with a handful of followers and they could at most coerce a small number of people to join them. In actual battles, those "soldiers" who had signed up under threat would scatter at the first opportunity.

ABUSE OF POWER AT EVERY LEVEL

Some of the courtiers were charged with the task of interrogating criminal suspects. For the most part, facts and evidence were not their top priority. They might work on the basis of secret information from informers, or they might just need to find a reason to get rid of someone. Their priority was to get the suspects to confess to have committed the crimes, under torture if necessary, regardless of whether they had had any involvement. For that purpose, the interrogators invented many types of torture equipment and tried one after the other until the suspects said whatever the questioners wanted them to say. These courtiers were called cruel courtiers in the Chinese history book. There were a few cruel courtiers in Han Dynasty (206 BC–220), and there were some during the reign of Empress Wu, too. She used them against the many princes of the Li family and her other rivals, and anyone who stood in her way or opposed her intention to become sovereign empress. These cruel courtiers were especially useful in special cases, generally for treason. They were well-known for their brutality. But she never let the cruel courtiers have much power except as judges in the cases that suited her purpose. After there were no more political enemies left, she killed those cruel courtiers one by one. The cruel courtiers never judged cases involving the common people, so the populace as a whole never thought that Empress Wu was a merciless person because she used the cruel courtiers.

On the eighth day of the third moon in 686, Empress Dowager Wu ordered a bronze box to be made. She wanted to get a better sense of how the people were faring, the common people, the local governments and the courtiers A skilful man called Yu Baojia designed the bronze box for her. This is the Yu who secretly taught Xu Jingye how to make swords, spears, bows and arrows for Xu's rebellion; when Xu had failed, Yu had escaped.

On the eleventh day of the sixth moon, the bronze box was finished and placed in the front portion of the levee hall. The box had four compartments each with a respective slot in it. Anyone who had anything to say could slip in a memorial, in any category: ideas, criticism, complaints and "other." But an enemy of Yu Baojia threw in a memorial revealing the fact that Yu had made weapons for the rebels, by which many government soldiers had been slain. The bronze box was such a success that its creator was executed.

The magical appearance of the bronze box opened a door to all kinds of secret informers, who used it for all kinds of purposes. By the order of Empress Dowager Wu, anyone who wished to travel to the capital as an informer was to have lodging, food and transportation provided by the local government. All the missives inside the box were to be read by people appointed and trusted by Empress Dowager Wu, to whom they must report.

Some courtiers were named to interrogate and pass sentences on suspects exposed by the information contained in memorials. Some of the most famous in the history of the Tang Dynasty were Suo Yuanli, Zhou Xing, Lai Junchen and Wan Guojun. The latter two wrote a book titled "Instructions On How to Make False Accusations." Each of them detained hundreds of villains who had made false charges against those who opposed Empress Dowager Wu or others. If the suspects refused to confess to the false accusations, they would be tortured severely. Those courtiers invented quite a few new instruments and did their work diligently. Sometimes a suspect was just tortured to death.

Suo Yuanli (?–691) was the first cruel courtier employed by Empress Dowager Wu. He was a "foreigner" from a country to the west of the Tang Dynasty. His first invention was an iron cage. On the top side there was a hole through which the head of the prisoner was thrust out. Then wooden wedges were hammered into the head here and there, one by one, till the prisoner was willing to sign the papers describing the crimes he was to confess. Sometimes the papers were written by someone else and the prisoner was not even told what they said. Suo Yuanli's first case was Yu Baojia, the one who had made the bronze box. When Yu refused to own his crimes, Suo cried to his men, "Come! Get my iron cage." When Yu saw the cage, he signed the papers and was executed without the additional torment. But afterwards, when Suo was himself put in prison for taking bribes, he refused to confess.

Then the judge who interrogated him said, "Come! Get me his iron cage." Suo had to sign his crime papers and died in jail.

In the fourth moon of 688, a courtier Hao Xiangxian was executed. One of his slaves had reported (falsely) that Hao was planning treason. Empress Dowager Wu let Zhou Xing judge the case. His verdict was the death penalty. Family members went to complain to an imperial censor, Ren Xuanzhi. Ren handed in a memorial to Empress Dowager Wu saying that Hao was not guilty; he was removed from his official position. While Hao was being executed, in public, he cursed Empress Dowager Wu and shouted out some palace secrets. He snatched a stick from a by-stander and struck the executioner. But he was killed by the guards. From then on, every criminal to be executed would have a wooden ball stuffed in his mouth so that he could not reveal anything to the spectators.

In the ninth moon of 689, the cruel courtier Zhou Xing handed in a false accusation against prime minister Wei Xuantong, saying that as Empress Dowager Wu was growing old, Wei had told him he had better change his support to the emperor. Empress Dowager Wu was, of course, inspired into fury and ordered Wei to end his own life at home. Zhou had long harbored hostility against Wei because he thought Wei had impeded his promotion. He had been the mayor of Heyang (He means River and Yang means the Sun) Town when Emperor Gaozong had still been alive. The emperor had wanted to promote him, but someone told the emperor that he was not a good man and so no promotion order had been issued. Zhou had often waited in the waiting room for the courtiers before the levee. Other prime ministers had not said anything to him. Only Wei thought that it was useless for him to stay any longer and so he told Zhou he might as well leave. Therefore, Zhou thought that it was Wei who had hindered his promotion. Now, when the order came that Wei should die, someone advised him to let Empress Dowager Wu know that he had a secret to tell her so that he could have a chance to explain to Empress Dowager Wu and plead for himself. But Wei rejected the advice, saying that he accepted death; everyone would die, and he would never be an informer.

Wei Xuantong passed the government tests and received an official position. As he befriended Shangguan Yi, who offended Empress Wu and was put into jail, Wei Xuantong was exiled to a remote southern province. In 674, he was pardoned and appointed to be the administrator of Qichow (Qi here means Forked). Later he was promoted to the position of the vice minister of Official Ministry and finally to be a prime minister.

As now Empress Dowager Wu used her nephews Wu Chengsi and Wu Sansi as her main supporters, they became very powerful though their official positions were not the highest. Even prime ministers would listen to them.

Once in 690, a prime minister Wei Fangzhi was ill and they went to see him. Wei was lying in bed and did not even say hello to them. Someone advised him that he should not show his contempt so obviously, but he said that life and death was already destined and an upright man should not condescend to flatter those in-laws for his life. Before long, he was falsely accused by the cruel courtier Zhou Xing under the instruction of the nephews and was exiled to Danchow (Dan is the name of a place). His estate was confiscated. He died soon thereafter.

Besides the cruel courtiers, there were also just and upright courtiers who also worked in the Judicial Ministry. Xu Yougong (641–702) was one of them. He never used any torture instrument when he interrogated prisoners. Prisoners said that if they were judged by Xu Yougong, their chance of survival was great. He tried any case in justice to the prisoner. And Li Rizhi, another just and upright courtier, had once insisted in his sentence that a prisoner did not deserve death while Suo Yuanli, a cruel courtier, had persisted in the death verdict. They argued about the verdict for several days. Suo announced that as long as he worked in the Judicial Ministry, the prisoner would be executed at the last, but Li declared that as long as he worked there the prisoner would not be put to death. So there were two verdicts on the same case. However, the man was pardoned at length.

At the beginning of the seventh moon in 690, there was a special prison set up for rebels only. Empress Dowager Wu wanted to eliminate her political foe. In the ninth moon, the cruel courtier Zhou Xing trumped up a false charge against the general Heichi Changzhi for the crime to rebel against Empress Dowager Wu and put him into jail. In the tenth moon Heichi was hanged in the prison.

In the tenth moon, two brother officials would die under false accusation of treachery. The just courtier Xu Yougong pleaded the case for them. The cruel courtier Zhou Xing said to Holy Empress Wu that Xu should be beheaded because he wanted to release the criminals. Although Holy Empress Wu did not kill him, she demoted him. But she liked him so much for his uprightness that she restored him to the former position in a few days. When Xu wanted to resign, Holy Empress Wu would not permit it. Xu said, "If I don't want to twist the law, I will die in this position sooner or later." He meant that those cruel courtiers would not let him go since he opposed them. Holy Empress Wu insisted on it.

In the second moon of 691, as the courtiers had the strong opposition to the cruel courtiers, Holy Empress Wu had cruel courtiers Zhou Xing and Suo Yuanli put to death. A story in the history book went like the following about Zhou Xing, who was a close friend of another cruel courtier Lai Junchen. Holy Empress Wu received a report that Zhou Xing would rebel, and she wanted Lai Junchen to interrogate Zhou Xing about his crime. Lai knew that all his torturing instruments could not make Zhou confess his crime. So he delayed the arrest of Zhou, but invited Zhou to his yamen for dinner. While eating, Lai asked Zhou what he could do if a criminal would not make a confession even though he had exhausted all his methods of torture. Zhou said that he could put the criminal into a big pottery vat and start a wood fire round it. Thus no one could resist. Then Lai ordered his men to prepare such a vat with firewood ignited round it. When it was ready, Lai said to Zhou, "Her Majesty ordered me to interrogate you. Will you please get into the vat?" So Zhou knew that he had to plead guilty to whatever was the charge, just as he had made others do. According to the law, Zhou should have been sentenced to death, but Empress Dowager Wu commuted his sentence to exile to a southern district. However, he was killed on the way anyhow by a personal enemy.

On the second day of the first moon in 692, Wu Chengsi and the cruel courtier Lai Junchen made a false accusation of treason against seven honest courtiers who often had opinions different from theirs. They were Ren Zhigu, Pei Xingben, Di Renjie, Pei Xuanli, Lu Xuan, Wei Yuanzhong and Li Sizhen. The seven courtiers were thrown into prison. Lai wanted them to confess. Di Renjie confessed and was not tortured. Wei Yuanzhong was the one tortured most severely. Lai wanted to kill them all and made it look like suicide. So he faked seven memorials of thanks for the death sentences. (In feudal China, sometimes when a courtier received a death sentence or an order to die from the emperor, he would write a thank-you to the emperor to show that he was happy to die at his order. By not making any complaint, or even better by writing such a memorial, the loyal courtier showed that the emperor was right to order the courtier to die.) As Di admitted to his crime, he received better treatment. Then he wrote a letter on the lining of his winter gown and asked the jailor to notify his son that he wanted a change of clothes since it had become warmer. When his son received the letter with all the facts about the false accusation, he went to see Holy Empress Wu, who then came to know the truth. When Lai Junchen implored Her Majesty to execute the seven men, Holy Empress Wu did not consent. She sent for Di Renjie and asked him why he had admitted to the false charge. Di replied that if he had refused to admit, he would already have been tortured to death. Then the forgery of the thanks memorials of the seven courtiers was exposed, too.

On the fourth day of the same moon, Ren Zhigu was demoted to be the mayor of Jiangxia (Jiang here means River and Xia here means Summer) Town, Pei Xingben was banished to Lingnan (Ling here means Hill and Nan here means South), a remote southern place, and Di Renjie was demoted to be the mayor of Pengze (Peng here is a surname and Ze here means a Pool of Water) Town.

Then another cruel courtier Huo Xuanke, the nephew of Pei Xuanben, said to Holy Empress Wu, "If Your Majesty won't execute Pei Xuanben, I will die before Your Majesty." He wanted to show that his loyalty to Her Majesty was stronger than his relationship with his uncle. He then knocked his head on the steps of the dais on which Holy Empress Wu was sitting. His forehead was bleeding and his blood smeared the steps. But Holy Empress Wu did not give her assent. Later he bandaged his forehead but let the bandage show a little under his official hat so that Holy Empress Wu would know his loyalty when she noticed it.

On the last day of the ninth moon in 694, the cruel courtier Lai Junchen was found guilty of taking bribes and demoted to be a petty official in Tongchow (Similar District). Another cruel courtier, Wang Hongyi, was banished to a remote southern place. He made a false document showing that he was pardoned and summoned back to the capital. On his way back he ran into a courtier, Hu Yuanli, who knew him as they had worked together in the capital. His false document was exposed and he was beaten to death.

In the tenth moon of 697, Liu Sili, the magistrate of Jichow (Ji here means Dustpan), was learning the art of face-reading from the fortune-teller Chang Jingzang, who said to Liu that his face-reading showed that he would be in the highest position in the future. Liu was exhilarated and told it to the official Qi Lianyue. They sent a messenger to contact some of the courtiers in the capital and promised them promotions and fortune if they could support Liu. One of the courtiers under the name of Ji Xu reported it to Holy Empress Wu through the cruel courtier Lai Junchen (Ji Xu's position was too low at the time to report directly to Holy Empress Wu). Holy Empress Wu commanded Wu Yanzong, her nephew, to judge the case.

Wu Yanzong set a trap by lying to Liu Sili, saying that Holy Empress Wu needed a great many capable men to assist Her Majesty. Then he asked Liu to recommend capable men among the existing courtiers. Liu seized the opportunity to promote his co-conspirators to more important positions, and so he recommended thirty-six courtiers. All of them were arrested and executed together with Liu Sili on the twenty-fourth day of the initial moon next year. Their relatives and friends involved were exiled, a thousand in number.

Later the cruel courtier Lai falsely accused Ji Xu, who used the ruse of offering to report a secret. Holy Empress Wu sent for him and he pleaded the case. It must have been a good secret, as Holy Empress Wu pardoned him.

Later he was given a promotion and began to hate the cruel courtier Lai, who had already been summoned to the capital.

In the fifth moon of 697, the cruel courtier Lai Junchen wanted to make a false charge of treason against Holy Empress Wu's nephews and her daughter Princess Taiping, and also the crown prince and Prince Luling, the ex-emperor, both being the sons of Holy Empress Wu. If all those persons were imprisoned, Lai thought that he could have a chance to usurp the supreme power. But the nephews and Princess Taiping reported all sorts of unlawful things Lai had done to Holy Empress Wu. Therefore, Lai was imprisoned himself, and sentenced to death. But Holy Empress Wu still wanted to pardon him. When the courtier Ji Xu went to see Her Majesty, she asked him how things were going outside the palace. Taking the opportunity, Ji Xu replied that the people all wished Lai Junchen would be eliminated immediately, and he persuaded Her Majesty to approve the execution.

On the third day of the sixth moon, the last cruel courtier Lai Junchen was executed. When his body was left on the ground at the execution spot, people rushed forth to cut his flesh or stomp on his body. Soon nothing was left but a bloody pulp. After the death of Lai, those courtiers who had been his followers all came to Holy Empress Wu to confess their relationship with Lai in hopes that they would not be considered guilty of any offense. When Holy Empress Wu chided them for it, they said, "We are sorry if we are guilty. However, if what we did offends Your Majesty, Your Majesty will punish only ourselves; but if we had not obeyed Lai, everyone in our families would have been murdered under his false accusations." So Holy Empress Wu pardoned them.

A courtier called Hou Ming had always flattered Lai. His wife advised him to keep a safe distance from Lai because Lai would someday be caught and punished for his misbehavior. Hou listened to his wife and backed off from Lai. Lai was angry and demoted him to be the mayor of Wulong (Wu here means Martial and Long here means Dragon) Town far away from the capital. At first he refused to go, but his wife urged him to leave. Thus when all Lai's supporters were exiled, he got away without penalty.

In the ninth moon of 697, Holy Empress Wu said to the courtiers during a levee, "When Zhou Xing and Lai Junchen [both were cruel courtiers] were judges, there were several cases of treason among the courtiers. As these matters are governed by law I had to consent to their judgments. I had sent someone I trusted to ask the prisoners if they were guilty of treason, and all admitted it. But since Zhou and Lai are gone, no more treason cases are being brought. So I think that some of those cases must have been trumped up." A courtier said, "They all died on false accusations of treason. Zhou and Lai wanted to show that they had a keen ability to find betrayers. As for those prisoners who admitted their guilt, they did so because if they told the truth, they would be tortured severely and eventually found guilty anyway. They would rather die quickly than experience the worst torments, in vain. Your servant can guarantee at the risk of the lives of my family that there will be no traitors among the courtiers anymore. If any traitor is found henceforth, Your Majesty can execute everyone in my household." Holy Empress Wu said, "That sounds reassuring."

In the eleventh moon of 702, a courtier handed in a memorial, saying, "Now that Your Majesty knows the guilt of the cruel courtier Lai Junchen and you have executed him, Your Majesty should assign someone to reopen the cases he judged and right the wrong verdicts." Holy Empress Wu let another courtier to check all the cases and many of them were corrected.

In Chinese history, most of the cruel courtiers did not die a natural death because cruelty is against human nature. Even if a ruler used the cruel courtiers for a certain purpose, the ruler would desert them once he or she reached his or her goal and had no more use of them. Generally he or she would kill those cruel courtiers to appease the hatred of other courtiers against the cruel ones. The brutal actions were really a distortion of human nature.

CHAPTER 6. PICKING FAVORITES

NAMING A SUCCESSOR

As a rule, every sovereign ought to name a successor to the throne while he or she is still alive. So did Empress Wu when she had become the sovereign empress. At first she was wavering among her sons and nephews. But she did not have to make a decision right away; whom would she choose as her successor later?

In the tenth moon of 691, a courtier Zhang Jiafu encouraged courtier Wang Qingzhi, together with hundreds of others, to hand in a memorial to suggest that Wu Chengsi (nephew of Holy Empress Wu) should be the crown prince. Holy Empress Wu did not agree. When Wang importuned her several times, Holy Empress Wu lost her patience and ordered a prime minister Li Zhaode to beat him. Seizing the opportunity, Li told his men to beat him to death. Li Zhaode then advised Holy Empress Wu to make her son the crown prince. Li Zhaode said to Holy Empress Wu that a ruler should let the son, not the nephew, inherit the dynasty. Holy Empress Wu thought so, too.

In the sixth moon of 692, Li Zhaode said to Holy Empress Wu, "I'm afraid that Wu Chengsi is too powerful." Holy Empress Wu responded, "He's my nephew. So I give him the power." Li said, "Who is closer in relationship, nephew to aunt, or son to mother? In history, even sons have killed fathers for the throne; let alone a nephew." Holy Empress Wu said, "You are right. I didn't think of that." So she made her son the crown prince.

In 693, someone at the bidding of Wu Chengsi made a false accusation that the crown prince was planning a revolt. This was because if the crown prince was deposed, Wu Chengsi might have a chance to be made the crown prince. Holy Empress Wu let the cruel courtier Lai Junchen (died in 697) judge the case. Lai could not interrogate the crown prince himself, and so he cross-questioned those who waited on the crown prince. Most of them made false confessions about the charge. But one man denied it and said to Lai, "If you don't believe what I say, I'll cut myself open and take out my heart to show that the crown prince won't revolt." With these words, he drew out the knife he brought with him and cut deeply into his stomach region. He bled and the bowels were seen. When Holy Empress Wu got news of this, she ordered to bring the man into the palace and ordered the palace surgeon to sew up his wound. After the treatment, the man woke up next day. Then Holy Empress Wu came to see him and said, "I can't trust my own son and it has made you suffer so much." So the case was dismissed.

In the second moon of 698, Wu Chengsi was more determined to be the crown prince and hinted to his followers to persuade Holy Empress Wu to make a move. Someone said to Holy Empress Wu, "Since ancient time, all the successors to the throne should have the same surname as the sovereign's." By this he meant that as Her Majesty had the surname of Wu, the successor must have the surname of Wu, too, not of Li. But Holy Empress Wu still hesitated. Then Di Renjie, who was a prime minister now, came to see Holy Empress Wu and said to her, "Who are closer to Your Majesty, nephews or sons? Besides, when a nephew becomes the emperor, he will make libations only to his own parents. I have never heard of one who would do it for his aunt, even if she made him the emperor. It's tradition." Holy Empress Wu said, "It is my family matter as to whom I will make my successor." Di replied, "It is a family matter if it happens in ordinary families. But as for the imperial family the matter concerns the whole nation. So it is no longer a family matter. It is a national matter. Every one of Your Majesty's subjects should have a say to that effect." Holy Empress Wu was inclined to agree.

A courtier Ji Xu asked Zhang Yizhi, the favorite of Holy Empress Wu for his musical talent, to suggest to Holy Empress Wu to make Prince Luling the crown prince. (Prince Luling was the third son of Holy Empress Wu. He had once been the emperor, but was removed from the throne and made Prince Luling because he had joked about giving his father-in-law the empire.) He said to Zhang, "You don't have any merits for the benefits of the nation to deserve to be in such a high position. Therefore, as far as I know, many courtiers hate you. If you can persuade Her Majesty to summon Prince Luling back to the capital and make him the crown prince, people will be thankful to you. Then you will be safe." Zhang thought it was a good idea and repeatedly he took pains to instill the idea into Holy Empress Wu, till she gave her assent.

On the ninth day of the third moon, Holy Empress Wu sent for Prince Luling on the excuse that he was ill and must come back to the capital for treatment. When the courtier went to convey the order of his mother, Prince Luling thought he was being set up for another disaster. But to his surprise, he was being summoned back to the palace. So on the twenty-eighth day, Prince Luling reached the capital.

On the fifteenth day of the ninth moon in 698, the successor (the fourth son of Holy Empress Wu) petitioned to give his position to Prince Luling (the third son, i.e., his elder brother). Holy Empress Wu granted his petition and made Prince Luling the crown prince.

On the sixth day of the initial moon in 699, the ex-successor, the fourth son of Holy Empress Wu, was given the title of Prince Xiang.

On the twenty-fifth day of the winter moon in 699, the crown prince was re-surnamed Wu.

On the eighteenth day of the fourth moon, considering that the crown prince, Prince Xiang, Princess Taiping and her nephews might fight each other after her death, she ordered them to gather in the Ming Hall and vow that they would not fight each other. She had their vows engraved on a piece of iron plate and stored it in the building holding history records and books. But vows carved on an iron plate are nothing compared to things vowed in the heart, and this did not prevent them from killing each other.

Empress Wu's Favorites

Every emperor in China enjoyed having many women at his disposal. One of the women was designated his wife, titled empress, and the others were imperial concubines. He could in fact take advantage of any girl in the palace as well, title or no title. Thus as sovereign, Empress Wu might be considered to have had the right to take a lot of male concubines, but she had none. However, she did have a few favorite men who waited on her and entertained her, even when she was still the empress dowager.

Her first male favorite was a fake monk called Xue Huaiyi. On the first day of the tenth moon in 685, Empress Dowager Wu had the old White Horse Temple fixed up and appointed Xue Huaiyi as the head monk. His original name had been Feng Xiaobao. He started out as a hawker selling herbal medicines in the street. He was a handsome, well-built man and one day by chance he met Princess Qianjin, who recommended him to Empress Dowager Wu. Empress Dowager Wu wanted an excuse to enable him to come into the palace frequently and conveniently so she made him a monk. As she was known as a devout believer in Buddhism, it was reasonable for a monk coming into the palace to read the Buddhist sutras to her. To make it sound like he was from a noble family, Empress Dowager invented his biography as a relative of her son-in-law Xue Shao; hence he was renamed

Xue Huaiyi. Since he had become a favorite of Empress Dowager Wu, most of the courtiers were afraid of him, and some went out of their way to flatter him. Even the nephews of Empress Dowager Wu showed a certain esteem when they met him in the street. Common people would flee at his shadow, hastening to make way when he came strutting down the alley with his thug followers. Anyone who got in his way would be beaten.

In the sixth moon of 686, Xue Huaiyi, the monk, did not salute a prime minister called Su Liangsi, who flared up and ordered the attendants to slap his face. (In feudal China, everyone was required to salute those in higher ranks.) When the monk complained to Empress Dowager Wu, she said, "You should enter by the north gate. The south gate is for the prime ministers. Avoid that in the future."

Empress Dowager Wu sometimes called for the monk to come into the palace on the pretext that he was skillful and was needed for some artwork. A courtier Wang Qiuli handed in a memorial, saying, "If Your Majesty want to use his skills in the palace, he must be castrated to meet the palace rules." The memorial had no noticeable effect. In the fifth moon of 689, the monk Xue was appointed the commander-in-chief to attack the Tujue Clan. Since he did not in fact encounter any troops of the Tujue Clan, he returned to the capital victoriously. In the winter moon of 690, Empress Dowager Wu endowed the monk Xue Huaiyi with a title of Duke of Eguo and also another title as a general.

On the sixteenth night of the initial moon in 695, Heavenly Hall caught fire and the fire to the Ming Hall. By daybreak, both halls were reduced to ashes. According to the history book, it was the monk Xue Huaiyi who set fire to the halls as he wanted to vent his jealousy and wrath against Holy Empress Wu. The history book (written by men who, presumably, never did grow accustomed to having a woman as a sovereign) says that Holy Empress Wu had an affair with the monk Xue Huaiyi, but later she preferred an imperial doctor, Shen Nanqiu, thus fueling monk Xue's jealousy and rage. Holy Empress Wu did not need any of the background details leaking out, so she declared that the fire had been caused by negligence on the part of some workers. As a matter of course, she could not punish the monk Xue. On the contrary, she assigned to him the task of reconstructing the Ming Hall.

But on the fourth day of the second moon, the monk Xue Huaiyi was killed. This is the story: ever since Xue had become the favorite of Holy Empress Wu, he had become more and more unruly. Many local rogues came to him for protection, and he made them all monks till their number reached a thousand. The rogue-monks broke more laws than they observed. A courtier, Zhou Ju, reported this to Holy Empress Wu, who at first made some excuses to protect him. Zhou Ju began to collect evidence and then presented all the evidence before Holy Empress Wu, who agreed that Zhou Ju could banish all the rogue-monks to remote districts. But he could not touch the monk Xue.

After the Ming Hall had been burned, Holy Empress Wu was in fact furious with Xue Huaiyi, although she did not punish him immediately. She ordered Wu Youning, another nephew, to secretly capture Xue and kill him. He was told that Princess Taiping wanted to see him. So the monk Xue went there; a servant led him to the back garden. Then Wu Youning came out from the depths of a grove of trees, with some men. The men seized Xue and killed him. The corpse was sent to the temple, burned, and buried there in accordance with the normal treatment for a dead monk.

On the first day of the initial moon in 697, Holy Empress Wu gave a banquet for all the courtiers in Heavenly Hall. A young man by the name of Zhang Yizhi was there and soon became the favorite of Holy Empress Wu. Zhang Yizhi was handsome, versed in music. He had a brother called Zhang Changzong, who knew Princess Taiping, the favorite daughter of Holy Empress Wu. Princess Taiping recommended him to her mother. Zhang Changzong introduced his brother Yizhi to Holy Empress Wu at the feast. Both the brothers became her favorites and were granted official positions. Even Wu Chengsi and Wu Sansi, the nephews of Holy Empress Wu, would show respect to the Zhang brothers.

There is a difference between concubines and favorites. Holy Empress Wu was already pretty advanced in age; it flattered her to have attractive men around but it is not recorded that she enjoyed more than the brothers' entertainment in dance and music.

In the sixth moon of 700, Holy Empress Wu held a few palace banquets. Only the Zhang brothers and Wu family members attended. They cast all etiquette to the winds. They drank, laughed and joked with each other. Zhang Changzong donned a robe of feathers and played a fife, riding on a wooden stork in the yard before the banqueting hall. He was playing the role of Wang Zijin, a deity who had ascended to Heaven riding on the back of a stork and playing a fife.

The two Zhangs had a younger brother called Zhang Changyi, who was the mayor of Luoyang City. He would grant any request put to him if he could get money under the table. Once an official by the surname of Xue blocked his way to the levee. The man offered him fifty taels of silver and asked for a higher position, which he promised. When he reached the waiting room for the levee, he gave a promotion document to a courtier Zhang Xi, who kept it for several days and then lost it. He went to see Changyi and asked for the man's full name so that he could give him another promotion document. Changyi reprimanded him, saying, "How can I remember? Give it to a man surnamed Xue." Zhang Xi was afraid of him and retired to his office. He checked the list of the officials and found that there were over sixty officials with the surname of Xue. He had to give each of them a promotion document lest the one who had spent the money should file a complaint.

In addition to Holy Empress Wu, there were three persons so powerful that other courtiers were afraid of them. They were Wu Sansi, a nephew of Holy Empress Wu, and the two Zhang brothers. But a bold courtier called Wei Anshi often criticized them to their faces. Once when they were all at a feast in the palace, Zhang Yizhi brought with him some merchants from Sichuan (Four Stream) Province. Wei Anshi went down on his knees before Holy Empress Wu and said, "Merchants are in the lowest caste. How can they come to the palace feast?" Then he told the guards to drive them out. Many courtiers thought that it was not proper for him to do so without getting an order from Holy Empress Wu first. The Holy Empress appreciated his action and praised him. In feudal China, merchants were the lowest class, since they produced nothing but made money off other people's labor.

On the third day of the ninth moon in 701, Prince Shao, Princess Yongtai, sister of Prince Shao, and Prince Wei, husband of Princess Yongtai, were forced by Holy Empress Wu to commit suicide because they had secretly criticized the Zhang brothers for their administration of national affairs entrusted to them by Holy Empress Wu. As the Zhang brothers were quite unprincipled, Prince Shao, his sister and his brother-in-law spoke sarcastically about them among themselves, but someone told on them and the Zhang brothers complained to Holy Empress Wu. This Prince Wei was her grandnephew, son of Wu Chengsi. He had inherited his father's title.

In the seventh moon of 702, since the Zhang brothers had become so powerful, even the crown prince, Prince Xiang (the fourth son of Holy Empress Wu and the younger brother of the crown prince) and Princess Taiping wanted to please them. They sent in a memorial to suggest conferring on Zhang Changzong the title of prince, but Holy Empress Wu did not agree. A few days later, under the persistence of her two sons and the daughter, she gave him only the title of Duke of Yeguo.

In the ninth moon of 703, a prime minister Wei Yuanzhong had a servant of Zhang Yizhi beaten to death for the various offenses of the law. He was an upright man and never the flattered Zhang brothers. Once Holy Empress Wu summoned Zhang Changqi, the magistrate of Qichow (Qi here is the name of a mountain in Shaanxi Province), yet another of the Zhang brothers, back to the capital and wanted to promote him to be the administrator of Yongchow (Harmony District). During a levee, she asked prime ministers, "Who is fit for the position?" Wei Zhongyuan said, "No one among the courtiers is more suitable than Xue Jichang." Holy Empress Wu said, "Jichang is always working in the capital. I'd like to have someone else to fill it. How about Changqi?" Other prime ministers all said, "Your Majesty has selected the right person." But Wei Yuanzhong alone said, "Changqi is not fit for the position." Holy Empress Wu asked, "Why not?" Wei replied, "Changqi is too young and does not know official business. When he worked in Qichow, many people fled from there. Now Yongchow is a more important district. The administrator has more responsibilities. Xue Jichang is a man of ability and is familiar with official affairs." Holy Empress Wu was silent and said nothing more. But she was unhappy, and the Zhang brothers hated Wei Yuanzhong all the more.

Another courtier, Gao Jian, was the favorite of Princess Taiping. When Holy Empress Wu came down with a little ailment, it occurred to Zhang Changzong that if Holy Empress Wu died, Wei Zhongyuan would kill him. So he lied to Holy Empress Wu that Wei Yuanzhong and Gao Jian were privately saying, "As Her Majesty grows old, we'd better support the crown prince." Holy Empress Wu was enraged and put Wei and Gao both into the prison. She would stage a confrontation in her presence between Zhang Changzong and Wei and Gao. Zhang Changzong secretly met a courtier called Zhang Shuo. Zhang Changzong promised Shuo a promotion and asked him to be a witness. Shuo agreed.

Next day, Holy Empress Wu sent for the crown prince, Prince Xiang and all other prime ministers to come into her presence. She let Zhang Changzong confront Wei and Gao. Since both sides stated different things, Holy Empress Wu could not decide who was right. Then Zhang Changzong said, "Zhang Shuo heard what they had said. Your Majesty can send for him." So Holy Empress Wu summoned Zhang Shuo to her presence.

Before Zhang Shuo went in, another courtier, Song Jing said to him, "A good reputation is most important. No one can cheat gods and ghosts. So you mustn't side with the corrupt courtiers to save your own skin. Even if you offend them and are exiled, you have at least a good reputation. If anything happens to you, I will go to see Her Majesty to plead for you. I even will die with you. Think about it." Another courtier said to him, "Don't leave a foul name in the history books and shame your posterity."

When Zhang Shuo entered the levee hall, Holy Empress Wu asked him if he had heard what Wei and Gao had said. Shuo kept silent. Wei was afraid and said to Shuo, "Do you want to make a false accusation against me together with Zhang Changzong?" Shuo said to him, "You are a prime minister. Why talk like a thug in the street?" Then Zhang Changzong forced Shuo to say what he had promised.

Shuo said to Holy Empress Wu, "Your Majesty can see, Changzong is forcing me like this, even in the presence of Your Majesty. What is he doing behind Your Majesty's back? Now in front of Your Majesty and all the others, I must tell the truth. I never heard Wei and Gao say such words. Changzong pressured me to give phony testimony."

Then the two Zhang brothers shouted, "Shuo is planning a rebellion with Wei." When Holy Empress Wu asked them to explain, they cited a tale from the Shang Dynasty (1765 BC–1122 BC). As the king was a tyrant and ruled the people mercilessly, Yi, a prime minister, banished the king to Paulownia Palace for three years. During his time in captivity there the king realized the errors of his ways and changed to a better man. So Yi released the king turned the power over to him again. "Shuo once said that Wei was like Yi and Zhou. Yi banished his king and Zhou acted as the prince regent, ignoring the king. Were they not rebels?" Shuo retorted, "The Zhang brothers know nothing about history. Yi and Zhou were loyal courtiers. When Your Majesty appoints a prime minister, whom does Your Majesty want him to learn from if not from the loyal courtiers? Besides, I know that if I say what Changzong wanted me to say, I will get promotion; if I say the truth, I will be killed. But I can't give false testimony." Holy Empress Wu said, "Shuo is speaking out of both sides of his mouth. Imprison him, too."

On another day, Holy Empress Wu asked Shuo about it again. Shuo insisted on what he had said before. Holy Empress Wu was angry and let the prime ministers and Wu Yanzong interrogate him, but Shuo refused to say what they wanted him to say. Quite a few courtiers handed in memorials to plead for Wei Yuanzong and Zhang Shuo. At length, Wei was demoted, and Gao Jing and Zhang Shuo were exiled.

Zhang Shuo (667–730) was a man of letters and could write beautiful essays. He was given his first official position at the age of twenty. This time, though he was exiled, he was summoned back after the death of Holy Empress Wu and was made a prime minister by the emperor. He was granted the title of Duke of YanGuo.

On the day when Wei was leaving the capital, eight courtiers went to see him off outside the city. Zhang Yizhi sent in a memorial of false accusation written by a man called Cai Ming, saying that Wei and the eight courtiers were plotting a mutiny. There was really no such a person called Cai Ming. Zhang Yizhi made it up.

Holy Empress Wu let the courtier Ma Huaisu interrogate them. She said to Ma Huaisu, "Everything is so obvious. You can just ask some questions and let me know the result." She sent messengers several times to urge Ma, saying, "It seems to be a pretty obvious case. Why the delay?" Ma came to ask for a confrontation with Cai Ming. Holy Empress Wu said, "I don't know where Cai Ming is. You can just judge according to the memorial." Ma told Holy Empress Wu the truth, but she flared up and demanded, "You want to free the rebels?" Ma said, "Your servant would not dare to free any rebels, but Wei was leaving and the others came to see him off on his way. So neither would I dare accuse them of rebellion. Your Majesty has the power to kill them. Your Majesty can just order them executed at will. But if Your Majesty wants me to interrogate them, your servant can only tell the truth." Holy Empress Wu said, "So you think they are not guilty?" Ma said, "Your servant is very stupid and cannot see where they are guilty." Holy Empress Wu was persuaded, and the eight courtiers were pardoned.

In 704, when Holy Empress Wu's health began to fail again, the Zhang brothers were afraid that she would die and then they would surely be killed. Therefore, they gathered their followers and plotted a rebellion of their own. Although Holy Empress Wu got word of it, she would not believe it.

Then a man called Yang Yuansi reported, "Once Zhang Changzong had a fortune-teller read his face. The fortune-teller told him that his face showed that he would be emperor." So Holy Empress Wu ordered three courtiers, Chengqing, Shenqing and Song Jing to interrogate Zhang Changzong. The first two reported, "Zhang Changzong says that he already told Your Majesty what the fortune-teller had said. So the fortune-teller is guilty of saying such words to Changzong. He deserves to be put to death." But Song Jing had a different view. "Changzong has such an elevated position and lives such a find life, yet he still asks a fortune-teller to read his face. What's his purpose? If he thinks what the fortune-teller told him is wrong, he should take the fortune-teller to the yamen. Though he said that he had reported it to Your Majesty, yet it shows that he harbors evil ambitions. According to the law, he should be executed and his estate be confiscated." Holy Empress Wu did not know what to say.

Although Song Jing frequently demanded that Zhang Changzong be imprisoned, Holy Empress Wu never made up her mind to it. On the contrary, she sent Song Jing out of the capital to be governor, once here, then there, then another place, but all the appointments were rejected by Song Jing for the reason that since nothing unusual was happening in these places, a prime minister should not leave the capital.

Song Jing (663–738) was a learned youth and well-versed in literature. He passed the government tests at the age of twenty. He was a brave and principled person, and always spoke out when he saw what he thought was wrong. Later he was made the vice minister of Official Ministry, then the minister of Official Ministry and then the minister of Judicial Ministry. In 729, he was appointed a prime minister. In 732, he retired and died at the age of seventy-five. He had a nickname of "Walking Spring," because everywhere he went to work, he brought the new warmth of spring to that place.

Quite a few courtiers said that Zhang Changzong had broken the law so many times that he had to be sent to prison. Holy Empress Wu had to send Zhang Changzong at least to be questioned. When the interrogation was still going on, Holy Empress Wu sent a messenger to deliver her pardon edict for Zhang Changzong. Song Jing sighed, "I hate myself for not having crushed his brain in time." Holy Empress Wu sent Zhang Changzong to see Song Jing to apologize, but Song Jing refused to see him.

In 705, the Zhang brothers were killed outside the chamber of Holy Empress Wu when a prime minister and other courtiers joined in a coup d'état to force Holy Empress Wu to abdicate.

Chapter 7. Relations with Other Nations

The Tang government had to contend with a variety of Central Asian or Altaic peoples to the north and west of their territory and also Korea in the east. Some turned out to be strong and betrayed the Tang government or even invaded its territory. The emperor had to send his troops to fight them. When the Tang army conquered some of them, the government divided the region into many districts and appointed quite a few governors to rule them. But some Khans of the local tribes often rebelled and the central government had to dispatch armies to subdue them. The problem lasted for the entire Tang Dynasty till the nation was split into several small kingdoms. The most important relationships with the neighboring peoples were those with Tibet, Korea and the Tujue Clan.

TIBET

Tibet was then an empire in it is own right, independent of China. Sometimes it was friendly to the Tang government and sometimes it invaded the Tang territory.

It was a leap year in 640. The lunar calendar has a double month in the leap year. There were two tenth moons in that year and in the bissextile tenth moon, the king of Tibet sent an envoy to the capital of the Tang Dynasty with five thousand taels of silver and hundreds of gems and other valuables, asking for the hand of one of the princesses in marriage. Emperor Taizong was on the throne at that time and agreed to marry Princess Wencheng to the Tibetan king.

On the fifteenth day of the third moon in 641, Emperor Taizong ordered Prince Jiangxia, by the name of Li Daozong, to escort Princess Wencheng to

Tibet for the wedding ceremony. When the princess arrived, the king was very happy and had a palace built for her in the Tang style. The king also liked the Tang style clothes and etiquette. Whenever he went to see the princess, he put on muslin clothes. According to the history records, the princess brought the Tang culture there together with silkworm eggs, which altered the life and customs of Tibetan people.

In the fifth moon of 650, the king of Tibet, the husband of Princess Wencheng and so the brother-in-law of the present Emperor Gaozong, died. His son had died early and so his grandson was made the king. (Strangely, the history book does not say anything about a message conveying the sad news of the death of the Tibetan king being sent to the Tang government.) As the grandson was a child, the prime minister Ludongzan had all the power to rule Tibet. He was a smart man and Tibet became strong, and began to invade Tang territory.

In the bissextile third moon of 676, as the Tibetan army invaded Tang territory, Heavenly Emperor sent Prince Xiang, the fourth son of him and Heavenly Empress Wu, as field marshal to resist the aggression.

In the fifth moon of 677, the Tibetan army invaded Linhe (Lin here means Facing and He here means River) Town (so called as the town faced a river.) and captured the Tang officer Du Xiaosheng. The Tibetan army leader wanted Du to write a letter to the governor of Songchow (Song here means Pine Tree) to persuade the governor to surrender, but Du refused to write such a letter. When the Tibetan army withdrew, the leader let Du go. Later Du was made a junior general.

In the ninth moon of 678, Li Jingxuan went with eighteen thousand Tang warriors to fight the invading Tibetan army. A general Liu Shenli led a detachment deep into the area occupied by the Tibetan army. While Liu Shenli was assailed by the Tibetans, Li Jingxuan did not go to his rescue. So Liu was captured by the Tibetans. Then Li beat a retreat and camped behind a trench. A junior general Heichi Changzhi made a surprise attack on the Tibetans at night and defeated them. The emperor promoted him to general.

Heichi Changzhi (?–689) was a brave Korean man. In 663, he came to join the Tang army and fought for them in various battles. Besides the above-mentioned struggle with Tibet, he went to defeat the Tujue troops in 686 and was granted the title of Duke of YanGuo for all his merits. However, he was finally sent to prison on a false indictment and hanged himself there.

The son of Liu Shenli implored the emperor to let him go to Tibet to replace his father as a hostage of the Tibetans. The emperor consented. But by the time the son reached Tibet, his father had died of disease. He cried so bitterly that the Tibetans let him take his father's body. The son carried the body on his back all the way back to the capital. (So it is recorded in the history book.)

In the second moon of 679, another king of Tibet died, and his son, eight years old, succeeded him. In the tenth moon, the sad news of the death of the Tibetan king, sent by Princess Wencheng, who was still alive, arrived in the capital of the Tang Dynasty. A courtier, Song Lingwen, was sent to attend the funeral.

In the seventh moon, General Heichi Changzi drove back the invading Tibetan army. Then he set up more than seventy beacon towers and had his men-at-arms cultivate five thousand acres of land to grow grain so as to avoid having to transport provisions from afar.

During the tenth moon of 680, Princess Wencheng died in Tibet.

In the fifth moon of 681, General Heichi Changzhi defeated the Tibetan army again.

In the third moon of 696, the Tang army under the command of Wang Xiaoji and Lou Shide was defeated by the Tibetan troops. Wang was deprived of all his official positions and Lou was demoted.

In the ninth moon of 696, Tibet sent a messenger to ask for the hand of another princess for their king. Holy Empress Wu was on the throne at that time and sent a courtier by the name of Guo Yuanzhen to Tibet to see what they wanted. A powerful Tibetan general, Qinling, asked the Zhou Dynasty government to withdraw the soldiers who were guarding four towns. Guo Yuanzhen retorted, "Are you asking us to withdraw our soldiers, so you can invade eastward to expand your territory?" Guo could not promise anything, so the powerful general sent an envoy to go back with Guo to see Holy Empress Wu.

Guo Yuanzhen (656–713) passed the government tests at the age of eighteen. He became a famous general of the Tang Dynasty. In 701, he was appointed the governor of Liangchow (meaning Cool District). In 711, he was made the minister of Official Ministry and then the minister of Military Ministry. He was granted the title of Duke of Daiguo and died a natural death.

Once back in the capital, before any decision was made, Guo Yuanzhen handed in a memorial analyzing the situation. "The request of Tibet puts us in a dilemma. We must deal with it carefully, not in a rush. We should not give them a flat refusal. We must think of a way to delay so that they won't get desperate. Tibet wants the four towns as much as we want the region of the Green Sea (now called Green Sea Province, in the western part of China) they are occupying. We can thus reply to them, 'The four towns are so distant, they are useless to China. We have sent soldiers to guard them in order to block any possible invasion. If Tibet has no intention of invading, we can withdraw the soldiers; but Tibet must return to us the region of the Green

Sea.' If Tibet refuses to return that region to us, they are up to no good." Holy Empress Wu agreed with him.

Then Guo Yuanzhen handed in another memorial, saying, "The Tibetan people are tired of wars. They wish to cement a relationship with us through marriage. Only the powerful general Qinling wants to wage wars, by which he can always stay in power. He's the one opposing the marriage policy. If we send a messenger there for that purpose every year and if Qinling always refuses, the Tibetan people will hate him all the more. Thus he cannot drive their people to war against us." Holy Empress Wu thought that sounded promising.

In the bissextile seventh moon of 700, the Tibetan troops attacked Liangchow. General Tang Xiujing had the command of the government army at that time. They met in the Hongyuan (meaning Flood Source) Valley. The Tibetan troops in array looked awesome with bright weapons and colorful banners. Tang said to his men, "Don't be afraid. I've learned that their commander is a green hand in martial arts and tactics. I can easily deal with them. I'll fight them first." He put on a coat of chain mail and helmet and rode his steed towards the enemy's formation. Six times, he rushed to attack and returned safe and sound. Under his fearless repeated assault, the Tibetan troops began to flee. The government army chased and killed two thousand five hundred Tibetans.

In the tenth moon of 702, more than ten thousand Tibetan soldiers invaded Maochow (meaning Flourish District). The governor Chen Daci defeated them and killed over one thousand Tibetan soldiers.

The battles between Tibet and China continued after the death of Holy Empress Wu.

KOREA

Unlike Tibet, Korea at that time was not independent, but was looked upon as a subsidiary nation of the Tang Dynasty. However, the Korean kings often defied the Tang government. So the Tang army invaded Korea with the aim of subduing their kings.

In 644, since Korea had disobeyed the Tang government, Emperor Taizong decided to invade it. In the seventh moon, he had four hundred ships built to transport grain and other equipment and had all other preparations made. On the fourteenth day of the tenth moon the emperor reached Luoyang (Luo here is the name of a river and Yang here means South Side) City where the army gathered.

On the twelfth day of the second moon 645, the emperor decided to go to war himself. He left the crown prince to take care of the day-to-day routines with the help of the prime minister Fang Xuanling. Then he led his army, a hundred thousand strong, marching toward Korea. A detachment commanded by General Li Ji reached Youchow (meaning Secluded District), which was close to Korea.

In the third moon, the emperor arrived in Dingchow (meaning Fixed District). Whenever the emperor saw a soldier was ill, he would console him and let him stay behind for treatment. All the soldiers were touched by this consideration and vowed to fight for the emperor to their last breath. Many young people, who had not been recruited, came forth to voluntarily join the army, bringing uniforms and weapons at their own expenses. But the emperor did not accept them into his army. The detachment under General Li Ji marched along a route to the north and Prince Jiangxia by the name of Li Daozong took another route to attack Korea.

The courtier Cen Wenben was also in the army, in charge of provisions. He worked so hard that the emperor was afraid that he would be taken ill. He said, "I'm afraid that he is coming with me, but won't go back with me." One day Chen Wenben suddenly did die of a disease. The emperor had to send for another courtier, named Xu Jingzong, to take over the charge of the provisions.

On the tenth day of the fifth moon, the Tang army entered Korea and defeated Korean army and conquered quite a few Korean cities. The winter there came early. The Tang army had fourteen thousand Korean captives, waiting to be distributed to the generals and courtiers to be their slaves. Thus, they would be separated from their families. The emperor sympathized with them and announced that the captives could redeem their freedom with money or scrolls of cloth. The captives were ecstatic and cheered the emperor for his mercy for three days. (So it says in the history book.)

In the ninth moon the emperor suffered from carbuncles and returned to the capital. He passed Yichow (meaning Easy District) on his way. An official Chen Yuanshou there had people grow vegetables in their cellars using fire to warm the vegetables like in a hothouse. When the emperor heard about it, he thought it was just a foolish act of flattery and terminated his official position.

In the fourth moon of 648, a general Guo Shaman took some ships to besiege Korea from the sea. After disembarking and marching inland to Mount Yi, he met the Korean cavalry and infantry, five thousand in all. He defeated them. At night the Koreans, ten thousand in number, came to attack his ships, but were ambushed. Then he sailed his ships back.

In the sixth moon of 658, generals Cheng Mingzhen and Xue RenGui assailed a town of Korea and took it over, slew more than four hundred Korean soldiers and captured more than one hundred of them. A Korean general came to counterattack with three hundred thousand strong. General Cheng Mingzhen made Xiedan (a small ethnic group in Northeastern China) war-

riors attack the Korean army, defeated it and killed two thousand five hundred Korean soldiers.

In the eleventh moon of 659, the general Xue RenGui had a battle with
Korean army at Mount Heng and defeated it. Xue RenGui (613–683) was a
renowned general in the Tang Dynasty. When Emperor Taizong ordered to
recruit for the invasion of Korea, Xue joined the army. He was very brave and
skilful in archery. He liked to wear white armor. Once he defeated Korean
army of two hundred thousand strong with fewer Tang soldiers. He fought
battles after battles against both the Tujue Clan and Korea. He died a natural
death at the age of seventy. The government made a special coffin for him as
thanks for his great merits.

In 660, Emperor Gaozong, the son of Emperor Taizong, wanted to invade
Korea again. A courtier Liu RenGui commanded the navy. His duties were to
transport provisions and other necessities. In the twelfth moon, the weather
was so bad that it was not safe to put the ships to sea. But Li Yifu, a bad
prime minister at the time, insisted on Liu's setting out on the voyage, as Liu
had offended him earlier. Liu RenGui had to set sail, but met a storm on the
sea and lost some ships and seamen. By law, Liu was liable for the losses. Li
Yifu said to the emperor that Liu should be executed. But a courtier pleaded
for Liu, saying that no one could do anything against the storm. The emperor
found that sensible and only removed Liu from the commanding position,
still letting him go with the army to gain some merits to offset his demerits.

In the first moon of 661, the government trained forty thousand recruits
and would send them to Korea. On the third day of the fourth moon, Emperor Gaozong felt better and wanted to lead the army himself to invade
Korea. On the twenty-ninth day, Empress Wu wrote to the emperor an official memorial to dissuade him from going himself and so on the second day
of the fifth moon, the emperor sent some generals to invade Korea.

In the third moon of 661, a general Wang Wendu was sent to Korea, but
died from a disease on the way. So Liu RenGui was sent instead. His troops
were well-disciplined and so were always victorious. However, while he was
attacking Pyongyang City of Korea, it snowed heavily. He could not conquer
the city and had to relinquish the attack. Then the emperor ordered him to
come back to China by sea, but Liu sent in a memorial to the emperor analyzing the situation. He suggested that he should stay where he was and sought
a chance to attack again. The emperor and other courtiers thought that he
was right and agreed to his suggestion.

Then at the request of Korea, Japan came to its rescue, but Japan's real
purpose was to defeat China and occupy Korea itself. In the eighth moon of
663, seven thousand Tang soldiers on one hundred and seventy ships fought
against ten thousand Japanese soldiers on one thousand ships on the sea. At

that time, Chinese warships were bigger and stronger than Japanese ones and they defeated the Japanese on the sea for four times. Finally Liu used fire to burn four hundred Japanese warships and the rest of the Japanese escaped home.

In the ninth moon of 666, the Tang army defeated Korean troops again. On the eighteenth day of the twelfth moon, Li Ji was appointed the commander-in-chief and was to lead the Tang army to attack Korea once more.

In the ninth moon of 667, Li Ji attacked a town belonging to Korea. He said that he had to take over the town first, before he could march to attack the other towns, because it occupied an important strategic location. At the severe attack the Koreans in the town surrendered. Then Li Ji conquered another sixteen towns as well. Another general had a run-in with the Korean army, but when he retreated the Korean army chased him. General Xue Ren-Gui came to attack the Korean pursuers from the side and slew more than fifty thousand.

General He Chujun set his camp before a Korean town. The Korean army came to attack him when he was sitting down to have his meal. When the message of the attack came, he did not even stir. But in a short time the Korean army was defeated because he had already posted a detachment to ambush and counterattack the Korean army.

In the second moon of 668, General Xue RenGui attacked a Korean town with three thousand soldiers. Other generals were afraid that three thousand men were not enough, but Xue said, "It does not depend on how many soldiers I have. It depends on how I use and maneuver my troops." When he battled against the Korean army, he beat them and killed more than ten thousand enemy soldiers. (The history book did not narrate how he maneuvered his troops.)

In the fourth moon, a comet was seen in the sky. People in ancient China called it a broom star as its tail looked like a broom. They thought that the comet was an ill omen shown to people by Heaven. Generally the emperor would criticize himself for something he had done wrong. Then he would cancel entertainments and think about doing some good for the people and the nation. This time, Xu Jingzong said, "It's a sign to show that Korea will soon be conquered." The emperor said, "It surely means I have done something wrong. How can you attribute it to the Koreans? Besides, the Korean people are my people, too."

On the twelfth day of the ninth moon, Command-in-Chief Li Ji subdued Korea, which was then included in the territory of the Tang Dynasty. He captured the king and some of the courtiers of Korea. This time Korea was entirely conquered.

On the second day of the tenth moon, the emperor held a banquet to celebrate the victory.

On the seventh day of the twelfth moon, Li Ji returned and brought the captives. All the generals and soldiers received rewards in accordance with their merits.

On the first day of the fourth moon in 669, the emperor ordered 38,200 families to be moved from Korea to the unoccupied regions to the south of Yangtze River and Huai River.

In the bissextile fifth moon of 673, Korea showed defiance again to the Tang government. General Li Jinxing was sent to fight them. He defeated the Koreans and captured several thousands of their men. But the Koreans attacked the town originally defended by Li Jinxing. Now Li was away fighting the Koreans somewhere else. But his wife took charge of the defense. Assaulting the town for a long time, the Koreans could not occupy it and they finally relinquished the efforts and went back. When the emperor was told about it, he granted the wife the title of Lady YanGuo.

Anyway, the Tang government never really beat Korea into total submission. The war between them went on and on.

The Tujue Clan

The Tujue Clan was a large non-Chinese group living to the north of the Tang Dynasty. At first they were a nomadic tribe, but later a state formed and their head was called the Khan. At the beginning of the Sui Dynasty, the Tujue Clan was divided into the East Tujue Clan and the West Tujue Clan. And one or the other often invaded Tang territory.

In the first and second moons of 630, the Tang army conquered the East Tujue Clan, who surrendered. Then many minorities in the north and northwest fell under the control of the Tang government. So Emperor Taizong received the title of Heavenly Khan, who was above all khans of the tribal groups.

In the sixth moon, Khan Chebi of the West Tujue Clan invaded Tang territory after the death of Emperor Taizong. Emperor Gaozong sent the general Gao Kan to fight him. General Gao made Khan Chebi his captive in a combat.

On the fourth day of the ninth moon in 650, General Gao Kan returned to the capital victoriously from the war with the Tujue Clan. That day, the general brought the captured Khan to the presence of the emperor in a martial ritual. A feast followed to celebrate the victory. To show his generosity, the emperor released the khan and made him a general to work for him.

On the twenty-third day of the sixth moon in 655, General Cheng Zhijie was made the commander-in-chief to fight the invading Tujue Clan, but only on the third day of the ninth moon in 656, the Tang army reached the battle-field and attacked the Tujue troops. The Tang army won the day and killed thirty-one thousand Tujue troops. Then between the twenty-second day of the twelfth moon in 656 and the nineteenth day of the first moon in 657, the Tang army met with forty thousand Tujue fighters on horseback. General Su Dingfang went ahead with five hundred cavalrymen as vanguard. He with his men dashed into the Tujue troops and fought so fiercely that Su put the Tujue horsemen to rout and chased them for twenty miles. One thousand and five hundred Tujue horsemen were either slain or captured.

But the vice commander-in-chief, called Wang Wendu, envied Su Ding-fang for his victory and said to the commander-in-chief Cheng Zhijie, "Though we won the victory, we also lost many cavalrymen. We must concentrate our army and allow them to rest, and fight only when the enemy came to attack us." By this, he wanted to prevent Su from gaining another such victory. As Cheng still wanted to continue fighting, Wang Wendu lied that he just received an edict from the emperor and let himself replace Cheng Zhijie to command the army. Then Wang ordered the soldiers to stop attacking, for the time being. General Su Dingfang said to Cheng Zhijie, "We came to fight the Tujue invaders. We will fail if we merely wait for them to come to attack us. If the generals and soldiers are all afraid of the enemy, how can we fight and win? Besides, since the emperor has let you be the commander-in-chief, how can the emperor let the deputy commander-in-chief replace you in the middle of war? It can't be true. You should hold Wang Wendu and write to the emperor to make sure."

But Cheng Zhijie did not listen to him. When the Tang army reached Hengdu (Heng here means Everlasting and Du here means Honesty) Town, many former Tujue fighters came to surrender themselves. Wang Wendu said, "These men were also our enemies. We must kill them and divide their belongings." Su Dingfang opposed it, saying, "If we do so, we will be like the Tujue invaders" (because Tujue soldiers always robbed the Tang people wherever they went.) But Wang Wendu did not listen to him and slaughtered all those who had surrendered and took their belongings. When they returned to the capital, Cheng Zhijie was removed from his position and Wang Wendu was sentenced to death because of his lying about the imperial edict, but later he was pardoned from the death sentence and only lost his official status.

Su Dingfang (592–667) was a celebrated general of the Tang Dynasty. At the end of the Sui Dynasty there were many rebels, some of whom would rob people of food and valuables. To defend their villages against the robbers, at the age of fifteen, Su and his father organized some thousand villagers. He was a fierce and brave fighter for one so young. When the Sui Dynasty collapsed, he joined in Dou Jiande's army. When Dou was killed, he went back to live in his village for a while. In the first year that Emperor Taizong was on the throne, he went to work for the Tang government. In 629, he was sent to fight the Tujue invaders under General Li Jing. In 655, he went to Korea in combat and in 656, he went again to fight the Tujue under General Cheng Zhijie, described above. All his life, he went wherever he was needed to fight. He was granted the title of Duke of Jingguo.

In 658, the Tang army subdued the West Tujue Clan. But the rest of the Tujue Clan still invaded Tang territory, because the conquest of a nation does not mean all its people were pacified.

In the tenth moon of 679, the Tujue Clan were coming to attack Tingchow. The magistrate, Prince Huo, ordered the town gate kept open, all the banners on the battlements taken down and every soldier hidden behind the walls. When the Tujue men came and saw it, they suspected an ambush and withdrew under the cover of the night. Then a man called Li Jiayun was detected to be working for the Tujue Clan. So he was arrested. When word of this came to the emperor, he ordered the magistrate to kill all those involved in the case. But the magistrate only executed Li Jiayun and let others go without any punishment. He reported this to the emperor, asking to be punished for not obeying the order of His Majesty, but by that time the emperor had regretted sending the order to kill everyone, and so now he praised the magistrate.

In the third moon of 680, General Pei Xingjian defeated the Tujue Clan and brought their chieftain back as a captive. Tujue warriors used to rob the Tang army of their provisions — and the covered wagons they were stored in. Therefore, Pei thought of a stratagem. He had three hundred covered wagons ready, in each of which five soldiers were hiding, and they were sent along as though they were loaded with provisions. As usual, Tujue soldiers came to steal the wagons and they pushed them to their camping ground. Then at night the hidden Tang soldiers jumped out and began to slaughter the Tujue soldiers, who ran off for their dear lives, but only to fall into another ambush.

In 684, the Tujue Clan invaded again and Empress Dowager Wu sent General Cheng Tingwu to the north frontier to push them back.

In the ninth moon of 686, the Tujue Clan invaded Tang territory again. But when they confronted the general Heichi Changzhi, they had to retreat under the cover of night. Then some other troops of the Tujue Clan invaded and General Heichi Changzhi fought them. Three thousand Tujue soldiers came as a vanguard. When they saw the Tang army, they got down from horseback. Heichi sent two hundred cavalrymen to attack. The Tujue tribesmen ran away. But at twilight, the main Tujue force came. Heichi had a bonfire burning in the campground. When the Tujue warriors came nearer, they saw another bonfire burning in the southeastern side to them. They thought that it might be an ambush and so they recoiled.

In 687, a general Cuan Baobi envied General Heichi Changzhi and wanted to earn some recognition in the martial arena. He volunteered to fight the Tujue invaders. Empress Dowager Wu told him to consult Heichi before he took any action. Heichi advised Baobi to wait for him before he launched an attack. But Baobi just went ahead to attack the Tujue invaders alone. Besides, he notified the Tujue warriors he was coming. Therefore, the Tujue were ready to meet him in battle formation. Baobi was defeated, and leaving his forces behind he escaped back alone. He lost all the soldiers he had foolishly led into combat. He did not escape the wrath of the Empress Dowager, who had him executed.

On the thirteenth day of the seventh moon in 687, there was an earthquake in the capital. That month, the Tujue Clan invaded again. General Heichi Changzhi vanquished them. Whenever Heichi received any reward for his merits, he would distribute it among the soldiers. Once, a soldier had hurt a good steed; an officer suggested that the soldier must be flogged. Heichi said, "How can I beat a man for the sake of a horse?" Since he treated his men with consideration, they were willing to risk their lives for him.

On the eleventh day of the fifth moon in 698, Mochuo, now the khan of the Tujue Clan, sent a messenger to the Zhou government. (The Zhou Dynasty was established by Holy Empress Wu.) He had a daughter and wanted to marry her to a nobleman of China.

On the sixth day of the sixth moon, Holy Empress Wu sent a courtier, Yan Zhiwei, to accompany Prince Huaiyang, Wu Yanxiu by name (son of Wu Chengsi, the grandnephew of Holy Empress Wu), to the tribe to marry the khan's daughter.

On the first day of the eighth moon, when Prince Huaiyang reached the place, he was detained by the khan. The khan said to courtier Yan, "I want to marry my daughter to a prince with the surname of Li, not of Wu. He is not the son of an emperor. The Li family had always treated our tribe so well. I have heard that almost all the descendents of the Li family were killed. Now only two are left (he had in mind the two sons of Holy Empress Wu). I will go with my cavalry to support the sons." So he imprisoned Prince Huaiyang and gave Yan Zhiwei the title of South Khan, by which he meant that when he conquered the territory of the Zhou Dynasty, South Khan Yan would rule there, but under fealty to him. In this way Yan was induced to betray the Zhou Dynasty and led the khan's army to invade China.

At the same time, the Khan wrote a letter to Holy Empress Wu stating his reasons for the invasion. He blamed Holy Empress Wu for five things: "1) you provided us with steamed grain seeds so that when we sowed the seeds they would not grow; 2) you gave us utensils of gold and silver, but not all were genuine; 3) when my messengers were given red or purple robes, you took them back; 4) the cloth sent us was all of inferior quality; 5) I wanted to marry my daughter to a son of the Li family, but you sent a member of the Wu family instead, who is no fitting match for my daughter."

Another courtier called Pei Huaigu had traveled with Yan Zhiwei. The khan wanted to give him an official position to work for him, but Pei rebuffed it. So the khan imprisoned him and planned to kill him later. But Pei succeeded in escaping. When he reached Jinyang (Jin here is the name of an ancient state in China and Yang here is the Sun) City, he was so thin and haggard that the patrolmen mistook him for a spy from the Khan. When they were about to kill him, one of the patrolmen recognized him, because the man had been falsely charged and Pei had saved him. Pei arrived in the capital and reported to Holy Empress Wu.

On the thirteenth day of the eighth moon in 698, Wu Zhonggui, Zhang Renbing and Li Duozuo were sent with a force three hundred thousand strong to resist the khan of the Tujue Clan.

On the eleventh day of the ninth moon, the khan surrounded Zhaochow (Zhao here is a surname). An official went over the town wall to meet the Khan's troops. The magistrate and his wife were prepared to commit suicide but were captured by the enemy. The Khan showed him a purple robe and a girdle of gold, saying that if he surrendered, he could be a high official under the Khan; if he refused, he would die. The husband asked the wife for her opinion. She said, "It's time we die for our nation." They just shut their eyes and made no answer. They were thus killed by the order of the Khan. When the Khan's troops retreated after much slaughter and pillage, the official who had gone to meet the khan was executed by the government army that reoccupied the town.

On the seventeenth day of the ninth moon in 698, the crown prince was sent as the commander-in-chief to fight Khan Mochuo. On the twenty-first day, Di Renjie was sent as deputy commander-in-chief, but in fact he served as commander-in-chief since the crown prince assumed the title of commander-in-chief only in name. Holy Empress Wu herself saw Di Renjie off when he was leaving the capital. Under so much military pressure, the Khan recoiled to the north. Di pursued him but did not catch him. Now the Khan had forty thousand fighters. The tribal groups in the northwestern regions all recognized his leadership.

On the seventeenth day of the tenth moon, the Khan released the traitor Yan Zhiwei, who had nowhere to go but home; he was executed along with his family and relatives.

In the eighth moon of 704, the Khan of the Tujue Clan allowed Wu Yanx-iu to return to the capital of the Zhou Dynasty.

Even so, the war between the Tujue Clan and China continued after the death of Holy Empress Wu.

JAPAN AND ARABIA

In 631, Japan sent their envoy to the Tang government for the first time. The next one did not arrive until 653.

Arabia sent an envoy to the Tang government for the first time on the fourth day of the eighth moon in 650, and brought the religion of Islam into China.

In the second moon of 654, a Japanese envoy came to China for the third time, and an envoy was sent again in the seventh moon of 659 and in 665. On the twelfth day of the eleventh moon in 669, Japan sent an envoy with gifts.

In the third moon of 696, a messenger came from Arabia and offered to send a lion to Holy Empress Wu. A prime minister said to her, "A lion eats meat. When it has to come from such a long distance, we must supply great quantities of meat, all of which will have to be taken from the people. Besides, Your Majesty doesn't even like to keep eagles and dogs for hunting. Why keep a useless beast?" So the offer was denied.

CHAPTER 8. FAMOUS LEGENDS ABOUT EMPRESS WU

There are always legends about great figures in history, no matter whether they were male or female. Empress Wu was certainly a distinguished, great woman. Make no doubt about it; there are plenty of legends about her. Here are just a few.

FACE READING

One legend goes like this. There was a famous fortune-teller as well as an astrologer by the name of Yuan TianGang, who had been summoned by Emperor Taizong to the capital. When he passed Lichow on his way there, Wu Shiyue, her father, who was the governor there, sent his men to invite him to his yamen and asked him to tell the fortunes of his family members. But Yuan only read their faces one by one. Fortune-telling in China is different from face-reading. Face-reading can go with palm-reading or be done alone. Fortune-telling requires knowing a person's birthday and birth time. The fortune is told based on certain fortune books that were written by ancient Chinese philosophers, because Chinese fortune-telling is deemed a sort of philosophy.

When Yuan read the wife's face he said, "Your Ladyship should have a son with a great future." But Wu did not have a son by this wife.

Then Wu sent for his two sons by his diseased wife and called them into his presence. After looking at them, Yuan said that they might be magistrates in the future, but would die unnatural deaths. Wu did not believe it, because he knew his two sons so well. They were quite ordinary, no talent, no learning. How could they become magistrates all by themselves? Then Wu sent for his two daughters by his present wife. At that time, Empress Wu was a baby wrapped up in swaddling clothes and no one could tell whether it was a boy or a girl. Yuan looked at the sister first and predicted, "She will be married into a rich noble family, but the marriage will bring harm to her husband." Then it was the baby's turn. When he set his eyes on the face, he was greatly surprised himself, and he said, "If this is a boy, he will be in the highest rank of officialdom with great power; but if it is a girl, she will be the sovereign over the country."

Yuan TianGang and another astrologer Li Chunfeng were co-writers of a famous picture book with ambiguous poems or words predicting the changes of the future dynasties. When they reached the sixty-fourth picture, Li Chunfeng pushed Yuan on the back to stop him. So the book had only sixty-four pictures in it and people thereafter called the book literally "Back-Push Picture Book," really a book of prediction. Every dynasty forbade the circulation of the book circulation lest people know how the dynasty would end and what dynasty would succeed it.

FLOWERS BLOOMING IN WINTER

A famous legend was handed down that said in the winter moon of 691, Holy Empress Wu wrote a poem titled "A Tour in the Imperial Garden on a Spring Day," It had four lines that may be translated loosely as follows:

I will go to the Imperial Garden tomorrow
Let the god of Spring immediately know:
All the flowers must be in bloom overnight,
No need for morning winds to blow.

The story indicates that one day during the cold weather Holy Empress Wu wished she could visit the Imperial Garden in its customary splendor. She wished that all the flowers should be in bloom and brighten her day. Therefore, she wrote the poem and had it posted in the garden, and, as the legend had it, when she went there the next day with all her favorite ladies and courtiers, the flowers did come out to greet her.

OTHER LEGENDS

There was a dam named after her: Zetian Dam (Ze here means Example and Tian, Heaven) (as "Heavenly Empress" she was called Empress Wu Zetian) and a tower called Tower of the Heavenly Empress.

Another legend was that one day her mother was rowing a boat alone on the Black Dragon Pond when she felt a dragon coming to her and then had a special sense inside her. Before long she was pregnant with Empress Wu. The belief of people at that time was that a female sovereign should not be born from a mortal father, but from something special. The dragon was considered a divine creature and also the impersonation of an emperor.

The history book recorded this event: in the seventh moon when Emperor Taizong was lying on his sickbed, the planet Venus appeared in the sky in the broad daylight several times. From the point of view of the ancient Chinese people, any unusual change in the movements of the stars in the sky had to be a sign from Heaven to foretell something good or bad. Therefore, divination was done and it was construed that this sign indicated the coming of a female sovereign.

The history book also says that a book was circulating among the common people, titled "Record of Secrets." There was a saying that after three emperors of the Tang Dynasty, a female sovereign surnamed Wu would reign. When Emperor Taizong was informed of this, he was troubled, but he did not believe that a female would rule the country. It had never happened before in all of history. He consulted some courtiers and one of them suggested that it might refer to a man who had once had a nickname at home that sounded like a girl's. The emperor thought that sounded like a good way to look at it. Therefore, he held a feast for all the courtiers to attend. During the feast, the emperor asked everyone to tell what his pet name at home had been. A courtier called Li Junxian said that at home they used to call him Wuniang (meaning Fifth Girl). The emperor was astonished to hear it, but feigned a smile, saying, "Where comes a woman, so strong!" After the banquet, the emperor thought that he might be the one that Heaven had pointed out, as a warning. So he had the courtier killed.

Then the emperor asked Li Chunfeng, the imperial astrologer, "Is the saying in the book 'Record of Secrets' credible?" Li answered, "I have watched the sky every night recently, and the omen shows that the person is already in the palace, and is your relative. Thirty years from now, the person will rule the country and will slay nearly all the descendents of the imperial Li family." Emperor Taizong asked again, "What if I kill all those who might be suspicious?" Li replied, "Once Providence has decided, no one can change it. The future sovereign won't die and you will just kill many innocent people. But thirty years from now, the person will grow old and may turn out to be lenient. So the disaster may not be as severe as it looks from today's vantage point. If you could get the person and kill her, Providence will send someone else. Now, if that second person is young, the disaster may be more severe."

Emperor Taizong took his advice and did nothing more about it. Fate would take its course.